The Business Organisation and its Environment

The Business Organisation and its Environment

BOOK 2

Second Edition

Matthew Glew
Michael Watts
Ronald Wells

Heinemann Educational Books

Heinemann Educational Books Ltd
22 Bedford Square, London WC1B 3HH

LONDON EDINBURGH MELBOURNE AUCKLAND
HONG KONG SINGAPORE KUALA LUMPUR NEW DELHI
IBADAN NAIROBI JOHANNESBURG
PORTSMOUTH (NH) KINGSTON PORT OF SPAIN

First published 1979
Reprinted with amendments 1980, 1982
Second edition, 1984

British Library Cataloguing in Publication Data

Glew, Matthew
The business organisation and its environment.
Book 2
1. Organization
I. Title II. Watts, Michael, *b.1943*
III. Wells, Ronald, *b.1947*
301.18'32'024658 HM131

ISBN 0-435-45904-X

Printed in Great Britain by Butler & Tanner Ltd
Frome and London

Contents

Preface

The two volumes of this book and their respective work books are specifically designed to assist students studying Common Core Modules 3 and 4 entitled 'The Organisation in its Environment' which represents an integral part of the Business Education Council National Award. The contents and its format closely follow the National Award Course Specification.

The book seeks to guide students towards an understanding of their roles within the business environment. Consequently it provides them with a basis for analysing the economic, legal, social and political problems that affect the business world. The material has been presented in such a way that it is in accordance with the underlying BEC philosophy of an interdisciplinary approach to business studies courses. A balance has been maintained throughout the book between the disciplines of economics, law, government and sociology, thus providing a complete view of the operations of the business organisation.

The book will also prove valuable for students requiring an introduction or conversion course to the BEC Higher National Award. In addition, students engaged upon professional and managerial courses will find that the wide perspective which it provides on the business environment can successfully augment their studies.

Matthew T. Glew
Michael G. Watts
Ronald M. Wells
July 1979

Preface to the Second Edition

Completely updated for the second edition, this book now takes account of the most recent economic, legal, social and political developments, and includes the latest statistics. In particular, chapters 5 and 6 on government policies and control of the economy and the importance of international trade have been substantially rewritten, while the remaining chapters, such as those on community pressures on the business organisation and contract and consumer protection, have been carefully revised.

The book will continue to help students preparing for the Business & Technician Education Council (BTEC) National Awards.

January 1984

Acknowledgements

The authors and publishers wish to thank all publications mentioned in the sources for permission to reproduce copyright material, and The Controller, Her Majesty's Stationery Office, for permission to use the following material from official publications:

Figs. 1.2, 5.10, 5.11, 5.13, 5.14, 5.16, 6.2, 6.3 and 7.1.
Tables, 1.1, 2.1, 2.4, 2.5, 2.6, 2.7, 5.1, 5.2, 5.3, 5.4, 5.5, 5.6, 5.7, 5.8, 5.9, 6.6, 6.7, 6.8, 6.9, 6.10, 6.11, 6.12, 6.13, 6.14 and 6.15.

1. Government Institutions which Affect the Business Organisation

The activities and affairs of every business organisation are influenced in some way by the institutions of government. This may be at a local, national or even international level. The various levels of government may have a direct impact on the organisation either through the creation and enforcement of legislation that regulates its behaviour, or through supporting and promoting its activities, or through offering it a wide range of advisory services. Government institutions may have an indirect effect on the organisation by creating an economic, social and political environment which is conducive to the success of its activities. The major institutions which impact on the organisation are illustrated in Fig. 1.1 (page 2).

Local government

Local government is responsible for the administration of a variety of services, including housing, planning, transport, education, the social services, the fire service, the police, consumer protection, environmental health, libraries, museums and the arts, recreational facilities, the encouragement of tourism, cemeteries and crematoria, footpaths, smallholdings and allotments.

The local authority's administration of these services is controlled by three central bodies. **Parliament** exerts its influence through the statutory powers which it confers on them, either in public general Acts or by local legislation promoted by the local authority itself. **Central government departments** have an administrative influence; for example, in England the Department of the Environment is largely responsible for local government. The **courts of law** exercise a judicial control and they have the power to award damages to an individual who has been mistreated by a local authority. They may also offer remedies to secure the performance by the local authorities of their statutory duties, and to restrain them from acting outside their jurisdiction.

Local authorities are left to create their own internal form of organisation. Major policy decisions are generally handled by the full council, and the administration of the different services is put in the hands of special committees; this enables councillors to specialise in particular areas. The actual operation and running of the services is carried out by local government officers and employees.

Local authorities finance their activities out of local rates, government grants, income from trading services and miscellaneous sources, such as council house rents and loans that they have raised to meet capital expenditure.

The structure of local government

The present system of local government has only been in existence for a relatively short period of time as the actual structure of local government has undergone a major reorganisation which started in 1965.

London was the first to be reorganised in 1965. The administrative area of Greater London was established covering about 610 square miles. It was divided into thirty-two London boroughs and the City of London. The actual local authorities are the Greater London Council, the Corporation of the City of London and the councils of the various London boroughs. The former is responsible for those services which require unified administration over the entire area. The borough councils and the City of London Corporation provide all the other services. This is clearly shown in Table 1.1 (page 3).

Northern Ireland was reorganised in 1973 into a single-tier structure of twenty-six district authorities based on main towns or centres. They are responsible for local public health services, entertainment, recreation, cleansing and sanitation, some regulatory services, cemeteries and crematoria, gas undertakings, and markets and abattoirs. There are also five area boards covering Northern Ireland which administer, on a local basis, education and the library and youth services. They combine with the districts to provide recreational, social, physical and cultural facilities. Local offices

Fig. 1.1: The major institutions of government which affect the organisation

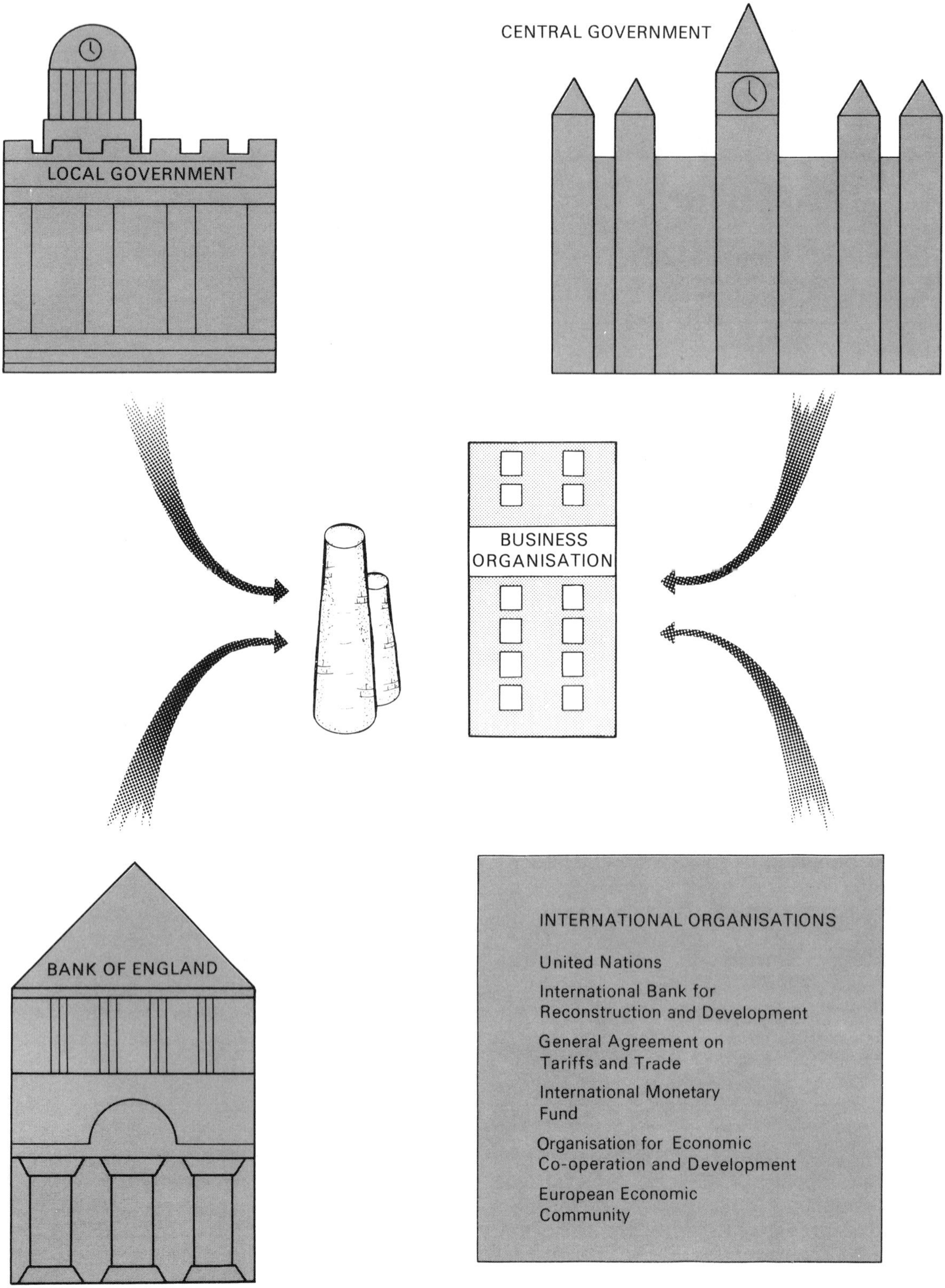

Table 1.1: The broad allocation of the main local government functions in England

FUNCTION	METROPOLITAN AREAS		NON-METROPOLITAN AREAS		GREATER LONDON	
	County Council	District Council	County Council	District Council	Greater London Council	London Borough Council
Planning						
structure plans	●		●		●	
local plans		●		●		●
development control		●		●		●
country parks	●	●	●	●		
national parks	●		●			
derelict land	●	●	●	●	●	●
Transport						
transport planning	●		●		●	
highways	●		●		●	●
traffic regulation	●		●		●	
road safety	●		●		●	
parking	●		●		●	●
public transport	●		●		●	
Education		●	●		● inner London	● outer London
Social Services		●	●			●
Housing		●		●	●	●
Fire Service	●		●		●	
Police Service	●		●			
Consumer Protection	●		●			●
Environmental Health						
building regulations		●		●	● inner London	● outer London
clean air		●		●		●
control of disease		●		●		●
food hygiene		●		●		●
refuse collection		●		●		●
refuse disposal	●		●		●	
street cleansing		●		●		●
Libraries		●	●			●
Museums and the Arts	●	●	●	●	●	●
Recreational Facilities	●	●	●	●	●	●
Encouragement of Tourism	●	●	●	●	●	●
Cemeteries and Crematoria		●		●		●
Footpaths	●	●	●	●		●
Smallholdings	●		●		●	
Allotments		●		●		●

SOURCE: *Local Government in Britain*, Central Office of Information, Reference Pamphlet 1 (HMSO, 1980).

Fig. 1.2

Note: Salop is now called Shropshire.

SOURCE: *Local Government in Britain*, Central Office of Information, Reference Pamphlet 1 (HMSO 1980).

of the central government departments concerned administer the health and social services, housing, the fire services, drainage and electricity.

England (apart from Greater London) was reorganised in 1974 into a new two-tier system as illustrated in the map in Fig. 1.2. Six metropolitan counties were established covering the main conurbations of Tyne and Wear, West Midlands, Merseyside, Greater Manchester, West Yorkshire and South Yorkshire. They were divided into thirty-six districts. The counties are responsible for strategic planning and those services requiring central control and the districts handle the other services. Table 1.1 clearly illustrates this division. The rest of England including the Isle of Wight was divided into thirty-nine non-metropolitan counties which were further divided into 296 districts. As Table 1.1 indicates, functions requiring planning and supervision over a large geographical area have been allocated to the counties and everything else to the districts. There are also 10,000 parishes, mainly in rural areas, which have their own parish councils and deal with the provision of very local services, such as allotments, arts and crafts, community halls, bus shelters and car parks.

In **Wales** a similar two-tier system to that established in the non-metropolitan counties of England was introduced. Basically there are eight counties, Clwyd, Dyfed, Mid Glamorgan, South Glamorgan, West Glamorgan, Gwent, Gwynedd and Powys. These are divided into thirty-seven districts. Many local communities which are similar to English parishes have been established for the whole country. The distribution of functions is very similar to that in England.

Scotland was reorganised in 1975 into the nine regional authorities of Highland, Grampian, Tayside, Central, Fife, Strathclyde, Lothian, Borders, Dumfries and Galloway. They were divided into fifty-three district authorities. Orkney, Shetland and the Western Islands are designated as all-purpose authorities. There is a similar division of functions between the regional and district authorities in Scotland as between the non-metropolitan counties and districts in England. Basically the regional authorities are responsible for strategic planning and related services and the districts for everything else.

Plans for the further reorganisation of local government

On 7 October 1983 the Conservative Government in a White Paper entitled 'Streamlining the Cities' put forward some proposals for **changes in the structure of local government**. In the White Paper it was proposed that the Greater London Council and the six metropolitan county councils should be abolished on 1 April 1986. Nearly all the functions of these authorities would become the responsibility of the boroughs and the districts. It was further proposed that joint boards composed of borough and district councillors would be established to control the police, fire services and public transport in the metropolitan counties and the fire services in London as a whole and the education service in Inner London.

The White Paper put forward the view that there was a need for change because the strategic role of both the GLC and the metropolitan counties had not proved to be fruitful but had merely brought them into 'conflict with lower-tier authorities or led them to promote policies which conflict with national policies which are the responsibility of central government'.

It was stated that the changes would be introduced under a bill which would be brought before Parliament early in the 1984–85 parliamentary session. During the intervening period there would be adequate time for discussions and consultations on the detailed proposals.

It is possible that the *range of services* under the control of local authorities may be reduced in the future. This is because the Conservative Government have expressed concern about the need for finding ways of improving the efficiency and cost effectiveness of local authority services. In fact the Conservative Government have actually encouraged local authorities to identify services or aspects of them which could appropriately be provided by private enterprise, while meeting the requirements of sound management and good value for money to the public. Some local authorities, such as Southend, Eastbourne and Peterborough have already contracted out their refuse disposal. The aspects of services that are most likely to be put out to private contractors are catering, laundry and cleaning. It is intended that the introduction of an element of competition between private contractors should help to improve efficiency and reduce costs, thus reducing overall public spending. Such changes would represent an aspect of the Conservative Government's policy of privatisation.

Local authority activities which directly affect the organisation

Many of the activities of local authorities have the indirect effect of creating a favourable environment for the operation of the organisation. However, some have a more direct influence on the operations of business organisations, as illustrated in Fig 1.3.

The **environmental health** departments try to control the effects of the business organisation on various aspects of the environment. They have the power to inspect an organisation for the detection of statutory nuisances, for example, the carrying on of offensive trades or the making of excessive noise. They may serve an abatement notice in order to stop the nuisance. If the organisation do not comply with this, then legal proceedings may be taken by the authority. The departments regulate standards of space, light, ventilation, sanitation and drainage for buildings. The 1955 Food and Drugs Act gives the Environmental Health Officer the power to investigate unsound food and drink and to take samples for analysis. Organisations selling food which is deficient or injurious to health may be prosecuted. The Clean Air Acts of 1956–1968 enable local authorities, with the sanction of the Secretary of State for the Environment, to set up smoke-control areas and then take action against those who pollute the atmosphere.

The **town and country planning authorities** are concerned with trying to ensure that land is put to the best use from the point of view of the community. Consequently they require an application before any development is undertaken, whether it is for an organisation's factory or office

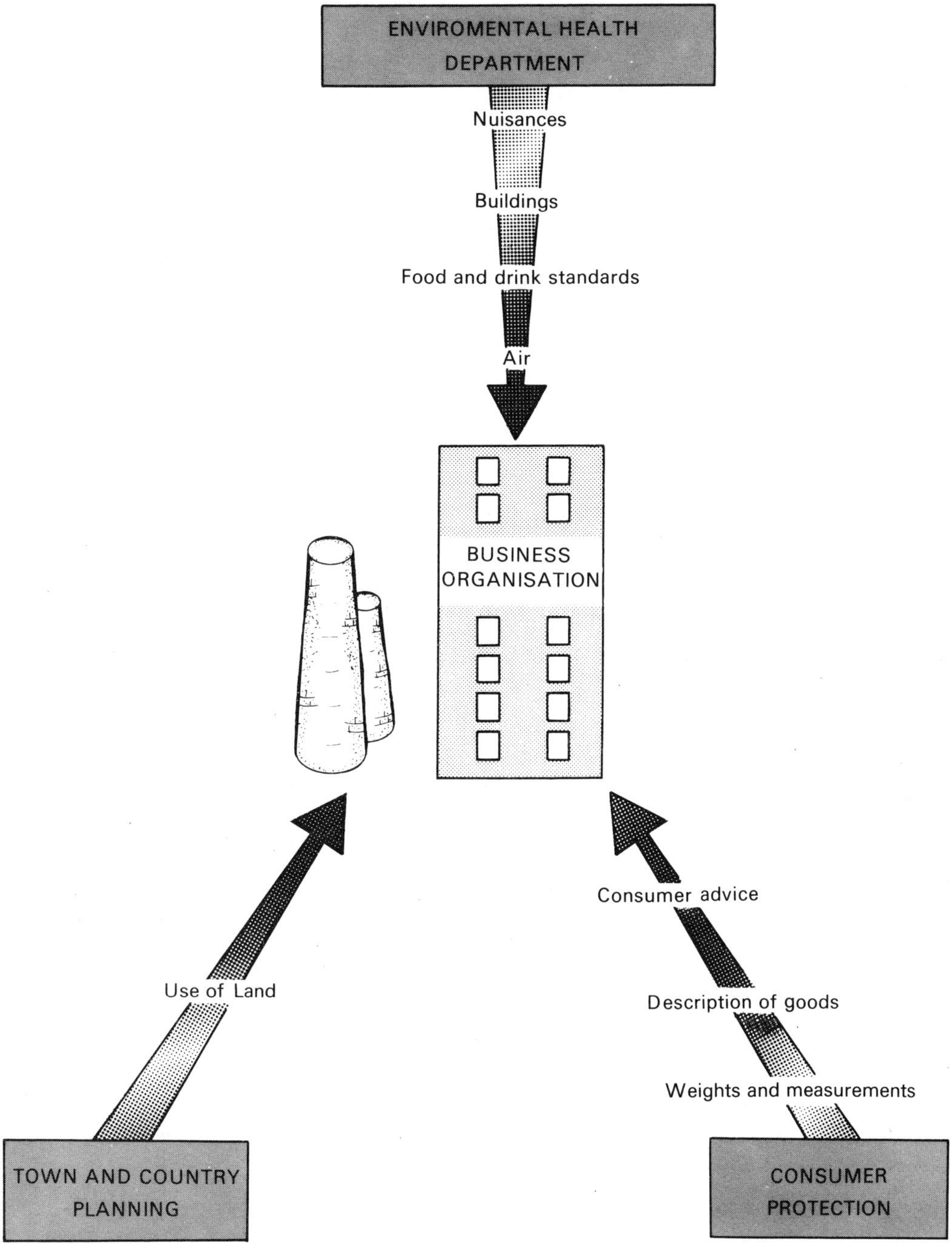

Fig. 1.3: Local authority activities which directly affect the organisation

block or even if it is for a domestic house extension. If a business organisation wishes to appeal against the authority's decision, they must go to the Secretary of State for the Environment.

In the field of **consumer protection,** the authorities carry out weights and measurements inspections. They also enforce the 1968 Trade Descriptions Act against anyone giving a misleading description of goods and services. The local authorities have the right to set up consumer advice centres, which may provide pre-shopping advice and information, and handle consumer complaints.

Central government

The central government is made up of the Prime Minister, who is appointed by the Crown, and his ministers, who are predominantly drawn from the House of Commons, with the remainder coming from the House of Lords. All appointments are made by the Crown on the recommendation of the Prime Minister. The Prime Minister is the head of the government and the position of the Prime Minister depends upon the maintenance of a majority in the House of Commons. The Prime Minister works through a personally selected Cabinet of ministers to formulate national policy.

The ministers in the Cabinet, in conjunction with the other ministers, are held responsible for the activities of particular government departments. After Parliament has passed the necessary legislation it is the government departments, operating through and with local authorities, statutory boards and other sponsored government bodies, which are the principal means of putting government policy into effect. Hence it is the activities of these departments which impinge most directly upon the business organisation.

Table 1.2: The main government departments which have an indirect effect on the business organisation

Department	*Function*
Civil Service Department	Deals with all aspects of the employment of civil servants. Responsible for ensuring that high standards of administration and management exist in government departments. Directly responsible for the work of the Central Office of Information and Her Majesty's Stationery Office.
The Home Office	Concerned with the administration of justice, criminal law, the police, prison and probation services, fire and civil defence services, race relations, immigration, public morals and safety and the control of explosives, fire-arms, dangerous drugs and gambling.
The Lord Chancellor's Office	The Lord Chancellor acts as speaker of the House of Lords and Custodian of the Great Seal. Concerned with the administration of the courts and of the law. Responsible for law reform.
The Law Officers' Department	Through the Attorney-General and Solicitor-General it represents the Crown in major civil, criminal and international proceedings. Provides legal advice for the government, and is ultimately responsible for the enforcement of criminal law.
The Foreign and Commonwealth Office	Through its diplomatic service it maintains relationships with foreign countries and represents British political and commercial interests abroad.
The Ministry of Overseas Development	Administers the aid programme to the Third World.
The Ministry of Defence	Administers and controls the army, navy and air force.
The Department of Education and Science	Promotes and supports schools, further and higher education establishments, research programmes, libraries, museums and the arts.
The Department of Health and Social Security	Administers the National Health Service, and the social services provided by local authorities. Responsible for the administration of social security payments and benefits.

Government departments
The government departments are generally organised under a Secretary of State or minister. The departments are financed by money provided by Parliament, and run by members of the civil service. A large proportion of the information on which they base their decisions may emanate from their own legal, economic and statistical advisers or in some cases from their own information division. In certain cases they may be helped by advisory bodies, such as councils or committees, whose function is to provide the information on which a decision might be based. The majority of these committees are formed on the orders of the minister concerned, although in some cases there may be a statutory obligation for him to consult a standing committee. Departments may also derive information about a particular issue from a Royal Commission like that which considered the siting and timing of the third London airport.

If there is a change in government this will be unlikely to affect the actual function of a particular department, although it may influence its organisation and the general direction of its policy.

The activities of some government departments cover the whole of the UK. The Ministry of Defence falls into this category. Other departments—such as the one dealing with employment—cover just Great Britain. Certain departments—for instance, the Department of Education and Science—cover just England and Wales. Finally, the activities of some departments—such as the one responsible for the environment—are restricted to England. This apparent gap in the coverage of some departments is bridged by the existence in Scotland and Northern Ireland of their own government departments, and in Wales by the Welsh Office which is responsible for the affairs of Wales. The areas of responsibility could be further influenced by any development on the subject of devolution for Scotland and Wales.

The administrative work of the various central government departments embraces every aspect of national affairs. It covers *economic* issues like inflation, unemployment, the balance of payments, economic growth and the distribution of income and wealth; *industrial relations* problems between employers and trade unions; *social* issues involving poverty, living standards, housing, education, general health and welfare; *environmental* questions concerning the use of land, pollution and the destruction of the countryside; *legal* matters embracing the rights of the individual, the employer and the business organisation. Finally, it includes Britain's *international* role in terms of giving aid to the Third World countries, influencing world political opinion, and trying to ensure stability and peace. All these activities have an impact on the business organisation, either by directly regulating, aiding or promoting its affairs or by indirectly creating a favourable social, political, economic and legal environment in which it may operate.

Government departments with an indirect impact
Table 1.2 summarises the indirect contribution made by the main government departments to the creation of a favourable business environment.

Government departments with a direct impact
The seven central government departments which have a direct influence on the business organisation are illustrated in Fig. 1.4 (page 8).

The Treasury is officially headed by the Lord Commissioners, with the Prime Minister as the First Lord, aided by the Chancellor of the Exchequer and five junior lords. In practice the Chancellor assumes overall control and is assisted by the Chief Secretary to the Treasury (a political post), the Financial Secretary and a Minster of State.

The Treasury formulates Britain's overall economic policy. It performs this function through four major sectors of operation.

1. The **Domestic Economy Sector** which designs and controls fiscal, monetary and counter-inflation policies.
2. The **Chief Economic Adviser's Sector,** which prepares forecasts on the state of the economy and advises on broad economic issues.
3. The **Overseas Finance Sector** which handles Britain's reserves of foreign currency, international monetary issues, and overseas aid.
4. The **Public Sector Group** which controls the level of public spending.

These activities impact on the business organisation in a number of different ways. Changes in overall economic policy are usually announced as part of the government's budget. These will directly influence levels of consumer demand, business confidence and the availability of capital finance, hence indirectly influencing the business organisation's investment plans, pricing, profitability, wages policies and employment prospects.

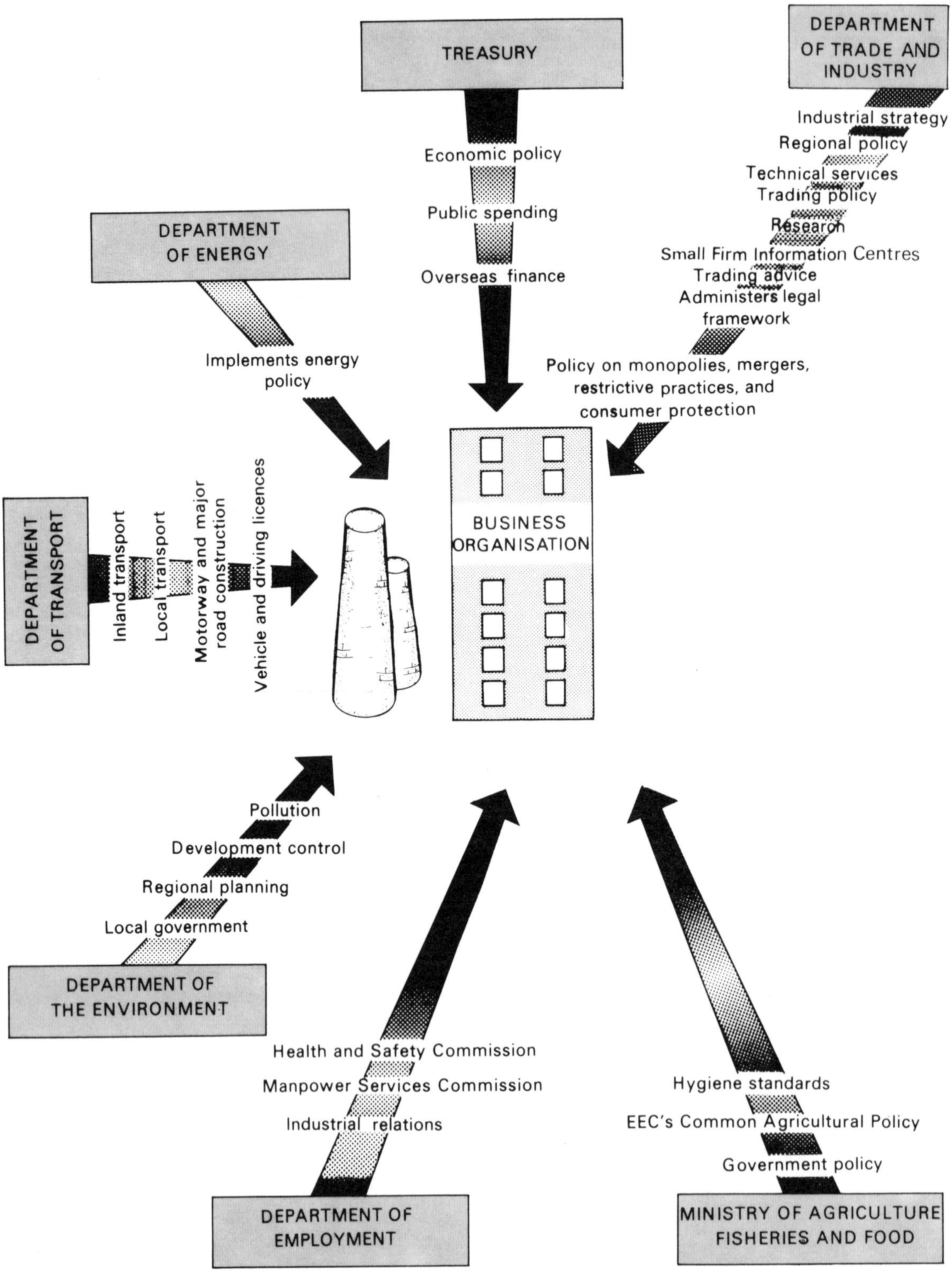

Fig. 1.4: Central government activities which have a direct impact on the business organisation

The Treasury may use its controls over public spending to stimulate particular types of business organisations—for example, in the October 1977 budget it was announced that an extra £400 million was to be spent by local and central government to boost the ailing construction industry, and to increase employment by 30,000 jobs. Many other examples of the impact of Treasury economic policy will be investigated in Chapter 5.

The Treasury ministers are responsible for two other institutions which have a direct impact on the business organisation:

1. The **Board of Inland Revenue** which is responsible for the administration of the laws concerning income tax, capital gains tax, corporation tax, capital transfer tax, petroleum revenue and development land taxes. It also operates stamp duty. It works with the Chancellor of the Exchequer and the Treasury on the implementation of any tax changes emanating from the budget.

Obviously the Inland Revenue will handle the business organisation's tax position. It may have further dealings with the business organisation as its duties include the valuation of real property for local authority rating and compensation for compulsory purchase.

2. The **Board of Customs and Excise** which is responsible for the collection and administration of value added tax and other customs and excise duties. Like the Inland Revenue it has to work closely with the Treasury on all these matters and comes into direct contact with the business organisation when establishing its tax liability.

The Board also carries out a number of functions for other government organisations. These include exchange currency controls, and the drawing up of UK overseas trade statistics.

The new **Department of Trade and Industry** came into being in June 1983 following the reelection of the Conservative Government. The department combines the functions of the previous Department of Industry with the commercial relations and trade functions of the Department of Trade. This means that it takes responsibility for general industrial strategy and the industrial aspects of regional policy. The Scottish and Welsh Offices exercise certain regional industrial policy functions in Scotland and Wales.

The department sponsors a large number of manufacturing industries ranging from paper, timber and board to machine tools and mechanical engineering. It offers certain technical services to industry and promotes industrial research and development. In association with the Scottish and Welsh Offices, the department runs a chain of twelve Small Firm Information Centres throughout Great Britain. The centres offer free advice to people wishing to establish a business and help established small firms to find the answers to their problems.

For business organisations in the private sector, the Department of Trade and Industry undoubtedly offers considerable guidance and support. In the case of the public sector, it is actually responsible for such organisations as the British Steel Corporation and British Shipbuilders.

The department supports British interests overseas by negotiating on trade and commercial matters—for example, it deals with questions arising out of membership of the European Economic Community (EEC). It also administers British protective tariffs.

These activities obviously help to create a favourable environment in which the business organisation may trade abroad, but in fact the department goes much further. Through the British Overseas Trade Board (which it sponsors) it attempts to encourage British export interests. The board offers specialist export advice to business organisations which are trying to sell abroad. For example, it provides them with information on the market prospects for particular types of commodities. It also helps with business visits abroad, the setting up of trading contracts and advises on overseas trade fairs. It even has a unit specialising in exports to Japan which provides organisations with advice on selling to the Japanese.

Under the direction of the Secretary of State for Trade and Industry a Minister for Corporate and Consumer Affairs takes responsibility for administering the legal framework within which business organisations operate. He also has responsibility for company law, all aspects of insolvency, patent, trade mark and copyright matters.

Another area of his work concerns the protection of consumers against any unfair practices or developments which might take place amongst various business organisations. He is responsible for policy on fair trading and in fact the department's Secretary of State appoints the Director-General of Fair Trading. The department is also responsible for policy on mergers, monopolies, restrictive practices (including competition rules) and home and consumer safety over the sale of such products as fireworks. Finally, it is concerned with standards and weights and measures, including metrication on which it liaises with the Metrication Board.

The **Ministry of Agriculture, Fisheries and Food** (MAFF) is responsible for the administration of government policy for the agriculture, horticulture and fishing industries. Consequently it exercises control over the business organisations which make up these industries. In the field of agriculture its responsibilities include the administration of market support schemes, and the EEC's Common Agricultural Policy. It also encourages research aimed at improving farming techniques and eliminating animal and plant diseases.

From the point of view of food, the MAFF is particularly concerned with hygiene standards, the composition of food, the use of additives, labelling and advertising.

The **Department of Employment** is primarily concerned with industrial relations policy and helping business organisations to make the best use of the nation's manpower resources. The latter is performed by assisting employees to find suitable jobs through the department's national network of Job Centres and the maintenance of a Professional and Executive Register. The department tries to improve the quality of the work force through its Manpower Services Commission, which operates an Employment Service Agency and Training Service Agency; these run public employment and training services and give the government general advice on manpower issues.

The department tries to improve industrial relations in the business organisation through its Advisory Conciliation and Arbitration Service (ACAS), which exercises certain moderating powers in settling disputes. It is also responsible for the Health and Safety Commission which guards the safety, health and welfare of employees and gives advice to industry on matters relating to these issues.

The Department of Employment provides useful statistical information for industry in the form of statistics on labour and industrial matters. Its main publication is the *Department of Employment Gazette*. It is also responsible for the computation of the cost of living index. These statistics are invaluable to organisations handling wage claims or dealing with conditions of employment.

The **Department of the Environment** (DoE) is responsible for a variety of different issues relating to the type of physical environment in which people live and work and business organisations operate. These issues include local government structure and finance, regional planning, development control and general land policy, the problems of the inner cities, new towns, commercial property, countryside property and minerals, housing and construction, and environmental pollution. The DoE is also responsible for guarding and administering historic buildings and ancient monuments.

The **Department of Transport** directly assists the business organisation by taking responsibility for both the main inland transport industries—including the railways, buses, freight and ports—and also local transport services. It is also responsible for motorway and major roadway contruction. Finally, it administers vehicle and driving licences and safety. All the department's activities should contribute towards the more efficient transportation of the business organisation's products and raw materials.

The **Department of Energy** is responsible for government policy relating to all sources of energy. It has over-all responsibility for the development and exploitation of gas and oil off the British coastline. It acts for the government in its dealings with the nationalised coal, gas and electricity industries and is responsible for the Atomic Energy Authority. Finally, it sponsors the government's energy conservation policy and so is likely to be instrumental in determining the type of energy that business organisations may use in the future.

The Bank of England

The position of the Bank of England

The Bank of England is at the centre of the nation's financial affairs. It plays a major role in controlling the monetary system and provides an important lead for the nation's financial institutions.

The Bank was founded in 1694 when it was established by an Act of Parliament and granted a Royal Charter as a corporate body in return for a loan to the government. Its present position as the state's central bank was formally recognised by its nationalisation in 1946. The nationalisation Act vested the affairs of the Bank in the hands of a Court of Directors headed by the Governor of the Bank of England. The Crown appoints the directors and all these officials work very closely with the Treasury to formulate monetary policy and control monetary affairs.

The nationalisation Act placed the Bank of England in a position of control over all the other banks. These powers were extended by the 1971 Competition and Credit Control Measures which increased the Bank of England's influence over both the commercial banks and the financial institutions. However, the controlling influence of the Bank of England is based not so much on statutory powers but rather a general acceptance amongst all financial institutions of its powers, responsibilities and status.

From its central position the Bank of England performs a number of very important functions which have a considerable impact on the affairs of the business organisation. The Bank influences the general monetary stability of the financial environment in which the business organisation operates. It also affects its ability to secure capital finance, the level of demand for its goods and the ease with which it may trade abroad.

The main functions of the Bank of England

1. *The Bank of England acts as the government's banker*

This function involves holding the central public accounts of the government, which include the Exchequer, the National Loans Fund, the National Debt Commissioners and Dividend Accounts and a number of minor associated accounts. All the receipts and payments of the various government departments are also channelled through the Bank of England. If the departments are short of money they may borrow overnight from the bank in the form of Ways and Means Advances.

All the borrowing carried out by the government is collectively referred to as the National Debt, and it is the Bank of England which handles this debt. This involves issuing government stocks and maintaining a register of stockholders and paying them any dividends as they fall due. The Bank is registrar for about 200 government, government-guaranteed, commonwealth and corporation stocks. About one-seventh of the Bank's total staff is engaged in this activity, which is probably one of its most time-consuming duties.

Apart from providing a means of borrowing for the government, the adjustment of the National Debt by these open market operations of buying and selling government securities also has important implications for monetary policy, in that they make it possible for the Treasury through the Bank of England to influence the availability and cost of credit.

Finally, like any good banker, the Bank of England provides financial advice to its customers. Due to its central position it obviously has the opportunity to derive a clear over-all picture of the financial system and thereby provide the government with extremely useful information for the formulation of its monetary policy.

2. *The Bank of England handles the nation's international financial affairs and relationships*

The Bank attempts to maintain the foreign exchange value of sterling through the operations of the **Exchange Equalisation Account.** It is in this account that the UK central reserve of gold and currency is held. This may be used to maintain the position of the pound in terms of foreign currencies (the mechanics behind these adjustments are discussed in Chapter 6).

The Bank of England represents the interests of the nation in the affairs of such international organisations as the International Monetary Fund, the International Bank for Reconstruction and Development and the EEC.

3. *The Bank of England controls the currency issue*

In consultation with the Treasury the Bank decides upon the required size of the **fiduciary issue** (those notes not backed by gold) and is also responsible for coinage. In England and Wales the Bank of England is the only issuing authority, whereas in Scotland and Northern Ireland their banks have the right to issue notes, although they are generally backed by Bank of England notes.

4. *The Bank of England acts as banker to the commercial banks*

All the commercial banks settle their transactions with each other through their accounts with the Bank of England. The existence of these commercial bank accounts at the Bank of England helps the London and provincial **clearing houses,** because they are able to draw cheques on a particular bank or to pay cheques in that have been drawn.

5. *The Bank of England acts as lender of last resort to the money market*

The Bank is pledged to help the London discount houses if they have become short of funds. It may do this in one of three ways. First, it may provide money by buying bills from the discount houses. Secondly, it may buy bills from the commercial banks thus releasing more funds for them to lend as call money to the discount houses. Finally, it may lend them money for seven days at a rate of interest which is in keeping with very short-term interest rate movements (Minimum Lending Rate).

6. *The Bank of England manages the government's monetary policy*
The unique position of the Bank of England as the fulcrum of the financial system, and its special relationship with discount houses, commercial banks and other financial institutions, places it in an ideal position to manage government monetary policy. This is performed with general guidance from, and in consultation with, the Treasury. By the use of a variety of monetary weapons the Bank of England is able to influence the size of the money supply and control the availability and price of credit. (These methods of control are discussed in detail in Chapter 5.)

International institutions which affect the organisation

There are a large number of international institutions which have some sort of influence on the organisation. Some of these institutions are basically political in nature, some economic, some social, some legal and some a combination of all four. This section will be concerned with major examples of such institutions.

The United Nations
The United Nations officially came into existence on 24 October 1945. Its main objective is to maintain world peace and security by creating those political, economic and social conditions which are conducive to such a situation. Obviously, through its efforts to maintain world stability the United Nations will be helping to create the type of environment in which the business organisation can prosper. Membership of the United Nations is open to any nation provided it has the recommendation of the Security Council. The United

Fig. 1.5: The major institutions of the United Nations

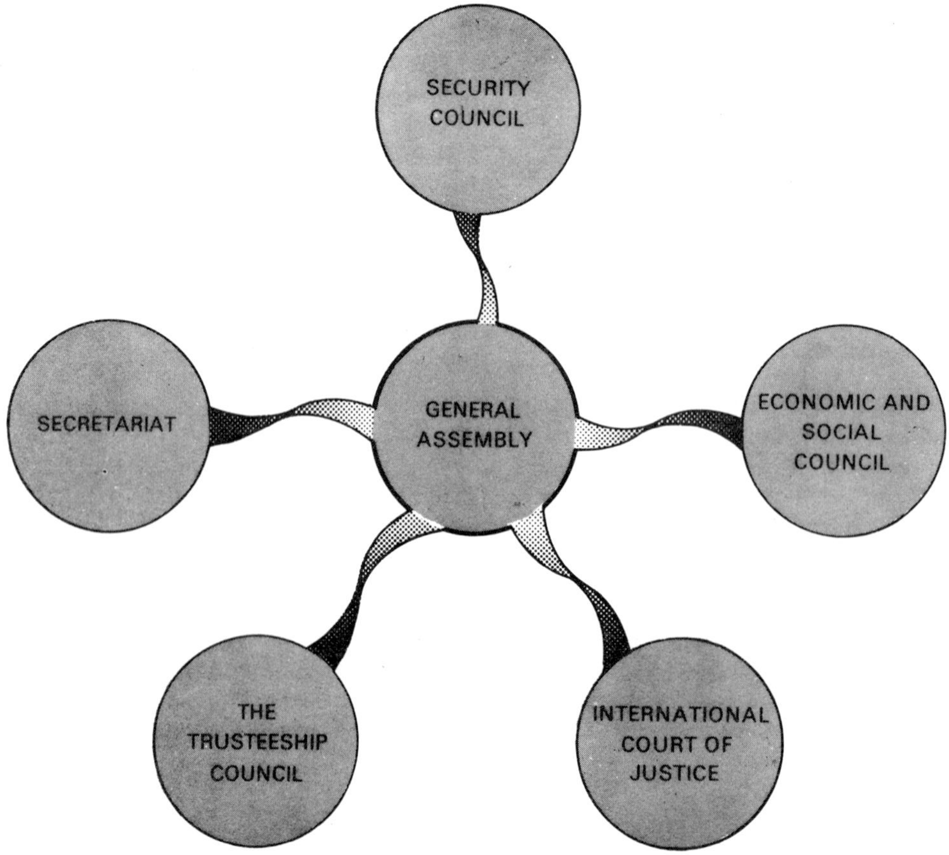

Nations Organisation tries to achieve its objectives through the operation of six major institutions, which are shown in Fig. 1.5.

1. The **General Assembly** is composed of all the members of the United Nations. Its basic function is to discuss any matter relating to the Charter on which the United Nations was formed. Discussions may cover such matters as political, economic and social security, humanitarian, cultural, legal and administrative problems. Decisions on major issues must be carried by a two-thirds majority, whereas for other matters a simple majority of those present is required.

2. The **Security Council** has the responsibility for maintaining international peace and security. The Council consists of five permanent members, namely China, France, the Soviet Union, the United Kingdom and the United States, and ten other members who are elected by the General Assembly for two-year terms. Each member has one vote. On issues involving procedure, decisions may be reached on the basis of an affirmative vote of at least nine of the fifteen members. However, on substantive matters nine votes are still required, but they must include the agreement of the five permanent members. This effectively gives the permanent members the power of **veto** on any decision.

The Council has the right to investigate any dispute or situation which might lead to friction between two or more countries, and may even call on the assistance of armed forces where it is felt to be necessary.

3. The **Economic and Social Council** administers the functions of the United Nations concerning international, economic, social, cultural, educational, health and related matters.

4. The **International Court of Justice** is made up of fifteen independent judges, who have been elected for periods of nine years by the General Assembly and Security Council. The court exercises its jurisdiction on all matters relating to the United Nations Charter, and then any matters concerning treaties or conventions which are referred to it.

5. The **Trusteeship Council** was set up to look after the interests of countries who have yet to achieve complete self-government and have been placed under the guidance of the United Nations during the intervening periods.

6. The **Secretariat** is headed by the Secretary-General who is assisted by an international staff.

The International Bank for Reconstruction and Development

The idea for such a bank was conceived at the Bretton Woods Conference of 1944, and the bank actually came into being in June 1946. It operates within the United Nations Organisation and its basic objective is to provide finance and technical assistance to encourage the development of the Third World.

The bank is a self-supporting organisation drawing its funds from the capital subscribed by its member countries, sales of its own securities, sales of parts of its loans, repayments and net earnings.

During the first thirty-five years of its operations it lent a total of $68,150·3 million for schemes concerned with education, agriculture, industry, water, energy and transport development. It also backs up this financial assistance by providing expert advice for member countries on all development programmes.

Through the affiliated **International Finance Corporation,** which was established in 1956, it attempts to encourage business organisations to set up, develop or diversify in the underdeveloped world. Encouragement may be offered by subscribing to share capital or offering long-term loans.

General Agreement on Tariffs and Trade (GATT)

The GATT was signed in 1947 and came into force in 1948. It operates within the United Nations Organisation and it is basically an informal arrangement of countries whose objective is to reduce barriers to international trade. Obviously such efforts are likely to confer considerable benefits on the overseas trading position of business organisations.

There are three provisions of the agreement that stand out above the rest. First, member countries must not discriminate in matters of trading against other members. Secondly, where a member country feels that it must protect its domestic industries it may use only tariffs and this must be after consultation with other countries. Thirdly, continuous efforts and negotiations should be held to reduce tariff barriers. With regard to this third provision the most successful recent negotiations to reduce tariffs was the Tokyo Round of talks from 1973 to 1979 which involved about one hundred countries and resulted in an agreement that over a period of seven years beginning on

1 January 1980, there should be an average cut in tariffs amongst industrialised countries of 34 per cent on manufactured goods.

In 1964 GATT established the **International Trade Centre** whose function is to furnish information and provide training to the developing world on the marketing of their exports.

The International Monetary Fund (IMF)

The IMF was established in 1945 as a result of the Bretton Woods Conference of 1944. It operates within the United Nations Organisation and its main purpose has been to try to establish stability in international financial affairs, thus facilitating orderly financial trading arrangements for countries and their business organisations. This has been done by trying to promote international co-operation and exchange-rate stability, and by providing loans from the IMF to countries experiencing balance of payments problems. For example, in 1976 the IMF helped the UK stop the slide in the value of sterling. The IMF is controlled by a Board of Governors on which each member government is represented. The board has delegated many of its powers to twenty executive directors who are based in Washington and who are responsible for the administration of the IMF.

The IMF operates on a **'quota' basis,** which is the method by which a member's voting rights, voting powers and contribution to the fund are established. The quota is determined by the IMF and adjusted every five years. Member countries have to contribute 25 per cent of their quota in the form of reserve assets and 75 per cent in their own national currency. They may then automatically borrow up to 25 per cent of their quota to finance, for example, a balance of payments deficit. If they need any more they have to seek the approval of the directors of the IMF. This will probably be given only if the country pledges itself to putting its domestic house in order. This was the situation in 1976 when the UK had to undertake to reduce the size of its public sector borrowing requirement and the volume of domestic credit expansion. Interest and service charges are payable on any borrowing, and the loan usually runs for a period of 3–5 years.

The IMF also significantly influences world liquidity through its **special drawing rights** scheme. Special drawing rights are international assets introduced in 1970 to help member countries to finance balance of payments deficits. Basically each member country is allocated special drawing rights in accordance with the size of its quota and they may be used to obtain currency to settle the country's debts. This may be done either directly by participants in the scheme and treated as a kind of overdraft, or indirectly through the IMF, in which case the IMF will designate to the applicant a country with a strong currency in exchange for special drawing rights. These special drawing rights are treated as part of the donor country's reserves and must be repaid at a later date in the form of foreign currency or gold.

Organisation for Economic Co-operation and Development (OECD)

The OECD developed in 1961 out of the strictly European Organisation for European Economic Co-operation. This heralded the membership of Canada and the United States of America. The other member countries are Australia, Austria, Belgium, Denmark, Finland, France, West Germany, Greece, Iceland, the Irish Republic, Italy, Japan, Luxembourg, the Netherlands, New Zealand, Norway, Portugal, Spain, Sweden, Switzerland, Turkey and the UK.

The basic objective of the OECD is to encourage economic and social welfare by helping member governments to formulate policies with this aim in mind. Obviously the achievement of such an objective will help to improve the environment in which the business organisation operates. The OECD also attempts to encourage its members to help the developing world.

The OECD is headed by a council which is composed of representatives of each member country and is responsible for the formulation of policy. It is assisted by an executive committee, plus numerous other committees who are responsible for a particular aspect of its work, such as, for example, economic planning, the environment or agriculture.

The European Economic Community (EEC)

The EEC was set up by the Treaty of Rome which was signed on 25 March 1957. It was originally composed of six countries: Belgium, France, Germany, Luxembourg, Italy and the Netherlands. On 1 January 1973 these six were expanded to nine by the inclusion of the UK, the Irish Republic and Denmark. It was further expanded in 1981 when Greece became a member.

The basic objective of the community is to promote economic, social and political union in order that Europe may be strong enough to influence world affairs. The Treaty of Rome laid down a number of specific objectives through which this over-all aim was to be achieved. These included:

1. The creation of a **Customs Union** and the phased adoption of a common external tariff against non-members.
2. The creation of a situation which would facilitate the **free movement** of labour and capital within the community.
3. The acceptance of a **Common Agricultural Policy,** which aimed at achieving an improvement in productivity, a fair income for the farmer, stable markets, security of supply and reasonable prices for the consumer.
4. The achievement of **economic union** by the creation of common transport and trading policies and the co-ordination of financial, commercial, economic and social obectives. The Treaty forbids any trading practices or arrangements which restrict free competition.
5. The eventual achievement of some degree of **political union.**

The following institutions have been established and developed by the community in order to achieve these objectives.

The **Council of Ministers** takes all the major decisions concerning community policy. It is composed of one minister from each country representing the particular field of discussion. The presidency of the council alters every six months. Unanimous support is required from all members of the council for any decision involving a very important issue. However, issues of less importance may be carried by a 'qualified majority' of weighted votes. The votes are weighted as follows:

Germany	10
Italy	10
Britain	10
France	10
Greece	5
Belgium	5
Netherlands	5
Irish Republic	3
Denmark	3
Luxembourg	2
Total	63

A 'qualified majority' usually requires forty-five votes from not less than six countries. However, if the point at issue has been referred to the council by the commission then any forty-five votes will be considered as a majority.

The **Commission** of the EEC acts as its executive body. It guards the EEC's interests, puts into practice the decisions of the council and puts forward proposals concerning the operations of the EEC. It also manages the Regional Fund, the Social Fund, the Customs Union and aspects of European agriculture and steel. The commission is composed of fourteen commissioners drawn from the member countries. Two are taken from Germany, France, Italy and Britain and one from each of the other member countries. They are appointed by the council as a whole on the recommendation of the ten governments of the member countries. The commissioners take an oath to serve the EEC first and to accept no instructions from their own governments or any outside body. The commission is assisted in the performance of its duties by a staff of international civil servants.

The **European Assembly** is referred to as either an assembly or parliament, although its major function is consultative in that it has to comment on the proposals put forward by the commission and the council. It also acts as a forum for discussion and criticism of the EEC's activities. In fact, it has developed considerable powers by which it may debate and question the EEC's budget and expenditure. It is made up of directly elected representatives drawn from each of the member countries.

The **Economic and Social Committee** is a consultative body, made up of representatives from each country, which is concerned with the position and status of employers, trade unions, the professions and farmers. Like the assembly its function is to comment on the proposals put forward by the commission and council.

The **European Court of Justice** is one of the most important institutions of the EEC. The Community's Treaty defines its task as that of ensuring 'the observance of law and justice in the interpretation and application of the Treaty'. This involves ensuring that the EEC's treaties and legislation are complied with. This may require the court to deal with a complaint from the commission against a member country, or handle a dispute between member states, firms or community institutions. The court sits in Luxembourg and is made up of one judge drawn from each member state. The judges are re-appointed every six years.

The Court of Justice is the EEC's highest court. However, as it has no enforcement agency its judgements have to be carried out through the national courts. The Treaty limits it to dealing with constitutional and commercial matters. It has no real jurisdiction over criminal or civil issues.

Very often issues are raised in the national courts involving community law. Under these circumstances the issue may be referred to the European Court of Justice for a preliminary ruling. However, if there is no possibility of an appeal being made from the national court, it is compulsory to refer the matter to the Court of Justice. In 1975 sixty-nine cases were referred by national courts to the European Court of Justice for a preliminary ruling. Britain submitted only one, whereas Germany submitted the most—twenty-six. This probably reflects the fact that Britain has yet to become European-minded on legal matters; however, this situation is likely to change in the future. The majority of the sixty-nine cases submitted involved issues connected with farm policy, trading practices, the social security position of migrant workers and common tariffs.

Unlike a great deal of international law, which usually has very little direct effect on firms and individuals, community law ruled through the European Court of Justice may have a significant impact on their actions. The business organisation may be directly influenced on such matters as engaging in unlawful trading practices. For example, in 1966 the Grundig–Consten case concerning anti-cartel rules was eventually dealt with by the European Court of Justice. Grundig had granted Consten, a French company, exclusive dealer rights on the sale of its recording machines. NEF, another French firm, was able to import the machines and to sell them at a lower price than Consten. Consequently, Consten took NEF to the French courts and sued them over the infringement of their private rights as exclusive dealers. NEF took the matter to the EEC Commission which ruled that the exclusive rights contravened Article 85 of the Treaty of Rome. Consten and Grundig took the case to the European Court of Justice who upheld the Commission's findings and so the agreement had to be terminated.

Membership of the EEC has had a tremendous impact on the UK business organisation.

Advantages of membership of the EEC

Membership of the EEC has produced a number of positive advantages:

1. It has placed the business organisation in a more dynamic, faster-growing environment, experiencing a higher standard of living and higher wages than the UK. Inevitably this should result in some beneficial spin-offs to UK organisations, especially those with initiative who should be able to expand and develop to their full potential.

2. Europe offers the business organisation a larger potential market of over 250 million people, which is almost five times the size of the UK domestic market. Entry into this larger market should help to stimulate the growth of those organisations who have the potential to enjoy considerable economies of scale from larger operations.

3. The removal of trade barriers should help to encourage the growth of exports to community countries and also create more competition from community industries, which might put inefficient UK industries out of business, thus redirecting national resources towards the more productive sectors of the economy.

4. The freer movement of factors of production, and in particular capital, should facilitate better investment opportunities for business organisations, which may result in the creation of technological and managerial improvements and the possible creation of more jobs.

5. Business organisations should benefit from the collaboration between member countries on technological, industrial and research projects. The enlarged EEC should provide the strength, resources, and markets which EEC organisations require if they are to embark confidently on development projects in such fields as aerospace and computers, in order to compete with economic giants like the USA and USSR.

6. Business organisations may benefit from the activities of, and sources of finance made available by, the European Investment Bank, the Regional Development Fund and the European Social Fund.

The **European Investment Bank** was set up under the Treaty of Rome in 1958. Its basic function is to provide finance for projects which benefit less developed regions, projects which are outside the scope of individual member states, and projects which are of common interest to a number of member countries. The bank is controlled by a board of governors drawn from the member states.

The **Regional Development Fund** was set up

in 1975 in order to help member countries with their regional problems. The financial assistance that it provides for member countries is allocated on a quota basis, with the quota reflecting the community's assessment of the nation's needs. In 1977 Italy had the highest quota at 40 per cent and the UK the second highest at 28 per cent. The amount of finance involved is still relatively small and so does little more than supplement member countries' other sources, for example the fund's total budget in 1977 was only £263 million.

The **European Social Fund** was set up in 1957 to help with the problems of redeploying redundant workers. It performs this function, for example, by providing assistance with retraining programmes.

Disadvantages of membership of the EEC

Membership of the EEC has had a number of disadvantages for the UK business organisation.

1. The benefits listed above will be realised only if the UK business organisations respond quickly enough to the new potential markets. Failure to do this might mean that UK businesses would be in danger of being swamped by competition from European firms. If this were to happen the resultant increase in imports would have an extremely adverse effect on the UK balance of payments.
2. Business organisations operating in Europe have the problem of dealing with new and different legislation concerning competition policy, transport standards and technical requirements.
3. There is a danger that if complete economic, social and political union were to be achieved, it might result in a sacrifice of national sovereignty which in turn might lead to a situation where the national government could not truly or effectively represent the interests of the UK business organisation.
4. It is felt that the Common Agricultural Policy will result in a higher cost of living for the UK resident and will pose an increasing burden on the balance of payments.

It is still too early to say whether membership of the EEC has conferred more benefits than disadvantages on the UK business organisation.

2. The Government's Relationship with the Business Organisation

The UK's mixed economy

The type of environment in which the business organisation operates in the UK is largely determined by its relationship with the government. An investigation of this relationship must include a consideration of the degree of respective responsibility taken by the government and the business organisation in decisions involving the allocation of scarce resources, the methods by which those resources are turned into goods and services, and the way in which the rewards from production are distributed.

In the UK responsibility for all these decisions rests with both the government and business organisations; therefore they are said to be operating in a mixed economy. Further study of this relationship between the government and the business organisation should include a consideration of two of the most important factors in the relationship—money and national income. The former provides the means by which the government and the business organisation are able to carry on their activities in a modern highly specialised industrial society. The size of the latter is determined by the combined efforts of both business organisations and the government, and therefore represents a measure of their effective performance and also ultimately determines the standard of living of the nation.

Types of economic systems

A mixed economy is composed of aspects both of a completely free-enterprise, capitalist system, and of one that is centrally controlled. Therefore, in order to appreciate the characteristics of this essentially middle stage, it is necessary to consider how the basic decisions at the core of the relationship between the government and the business organisation are made in both these two extreme systems.

A completely **free-enterprise, capitalist system** is where the factors of production (apart from labour) are owned privately and are used to earn profits for their owners (the entrepreneurs) who bear the risks associated with combining them with labour for the production of goods and services which are to be sold. Decisions concerning the allocation of resources are governed entirely by free market forces. Competitive pressures determine the methods of production employed by the business organisations. The distribution of rewards to the factors of production are decided entirely by their respective scarcity value. There is no country in the world which operates a pure capitalist system, although West Germany is probably the nearest to approaching it.

The completely free-enterprise system has been criticised for a number of reasons:

1. An allocation of resources which is based entirely upon free market forces is unlikely to satisfy all public wants, such as law and order and defence.

2. There may be a wastage of resources as the market may be divided between a large number of small competitive units all producing a similar product. These conditions may result in production inefficiencies as the small units are unable to enjoy economies of scale. (The converse to this might apply where one or two firms tend to dominate the market, which might create a threat to consumer sovereignty, a wastage of resources on advertising and a barrier to the entry of new firms into the market.)

3. Under an unregulated free market system fluctuations are likely to appear in the level of economic activity in the economy. This may result in slumps and depressions and associated problems of unemployment, lack of growth, poor investment, price instability and balance of payments difficulties.

4. The system by which income and wealth are to be distributed will probably foster tremendous

inequality which is likely to result in a failure to maximise social welfare and could lead to serious hardship and deprivation for families on very low incomes.

A **centrally controlled system** is one where all decisions concerning the allocation of resources, methods of production and distribution of the rewards of production are taken by the central administration. This would result in a situation where the factors of production, including labour, would be directed by the state and the state would decide what should be produced, in what quantities and by which production outlet. The central administration's decisions on these matters would be based upon the planner's view as to what would be beneficial for the community and the state as a whole. Obviously, it would be easier for the central administration to achieve its objectives if it actually owned all the available resources. Consequently, it is usual under a controlled economy for there to be considerable, if not total, public ownership of wealth and very little, if any, activities influenced by market forces. The nearest system to reflect this 'command economy' is that operating in Russia, although even this has traces of free choice and market forces in operation.

The centrally controlled system is often criticised on the grounds that because of its centralised nature the decision-making process reflects the views of a small group of officials rather than the wishes of society in general. This lack of sensitivity is aggravated still further by the removal of the market mechanism, thus destroying the consumer's means of expressing his wishes. The system is also criticised on the grounds that it requires a very large bureaucratic machine to collect the information on which over-all planning decisions might be based. Inevitably such a system is susceptible to corruption and inefficiency.

The **mixed economy**, which is made up of elements of both the free-enterprise, capitalist system and the centrally controlled system, is one where the ownership of the means of production is vested in both private and government hands. Decisions concerning the allocation of scarce resources are decided by a combination of market forces and government intervention and control. Decisions regarding methods of production are regulated by government controls and are made by a combination of government public sector organisations and private sector organisations. The distribution of the rewards of production are determined by the personal accumulation and inheritance of wealth, the share of rewards accruing to the different factors of production, taxes and social payments and services.

The mixed economy in the UK combines elements from these two extreme systems, and therefore gives rise to a situation where there are state-controlled, central government and local government services, public-sector nationalised industries, and the National Enterprise Board, operating alongside free enterprise and private companies, partnerships and sole traders.

The development of the UK mixed economy

The UK mixed economy developed from what was essentially a free-enterprise system which had been in operation between the seventeenth and the nineteenth centuries. During this period the main function of the government had been to provide law and order and defence on a national basis, and locally it had concerned itself just with the administration of justice and the relief of the poor.

The **Industrial Revolution** of 1760–1830 resulted in the development of an urbanised society, which was employed in the factories rather than on the land. This development led to the creation of social and economic problems which could be handled only by central government action. The newly created urban society lived under terrible conditions in towns whose growth had been totally unplanned, and which consequently lacked any basic amenities. The expanding market economy suffered wild fluctuations in activity rates and there were resultant problems of unemployment.

In the second half of the nineteenth century a **social reform** movement developed in response to these problems. The movement was supported by the enlightened factory owner Robert Owen and the important administrator Edwin Chadwick. The movement was particularly concerned with public health, Poor Law reform and working conditions.

However, it was not until 1906 that the **Liberal Government** introduced a number of very important measures which heralded the acceptance by the government of a more significant and active role in the economy. In 1908 they introduced the Old Age Pensions Act, in 1910 the first Employment Exchange, and in 1911 National Insurance.

The government's role in the developing mixed economy took a significant leap forward when the depression of the 1920s and 1930s encouraged the economist, **J. M. Keynes,** to change the direction of economic thinking by the publication in 1936 of his *General Theory of Employment, Interest and Money*. In this book he took the unprecedented view that economic stability and a reduction of unemployment could be achieved only by greater government intervention. His ideas were not fully accepted until the publication in 1944 of the 'Employment Policy' White Paper, in which it was acknowledged that it was the government's responsibility to intervene in the economy in order to achieve full employment.

The mixed economy as the UK knows it today was finally established in 1945 when the Labour Government introduced the **welfare state** and nationalised the railways, coal, steel, the power industries and the Bank of England. Since that time the degree of respective responsibility taken by the government and business organisations on the major issues of allocation, production and distribution have varied according to the political environment of the day.

Treatment of the major decisions in the UK mixed economy

The allocation of resources is determined by both free market and government forces. Government intervention is necessary because if the allocation of scarce resources was left entirely to free enterprise business organisations there is a danger that certain needs of society would never be satisfied. This is because in practice the free market system reflects only private monetary costs and benefits. This means that decisions concerning the allocation of resources are based entirely upon whether they are viable in economic terms. Obviously the provision of law and order and defence, or health, education and housing services cannot be considered in these terms. There are very few people who would refuse anybody medical treatment if they were desperately ill but could not afford the cost of treatment, or who would claim that a child should only be housed and educated if his parents could afford to pay for it. Consequently, there are some areas where the market mechanism seems to have failed and so it is necessary for the government to step in and to provide the necessary services.

The first of these areas involves the satisfaction of **'social' wants,** that is, those which arise out of the general needs of society. They include such services as law and order, and defence, which the market mechanisms is incapable of providing because individuals who do not pay for the services cannot be excluded from the benefits. Obviously no one is going to pay for an army from which everyone benefits, including those people who have not necessarily paid for it. Therefore it is necessary for the government to intervene and to satisfy such wants out of public revenue.

The second area where the market mechanism seems to have failed is over the satisfaction of **'merit' wants.** This is a highly controversial area of government intervention as they involve wants such as housing, health and education which could conceivably be satisfied in the private sector. However, as some individuals or their guardians might be unable to afford these services, and as they confer benefits on both the private individual and also society at large, it is felt desirable for the government to provide them. For example, an individual benefits from the education that he receives and so does society in the sense that a better-educated individual is capable of contributing more to general welfare. The fundamental problem with this type of government intervention is that there is no mechanism by which the government may assess the general public's desire for services. Obviously the public's feelings are partly reflected in the voting mechanism, but this lacks the final judgement of the price mechanism as operated in the private sector.

Methods of production are controlled by the government for three main reasons: to protect the consumer, to improve efficiency, and to protect the worker in his working environment. In the first case the government feels it necessary to protect the consumer from exploitation arising out of unfair trading practices. These might occur as a result of the development of a monopoly, the establishment of a merger, or the use of a restrictive trade practice. These are controlled by appropriate legislation such as the Fair Trading Act and the activities of such bodies as the Monopolies and Mergers Commission. The government also attempts to reduce the bargaining disadvantage the consumer suffers due to his lack of knowledge about a particular product by offering him consumer advice, and ensuring that certain production standards are maintained.

To improve efficiency the government may provide direct assistance to industry in terms of advice or finance, or alternatively it may go a stage further and actually take the industry under public control. This may be carried out by nationalisation or by purchasing a share in the industry through the National Enterprise Board. (The motives behind this type of action have already been outlined in the opening chapters of Book 1.) Finally, the government feels that it is necessary to protect the work force in its working environment by legislation such as the 1974 Health and Safety at Work Act, and by the work of the central and local government departments.

The **distribution of income and wealth** in a completely free market economy would depend almost entirely upon such factors as the laws of inheritance, the distribution of innate talents, the availability of educational opportunities, social mobility and the structure of markets. However, such a distribution will not necessarily be acceptable to the bulk of the population. The majority of the members of any society would advocate some form of redistribution if it was found that a small minority of the population were living in splendour whilst the vast majority were existing in a state of abject poverty. In the UK mixed economy there has been a gradual equalising of the distribution of income and wealth. In fact the Green Paper on the 'Wealth Tax' (Cmnd 5704) in 1974 revealed that the wealthiest 1 per cent of the population held 38 per cent of the wealth in 1960 but only 25 per cent in 1973, and the wealthiest 5 per cent held 64 per cent of the wealth in 1960 but only 53 per cent in 1973.

The extent to which this is felt to be desirable is obviously a political issue, although all governments whatever their political persuasion have always employed a number of devices to create a degree of equality. First, the tax system has been used to level down incomes, wealth and capital. For example, the UK has a progressive income tax system. In April 1983 income tax operated in progressive bands from 30 per cent for income between £1 and £14,600 then rising through five additional bands to a top rate of 60p in the pound for taxable income in excess of £36,000. In addition to this 60p in the pound there was an additional surcharge on levels of investment income over £7,100 of 15 per cent.

Secondly, some of the income which has been collected in taxes has been transferred to other sectors of the economy through transfer payments such as grants and social benefits and the provision of free services. This is reflected in Table 2.1 (p. 22) which indicates how the UK system generally takes a larger percentage of income in tax and other contributions from the wealthier groups and those with fewer personal commitments, and redistributes it as benefits in kind, indirect benefits and cash benefits to those who are less well off.

The **stability of the economy** may be maintained by planned government intervention. Experience has shown that an unregulated economy, where free market forces operate unchecked, is likely to follow a fluctuating path through time, pitching violently from boom to depression with resultant disastrous effects on employment, growth, prices and the balance of payments. Consequently, it is felt to be necessary for the government to try to check these tendencies by direct intervention in the economy. This may be undertaken by operating policies to direct the behaviour of business organisations, by adjusting government spending or taxation, or by influencing the financial and monetary system in order to create that level of activity which maintains full employment, stabilises prices, encourages economic growth and creates a balance of payments equilibrium.

One of the most important factors for the working of the mixed economy is money; therefore in the next section it will be necessary to consider its function and significance.

Money and consequences of changes in its value

Money is basically anything which is generally accepted as a means of exchange and a standard of value in payment for goods and services or to settle debts or other obligations. It provides the essential means by which the government and business organisations carry on their activities. Due to its immense importance changes in its value seriously affect the business environment.

The characteristics of money

The main qualities or attributes of money may be classified under two main headings—those which influence its acceptability and those which relate to its physical nature.

Acceptability

Money will only be acceptable if it is easily recognised by those people who are to use it. People must have confidence in its value, and so similar units of money must be of a consistent standard, that is, a battered £5 note must be worth as much

Table 2.1: Redistribution of income through taxes and benefits, 1979, all households[1]

United Kingdom											*£ per year[2] and numbers*
	Decile groups of original income										*All house-holds*
	1	*2*	*3*	*4*	*5*	*6*	*7*	*8*	*9*	*10*	
Average for each decile group of original income (£ per year[2])											
Original income	10	270	1,390	3,160	4,380	5,430	6,460	7,670	9,360	14,040	5,220
+ Direct benefits in cash	1,720	1,630	1,430	820	530	500	430	370	380	380	820
Gross income	1,730	1,900	2,830	3,980	4,910	5,930	6,880	8,040	9,740	14,420	6,040
− Direct taxes[3]	—	20	170	550	850	1,080	1,330	1,570	1,990	3,250	1,080
Disposable income	1,730	1,890	2,660	3,430	4,050	4,850	5,560	6,470	7,750	11,170	4,960
− Indirect taxes[4]	380	440	670	880	1,060	1,200	1,340	1,550	1,770	2,320	1,160
+ Benefits in kind[5]	780	680	740	870	960	980	960	960	970	1,010	890
Final income	2,120	2,130	2,730	3,420	3,950	4,630	5,190	5,880	6,960	9,860	4,690
Average per household (numbers)											
People	1·6	1·6	1·9	2·5	2·9	3·1	3·1	3·2	3·3	3·8	2·7
Adults	1·3	1·5	1·6	1·8	1·9	2·0	2·1	2·3	2·5	3·0	2·0
Children	0·3	0·1	0·3	0·7	1·0	1·1	1·0	0·9	0·8	0·8	0·7
Workers	0·1	0·1	0·6	1·1	1·4	1·6	1·7	2·0	2·1	2·6	1·3
Retired people	1·0	1·2	0·8	0·3	0·2	0·1	0·1	0·1	0·1	0·1	0·4
Number of households in sample	678	677	678	678	677	678	678	678	677	678	6,777

[1] These estimates are based on the Family Expenditure Survey.
[2] Rounded to nearest £10.
[3] Income tax and employees' national insurance contributions.
[4] Domestic rates, VAT, excise duties, etc, as well as taxes paid by industry and passed on to consumers, such as employers' national insurance contributions and commercial rates.
[5] Imputed benefits from government expenditure on education, health, housing, etc.
SOURCE: *Social Trends*, 1982, CSO (HMSO).

in terms of its purchasing power as a newly printed one. This confidence is usually enhanced by legal backing or authorisation from the state, which by performing this function is endorsing the money's value and thereby establishing its acceptability.

Durability
Physically money must be durable, that is, it should be capable of making a large number of transactions over a relatively long period of time without suffering physical deterioration. Money

which could be easily destroyed, lost or needed constant replacement would be incapable of performing its basic functions. Money must also be portable. Obviously notes and coins which can be carried in a pocket, purse or wallet fulfil this requirement. Finally, money must be easily divisible into a range of descending units of value. Thus it will be possible to make transactions involving both thousands of pounds and also a few pence.

The main functions of money

1. *Money acts as a medium of exchange* in that it may be accepted in exchange for goods and services. Acting in this way it removes the need for barter, because instead of having to exchange goods and services directly for each other a single intermediate transaction may be made. In a modern economy, practising the division of labour, this monetary system of exchange is vital. The alternative of a barter system suffers from such problems as the difficulties associated with matching large indivisible units, coping with inconsistencies in quality, establishing a rate of exchange, and the physical problems connected with the perishable nature of the goods being bartered and the difficulties of transportation and storage.

2. *Money acts as a unit of account or measure of value.* It performs this function operating as a measuring rod or standard by which the relative exchange values of various goods and services may be expressed and measured. For example, a shirt may be said to be worth £5, and a pair of trousers £15, so that the pair of trousers is said to be worth three times as much as the shirt. Money also has the advantage of making it possible to measure output not just in terms of the number of items produced but rather in terms of so many £millions worth of goods and services. This is vital for the calculation of national output, which is composed of an extremely varied and diverse range of goods and services.

3. *Money acts as a standard of deferred payment,* which means that it is possible for debts and future payments to be measured and recorded. Consequently, payments may be made in the future with the reasonable assurance that the value of money that they represent will not be less than at the time of the transaction. This function of money makes it possible to operate a credit system without which the activities of the government and business organisations would flounder. For example, in the case of the government the whole of the national debt represents the credit of the nation. In the case of a business organisation such as a builder, he is totally dependent on credit; he generally buys his materials on credit and pays for them only when the project is completed and he has been paid.

4. *Money acts as a store of value.* Money will only perform the previous function satisfactorily if its value does not seriously deteriorate with time; therefore it must be capable of retaining and storing its value in exchange. This function provides people with the confidence to save and to defer demands for payment.

Money in the UK

In the UK money takes the form of **notes and coins,** which are legal tender up to a certain amount. The 1844 Charter Act gave the Bank of England the right of sole issue of notes and coins. (The banks in Scotland and Ireland are allowed to issue some money of their own provided it is backed by the Bank of England.) Originally the Bank Charter Act stipulated that all the notes and coins issued by the Bank of England should be backed by gold with the exception of a fiduciary issue of £14 million which would be issued in trust. Since 1844 this fiduciary issue has gradually increased until with the abandonment of the gold standard and the transfer in 1939 of the Bank of England's gold reserves to the Exchange Equalisation Account the whole note issue has become largely fiduciary.

The existence of a **commercial deposit banking system** facilitates the creation of credit. This means that the number of transactions that money is capable of carrying out is restricted not by the physical quantity of money but rather by the limits imposed on its ability to sustain and create credit through the deposit banking system. Deposit banking is the method by which commercial banks accept deposits, and then allow their customers to draw cheques and bills in excess of their balances. There are a variety of ways in which this may be done, although the most usual is either through an overdraft on a current account, or alternatively a loan account may be opened for the customer and credited with a set amount of money. Therefore the ability of the commercial banks to create credit which may be used to settle transactions is limited not by the amount of notes and coins that they hold, but rather by the amounts they need to keep in reserve in order to meet the demands of customers.

A simple example will help to clarify this point. If all the commercial banks in the economy held 10 per cent of all the money deposited with them in the form of cash and highly liquid assets to meet the demands of depositors, also if customers demanded all the credit they could possibly have, then in this situation the effect of a £2,000 cash deposit with one of the banks would be to create a total of £18,000 worth of credit. This is because the bank which received the original £2,000 deposit would be in the following position. It would have to hold 10 per cent of the £2,000 (that is, £200) to meet any demands from customers, which would mean that it would be able to lend or advance £1,800 to its customers. If this was carried out, the bank's balance sheet would read as shown in Table 2.2.

Table 2.2: Balance sheet

Assets		*Liabilities*	
Cash	£200	Deposits	£2,000
Advances	£1,800		
Total	£2,000	Total	£2,000

The customer who borrowed the £1,800 might then use it to buy goods and services, and the recipients of the cheques might then deposit them with a second bank with a similar requirement for maintaining a reserve of 10 per cent. If this were the case, £180 would be held in a cash form and £1,620 advanced. Taken to its logical conclusion this would result in the situation depicted in Table 2.3. Therefore, on the basis of the original deposit of £2,000 the deposit banking system would have effectively created an additional £18,000 worth of spending in the form of credit. Credit would have been created in exactly the same way if it had been the government rather than a private customer who had been undertaking the borrowing.

Consequently, in the UK economy bank deposits are used via the cheque system to settle transactions, and their structure and ability to support a credit system determines the number of transactions which may be carried out by this means backed up by a given volume of notes and coins.

Table 2.3: Credit creation

	Deposits	*Advances*	*Cash*
First bank	£2,000	£1,800	£200
Second bank	£1,800	£1,620	£180
Third bank	£1,620	£1,458	£162
Sum for an indefinite number of banks	£14,580	£13,122	£1,458
Totals	£20,000	£18,000	£2,000

Measuring changes in the value of money

It is very difficult to define exactly what is meant by the value of money, because it varies between individuals according to their personal circumstances, nature, income and tastes. Consequently, it is necessary to generalise and state that the value of money depends upon its ability to command goods and services in exchange. Therefore the major factor that will be responsible for alterations in its value will be changes in the general price level. This means that during a period when prices are falling, the value of money will be increasing as its purchasing power will be increasing, whereas during a period when prices are increasing, the value of money will be decreasing as its ability to command goods and services will be decreasing.

The situation where prices are falling is referred to as **deflation.** It is characterised by falling total monetary demand, which causes a reduction to occur in the output of goods and services, in the level of aggregate demand, in money incomes and in the general price level. It may be triggered off by a fall in government expenditure, a reduction in consumer demand, or a fall in business confidence and hence investment.

The situation where prices are rising is referred to as **inflation.** This is caused by two basic factors:

1. **Cost–push factors,** which relate to increases in the costs of production, such as labour and raw materials, which tend to push up the price of the product.
2. **Demand–pull factors,** which refer to pressures on demand which cannot be satisfied and so prices are pulled up. This pulling effect may very often be caused by an increase in the money supply, which has not been matched by a comparable increase in the production of goods and services.

Index numbers are the most important method of measuring changes in the value of money. An index number is a measurement over time designed to show average changes in the price, quantity or value of a group of items. A price index is constructed by selecting a typical representative group of items, whose prices are recorded in a particular year. This year is designated as the base year, and is referred to as 100. If prices in subsequent years increase by, say, 24 per cent then the index will move up to 124, and if they were to fall by 16 per cent then it would stand at 84. Therefore increases in prices are denoted by figures greater than 100 and reductions by figures less than 100.

As the index deals with a group of items whose relative importance to the consumer will vary, it is necessary to weight the respective items used in the calculation of the index. This may be done by measuring the relative importance of each item to the consumer's total expenditure. For example, suppose that he spends 25 per cent of his income on food, 10 per cent on clothing and 30 per cent on housing; then if the price of food rose by 20 per cent, clothing by 15 per cent and housing by 30 per cent, the increase in living expenses for these items might be calculated as follows:

$$\text{Increase} = \frac{\text{Sum of increase in each item} \times \text{its weight}}{\text{Sum of the items' weights}}$$

$$\text{Increase} = \frac{(20 \times 25) + (15 \times 10) + (30 \times 30)}{25 + 10 + 30}$$

$$= 23{\cdot}85 \text{ per cent}$$

If the starting point for these increases had been the base year of 100, the index would now stand at 123·85. There are four main price index numbers, which are of particular significance to both the government and business organisations.

(i) The **Index of Wholesale Prices** records the changes in the prices of materials which have been purchased, of output, and of commodities which have been wholly or mainly imported into the United Kingdom. The weighting system is based on the Census of Production, supplemented by short-term statistics for production, information supplied by trade associations, and various other sources. It is published in the Department of Trade's magazine, *British Business*, and also in the *Monthly Digest of Statistics*.

(ii) The **World Commodity Prices Index** shows movements in world prices of food-stuffs and raw materials. The *Economist* publishes the index and bases it on 28 different commodities, of which food contributes 55·6 per cent of the index and industrial raw materials 44·4 per cent.

(iii) The *Financial Times* **Index of British Industrial Shares** shows changes in the price of thirty industrial equity shares. It is calculated and recalculated almost hourly. It is of crucial importance as it reflects the state of the stock market and hence the level of business confidence in the economy. It also helps to guide investors and the institutions in their decisions concerning the buying and selling of shares.

(iv) The **General Index of Retail Prices** is the one with which most people are familiar. This deals with changes in the price of items which appear in the shops. It is prepared by the Department of Employment and appears in a number of publications, including the *Department of Employment Gazette*, the *Monthly Digest of Statistics* and *Economic Trends*. Table 2.3 (p. 26) shows the index as it appears in the *Monthly Digest of Statistics*. The table clearly shows that the main purpose of the index is to measure the monthly degree of change in the retail price of goods and services for the whole field over which households distribute their expenditure, ranging from food to transport and vehicles. The index is calculated in a number of stages:

(a) First the base year is established. As Table 2.4 shows, the current index relates to January 1974 = 100. The previous series shown were based on January 1962 and January 1956. It is possible to link the series by the use of statistical techniques. The base year has to be regularly altered to take account of changes in the nation's spending habits.

(b) Using information derived from the Annual Family Expenditure Survey a list is drawn up of the typical purchases of the average household. This does not include the 11 per cent of all households made up of pensioners, nor the 3–4 per cent of households made up of the very wealthy. The relative importance of the various items in the household's expenditure is then established and weights are applied accordingly. In Table 2.3 all the items have been allocated a total weight of 1,000 and this has then been divided between the eleven categories of expenditure. The weights are altered annually to reflect the changes in the pattern of households' expenditure. A comparison of the weights operating in 1962 with those of 1981 illustrates how the share of income going on food

Table 2.4: General index of retail prices

	All items	All items except items of food whose prices show significant seasonal variations	Food	Alcoholic drink	Tobacco	Housing	Fuel and light	Durable house-hold goods	Clothing and foot-wear	Trans-port and vehicles	Miscel-laneous goods	Services	Meals bought and con-sumed outside the home[1]
	17 January 1956 = 100												
Weights 1962	*1,000*	–	*350*	*71*	*80*	*87*	*55*	*66*	*106*	*68*	*59*	*58*	
1962 January 16	117·5	–	110·7	108·2	123·6	140·6	130·6	102·1	106·6	126·7	128·2	130·1	
	16 January 1962 = 100												
Weights 1971	*1,000*	*956·8–958·3*	*250*	*65*	*69*	*119*	*60*	*61*	*87*	*136*	*65*	*54*	*44*
1972	*1,000*	*958·6–960·4*	*251*	*66*	*53*	*121*	*60*	*58*	*89*	*139*	*65*	*52*	*46*
1973	*1,000*	*957·5–958·7*	*248*	*73*	*49*	*126*	*58*	*58*	*89*	*135*	*65*	*53*	*46*
1970 Annual averages	140·2	140·2	140·1	143·9	136·3	158·1	145·7	126·0	123·8	132·1	142·8	153·8	145·5
1971 Annual averages	153·4	153·5	155·6	152·7	138·5	172·6	160·9	135·4	132·2	147·2	159·1	169·6	165·0
1972 Annual averages	164·3	164·1	169·4	159·0	139·5	190·7	173·4	140·5	141·8	155·9	168·0	180·5	180·3
1973 Annual averages	179·4	177·7	194·9	164·2	141·2	213·1	178·3	148·7	155·1	165·0	172·6	202·4	211·0
1974 January 15	191·8	189·4	216·7	166·0	142·2	225·1	188·6	158·3	166·6	175·0	182·2	212·8	229·5
	15 January 1974 = 100												
Weights 1978	*1,000*	*966·5–969·6*	*233*	*85*	*48*	*113*	*60*	*64*	*80*	*140*	*70*	*56*	*51*
1979	*1,000*	*964·0–966·6*	*232*	*77*	*44*	*120*	*59*	*64*	*82*	*143*	*69*	*59*	*51*
1980	*1,000*	*968·8–969·6*	*214*	*82*	*40*	*124*	*59*	*69*	*84*	*151*	*74*	*62*	*41*
1981	*1,000*	*970·4*[2]	*207*	*79*	*36*	*135*	*62*	*65*	*81*	*152*	*75*	*66*	*42*
1974 Annual averages	108·5	108·8	106·1	109·7	115·9	105·8	110·7	107·9	109·4	111·0	111·2	106·8	108·2
1975 Annual averages	134·8	135·1	133·3	135·2	147·7	125·5	147·4	131·2	125·7	143·9	138·6	135·5	132·4
1976 Annual averages	157·1	156·5	159·9	159·3	171·3	143·2	182·4	144·2	139·4	166·0	161·3	159·5	157·3
1977 Annual averages	182·0	181·5	190·3	183·4	209·7	161·8	211·3	166·8	157·4	190·3	188·3	173·3	185·7
1978 Annual averages	197·1	197·8	203·8	196·0	226·2	173·4	227·5	182·1	171·0	207·2	206·7	192·0	207·8
1979 Annual averages	223·5	224·1	228·3	217·1	247·6	208·9	250·5	201·9	187·2	243·1	236·4	213·9	239·9
1980 Annual averages	263·7	265·3	255·9	261·8	290·1	269·5	313·2	226·3	205·4	288·7	276·4	262·7	290·0
1980 January 15	245·3	246·2	244·8	241·4	269·7	237·4	277·1	216·1	197·1	268·4	258·8	246·9	267·8
February 12	248·8	249·8	246·7	244·7	269·7	241·7	278·2	220·4	199·8	274·4	262·9	251·0	273·3
March 18	252·2	253·2	251·1	247·7	275·2	243·8	282·3	223·1	203·1	278·0	265·3	253·4	276·3
April 15	260·8	262·0	254·1	259·4	292·9	269·8	289·1	224·9	204·6	288·0	272·6	258·4	281·9
May 13	263·2	264·7	255·7	260·4	294·3	272·1	300·5	226·0	205·5	290·4	274·6	260·0	288·9
June 17	265·7	267·1	257·9	261·7	294·3	275·1	315·3	225·9	206·7	293·0	276·9	260·8	290·9
July 15	267·9	269·3	259·9	265·1	294·3	277·0	322·8	226·4	207·5	294·0	279·4	263·9	294·8
August 12	268·5	270·5	259·0	265·2	298·4	278·8	324·1	227·8	207·3	295·0	280·3	264·5	296·5
September 16	270·2	272·3	259·0	272·3	298·4	280·3	330·8	229·2	208·4	293·9	283·9	266·2	299·9
October 14	271·9	274·1	259·3	274·6	297·9	283·7	337·4	230·8	208·4	295·1	287·9	267·4	301·5
November 19	274·1	276·3	260·0	274·6	297·9	286·4	348·8	232·4	208·8	295·8	289·2	278·6	303·7
December 16	275·6	277·6	262·7	274·6	297·9	287·4	351·4	232·5	208·1	298·8	291·0	280·8	304·6
1981 January 13	277·3	279·3	266·7	277·7	296·6	285·0	355·7	231·0	207·5	299·5	293·4	289·2	307·5
February 17	279·8	281·8	268·9	283·0	308·0	284·7	357·4	234·2	207·0	303·6	295·3	291·4	309·2
March 17	284·0[3]	285·9[3]	270·6[3]	299·8[3]	315·2[3]	285·9	357·5	234·9	207·6[3]	316·4	296·1	292·3[3]	311·8[3]
April 14	292·2	294·1	274·2	306·5	362·2	317·7	363·0	236·2	207·6	319·0	298·2	296·1	312·9
May 19	294·1	295·8	276·7	306·5	362·2	320·4	373·3	236·6	207·5	320·1	299·0	298·0	315·5
June 16	295·8	297·3	280·0	306·5	362·2	321·7	384·2	236·4	207·1	322·6	297·7	298·5	317·4
July 14	297·1	298·9	279·6	311·0	362·2	322·6	389·2	236·8	206·9	325·7	299·8	299·4	319·7
August 18	299·3	301·8	277·3	311·0	375·7	324·0	393·0	238·3	208·4	334·5	301·3	301·3	320·4
September 15	301·0	303·3	279·6	313·9	384·9	325·5	393·2	240·6	209·4	333·8	303·8	303·0	322·6
October 13	303·7	305·7	282·7	318·5	389·7	334·5	396·4	240·3	210·7	331·1	306·6	304·3	325·0
November 17	306·9	308·9	285·5	319·3	389·7	345·6	398·5	240·9	210·0	332·9	308·1	314·2	326·3
December 15	308·8	310·4	288·5	319·3	389·7	351·0	398·6	240·4	209·3	332·3	309·3	321·9	328·1

[1] The Cost of Living Advisory Committee (now renamed the Retail Prices Index Advisory Committee) recommended in 1962 that until a satisfactory index series based on actual prices became available half the expenditure on meals out should continue to be allocated to the food group and the other half spread proportionately over all groups, including the food group. The index for meals out for 16 January 1968 implicit in this recommendation was 121·4. Since January 1968 an index series based on actual prices has been available and indices in this series have been linked with the implicit index for meals out for 16 January 1968 to obtain indices for meals out with 16 January 1962 taken as 100.

[2] Provisional.

[3] Estimated.

SOURCE: Monthly Digest of Statistics, January 1982.

has declined as the weights have moved from 350 to 207, whereas now people are spending more of their income on buying and running their cars with a movement from 68 to 152 in the transport and vehicles category.

(c) The eleven main categories are calculated from the prices of about 350 separate goods and services. Changes in their prices are based on approximately 150,000 separate quotations which are taken each month.

(d) This information is then used to compute the changes that have occurred in prices since the base period, the weights are applied, and a final all-items index is calculated.

Index numbers provide a vital barometer of price changes, and hence alterations in the value of money. Consequently, they play an important role in determining future policy decisions made by both government and business organisations.

For the government they reflect changes in the cost of living, and hence the standard of living, of the nation. It is on this sort of information that many social and economic policies may be based. For example, rapid increases in prices might push up the cost of living to a level which caused severe hardship to certain groups in the community. As a result the government might try to alleviate the situation by the application of subsidies on key items of expenditure or by providing the lower-income groups with direct financial benefits.

For the business organisation the indices indicate how its costs of production are likely to be moving, what its future pricing policy should be, and thus provide the type of information about the business environment which will encourage or discourage general business confidence and therefore investment plans.

Consequences of changes in the value of money on the business environment

Falling prices, as illustrated by **a deflationary situation,** will result in an increase in the value of money, which will have a number of important implications for the business environment.

On the positive side it may encourage savings—as interest rates are likely to be higher, and the value of money is not depreciating—and this could mean that more funds are available for capital investment. Lower domestic prices will mean lower export prices, which could have a favourable effect on the balance of payments.

On the negative side there seems to be a relationship between deflation and a depression in the economy, with resultant unemployment. This is because deflation is accompanied by a fall in demand, especially of goods and services traditionally purchased on credit. This lower level of demand will lead to a decline in business confidence and then to a fall in investment. This in turn will slow down the rate of growth of the economy and also the level of demand for labour; therefore unemployment is likely to occur.

Rising prices, as illustrated by an **inflationary situation,** will cause a fall in the value of money with resultant effects on the business environment.

On the positive side a level of inflation around 5–6 per cent can help to stimulate demand, thereby increasing profits and business confidence. This would result in a higher level of investment, economic growth and a movement towards full employment. Such a situation would also tend to help debtors, especially the government who are responsible for the National Debt, the burden of which would obviously fall due to the reduction in the value of money.

However, on the negative side, once inflation has moved above this level—perhaps into double figures—this effect could be reversed. In the UK throughout the 1970s it was apparent that inflation could push up costs and in so doing squeeze profits (especially if the government was trying to counter inflation by the use of price controls). This had the effect of reducing business confidence, which inevitably resulted in a fall in the level of investment and ultimately a decline in employment opportunities. This situation may be aggravated still further by the fact that inflation tends to deter saving, which means that the supply of loanable funds will be reduced.

Inflation may also have an adverse effect on the balance of payments. Higher domestic prices will result in higher export prices and a loss of competitiveness. Also, unless inflation is running at a similar rate in other countries, imports will become more attractive as they will tend to be cheaper than the equivalent home-produced goods.

Inflation will have a serious effect on the distribution and value of income and wealth. Inflation will be particularly severe on those with fixed incomes or those with an important part of their income fixed—for example, pensioners, those living on unemployment benefits, those receiving income from annuity schemes and those living off past savings. Inflation will bring about a redistribution of income in favour of those who have the bargaining power to secure the largest wage and salary increases. This is generally those workers who occupy key positions in industry and where industrial action has an immediate effect on their industry and the economy as a whole. Throughout the 1970s the power workers, the miners, the car workers and the transport workers were able to wield this sort of collective bargaining power.

Finally, inflation is likely to cause a distortion in relative wages and salaries which may cause the wage mechanism in the labour market to result in a misallocation of labour. There will be a tendency for existing labour and new entrants on to the market to seek those jobs which are 'inflation-proof'. These types of jobs will tend to be in key industries and services or where the output of an industry is in excess demand or in inelastic demand. Under these circumstances the employer may be prepared to pay the higher wages as he is confident that he can pass on the cost increase in terms of higher prices without having a marked effect on his sales. Consequently, it may produce a drift of workers away from occupations where the good or service is not in excess demand and where consumers may not directly pay a price, such as in the health, education and police services. Nevertheless, such services may be making a contribution to total welfare in excess of the additional welfare derived from the output of more consumer goods.

The main components of national income and their practical importance to the business environment

The importance of national income

The fundamental decisions in the mixed economy need to be based on information concerning the amount of income available in the economy for distribution, the type and quantity of goods being produced under the existing system of resource allocation, and the level and composition of total expenditure in the economy associated with this form of distribution and level of production. In other words, the nation requires to know the amount that it pays itself, which may be referred to as **national income;** the value of goods and services which it produces, which may be referred to as **national product;** and the amount that it spends on goods and services, which may be referred to as **national expenditure.**

These three concepts are obviously equal, as the amount that a country pays itself must be equal to the value of the goods and services which it produces, which in turn must be equal to the total amount that it spends. Therefore, by measuring any one of the concepts of national income, product or expenditure it is possible to establish what should be the value of the other two. By analysing changes in the components of national income, product or expenditure it is possible to establish likely changes in the state of the business environment. Such information is of considerable value for the planning activities of both the government and business organisations.

Three methods of measuring national income

The expenditure method

This involves calculating the total amount of national expenditure undertaken in the economy in one year. Table 2.5 illustrates how these calculations were made by the Central Statistical Office in collaboration with other government departments and the Bank of England for the years 1970–80. These groups were also responsible for computing national income by the other two methods.

Table 2.5 shows that the main components of total expenditure are:

1. Consumers' expenditure, which refers to the expenditure on goods and services undertaken by private households.
2. General government final consumption, which covers the direct demand by central and local government for goods and services.
3. Gross domestic fixed capital formation (GDFCF) which includes expenditure on fixed assets such as buildings, plant and machinery, which is either used for replacing or adding to the stock of existing fixed assests. Any expenditure on maintenance or repairs is not included.
4. The value of the physical increase in stocks and work in progress, which refers to investment in short-term capital assets, and measures by how much stock levels and work in progress have altered during the course of the year.

The sum of these four components gives the total domestic expenditure at market prices. The remainder of the table illustrates how this figure is

le 2.5: The expenditure method

£ million

	1970	*1971*	*1972*	*1973*	*1974*	*1975*	*1976*	*1977*	*1978*	*1979*	*1980*
enditure											
sumers' expenditure	31,778	35,599	40,183	45,759	52,668	64,749	74,952	86,001	98,947	116,717	135,403
eral government final nsumption	8,991	10,250	11,675	13,380	16,618	23,039	26,776	29,237	32,969	38,241	48,337
s domestic fixed capital mation	9,470	10,517	11,606	14,238	16,833	20,416	23,567	25,753	29,741	34,251	40,050
e of physical increase in cks and work in progress	421	158	44	1,448	1,263	−1,483	847	1,950	1,075	2,539	−3,596
domestic expenditure at arket prices	50,660	56,524	63,508	74,825	87,382	106,721	126,142	142,941	162,732	191,748	220,194
rts of goods and services	11,594	13,008	13,725	17,233	23,130	27,197	35,430	43,572	47,705	55,183	63,198
s Import of goods and services	−11,147	−12,193	−13,772	−19,033	−27,398	−29,011	−36,916	−42,602	−45,536	−54,602	−57,832
s Taxes on expenditure	−8,417	−8,788	−9,267	−10,121	−11,457	−14,134	−16,532	−20,261	−23,221	−30,254	−37,287
idies	884	939	1,153	1,443	3,004	3,702	3,461	3,293	3,624	4,389	5,215
ss domestic product at ctor cost	43,574	49,490	55,347	64,347	74,661	94,475	111,585	126,943	145,304	166,464	193,488
property income from road	554	502	538	1,257	1,415	773	1,365	104	592	846	−38
ss national product	44,128	49,992	55,885	65,604	76,076	95,248	112,950	127,047	145,896	167,310	193,450
s Capital consumption	−4,428	−5,109	−5,900	−7,011	−8,648	−11,112	−13,415	−15,869	−18,686	−22,144	−27,045
onal income	39,700	44,883	49,985	58,593	67,428	84,136	99,535	111,178	127,210	145,166	166,405

RCE: Adapted from *National Income and Expenditure*, 1981, CSO.

transformed into national income in four main stages:

1. Trading activities abroad are included. Export expenditure on goods and services is *added* to total expenditure and imports are *deducted*; this is because the former brings income into the economy and the latter removes it.

2. Taxes on expenditure are *deducted*, and subsidies *added*, to the total figure to change it from one showing market prices to one showing factor costs. This then gives gross domestic product (GDP) at factor cost.

3. To turn this into a national figure it is necessary to adjust it for net property income from abroad. This refers to the balance between the receipts from abroad of rent, interest, profits and dividends and those paid abroad.

4. Finally, to turn this gross national product (GNP) figure into one representing national income it is necessary to make an adjustment for capital consumption, which refers to the amount of capital goods which have been used up during the productive process, and so represents a loss of real wealth to the country.

The expenditure figures are drawn from a variety of different sources. Consumers' expenditure is based mainly on the Census of Distribution, the Family Expenditure Survey, plus information from the Customs and Excise Department and the Department of Trade. The Census of Production provides information concerning GDFCF, stocks of raw materials and work in progress. Government departmental records provide the information concerning general government expenditure, taxes and subsidies. Import and export expenditure are taken from the balance of payments accounts.

There are a number of difficulties associated with the compilation of national income by this expenditure method. One of the greatest problems is that of trying to avoid **double counting.** This may arise when a product is included in total expenditure both in its final finished form and also in a semi-finished state. For example, double counting would occur if both the cloth from which a suit was made and also the suit itself were included in any calculation of national expenditure. The statisticians responsible for the compilation of national income try to avoid this danger

Table 2.6: The income method

£ m

	1970	*1971*	*1972*	*1973*	*1974*	*1975*	*1976*	*1977*	*1978*	*1979*	*19*[illegible]
Factor incomes											
Income from employment	30,546	33,481	37,836	43,773	52,263	68,195	77,598	86,037	98,477	115,330	137,
Income from self-employment	3,822	4,527	5,625	7,188	7,736	8,507	10,077	11,248	13,654	16,502	18,
Gross trading profits of companies	6,035	6,907	8,072	10,325	11,469	11,961	15,530	19,061	21,594	26,776	24,
Gross trading surplus of public corporations	1,447	1,520	1,681	2,063	2,558	3,091	4,502	5,087	5,384	5,543	6,
Gross trading surplus of general government enterprises	152	177	146	139	148	141	110	147	163	186	
Rent	2,769	3,082	3,530	4,178	5,299	6,315	7,388	8,443	9,578	11,286	13,
Imputed charge for consumption of non-trading capital	361	419	481	592	719	918	1,092	1,244	1,414	1,689	2,
Total domestic income	45,132	50,113	57,371	68,258	80,192	99,128	116,297	131,267	150,264	177,312	202
less Stock appreciation	−1,061	−1,055	−1,300	−2,835	−5,794	−5,373	−6,417	−4,850	−4,299	−8,649	−6,
Residual error	−497	432	−724	−1,076	263	720	1,705	526	−661	−2,199	−2,
Gross domestic product at factor cost	43,574	49,490	55,347	64,347	74,661	94,475	111,585	126,943	145,304	166,464	193
Net property income from abroad	554	502	538	1,257	1,415	773	1,365	104	592	846	
Gross national product	44,128	49,992	55,885	65,604	76,076	95,248	112,950	127,047	145,896	167,310	193,
less Capital consumption	−4,428	−5,109	−5,900	−7,011	−8,648	−11,112	−13,415	−15,869	−18,686	−22,144	−27
National income	39,700	44,883	49,985	58,593	67,428	84,136	99,535	111,178	127,210	145,166	166

SOURCE: Adapted from *National Income and Expenditure*, 1981, CSO.

by including goods only at the final stage of their consumption.

Another difficulty arises over the treatment of **transfer payments,** such as pensions or grants, which should not be included as part of general government expenditure as they do not represent a purchase of output but merely a transfer of ownership of spending power. Finally, it should be ensured that the transfer of the ownership of bonds and shares is not included as part of GDFCF as they do not represent an increase in the nation's durable capital equipment.

The income method

This involves calculating the total amount of income received each year by UK residents. Table 2.6 illustrates how these calculations were made between 1970–80. The table shows that total domestic income is made up of four main classes of income: income from employment, income from self-employment, profits or trading surpluses, and rent. The item entitled 'imputed charge for consumption of non-trading capital' is really a form of rent as it represents the imputed income of general government and private non-profit-making bodies from owner-occupied non-trading property. These different forms of income accrue to individuals and organisations in both the public and private sectors.

In order to arrive at the figure for GDP at factor cost, total domestic income is adjusted for stock appreciation and the residual error. **Stock appreciation** is deducted because it measures the increase in the value of stocks due to price changes occurring during the year, as distinct from changes in physical quantities of stocks held, and therefore does not relate to income earned from current physical output. The **residual error** is a balancing item between the estimates for the expenditure and income methods.

The fact that it is the income method which is adjusted is purely for convenience of presentation and does not imply that the estimates of expenditure are necessarily superior in accuracy to the estimates of income. The remainder of the table merely repeats the same adjustments for net property income from abroad and capital consumption as were employed in the expenditure method to arrive at a figure for national income calculated by the income method.

ble 2.7: The output method

£ million

	1970	1971	1972	1973	1974	1975	1976	1977	1978	1979	1980
riculture, forestry and ishing	1,266	1,435	1,556	1,972	2,075	2,549	3,109	3,343	3,639	3,935	4,296
roleum and natural gas	24	−15	35	26	−7	−30	521	1,845	2,488	5,144	7,649
ıer mining and quarrying	615	656	749	823	1,064	1,518	1,752	1,937	2,153	2,682	3,222
nufacturing	14,309	15,712	17,244	19,847	22,252	26,953	31,363	36,803	41,729	44,989	48,060
nstruction	3,050	3,431	4,328	5,383	5,912	6,730	7,539	8,141	9,831	11,743	13,025
s, electricity and water	1,385	1,572	1,751	1,912	2,141	2,681	3,416	3,828	4,222	4,552	5,803
nsport	2,749	2,933	3,324	3,803	4,120	5,165	5,939	6,869	8,052	9,333	10,084
mmunication	1,005	1,166	1,345	1,602	2,101	2,733	3,385	3,442	3,897	4,316	5,326
tributive trades	4,603	5,321	6,158	7,094	7,941	9,610	11,033	12,871	15,180	17,519	19,328
urance, banking, finance nd business services	3,097	3,631	4,346	5,574	6,148	7,197	8,534	9,928	11,286	14,169	18,288
nership of dwellings	2,368	2,627	3,011	3,572	4,609	5,581	6,633	7,670	8,685	10,218	11,996
fessional and scientific ervices	4,491	5,044	5,986	6,994	8,495	12,007	13,769	15,245	17,436	19,970	25,467
scellaneous services	3,645	3,746	4,350	5,191	5,786	7,769	9,426	11,217	13,495	16,266	18,734
blic administration and defence	2,874	3,385	3,852	4,342	5,303	6,999	8,148	8,668	9,641	11,165	13,987
al	45,481	50,644	58,035	68,135	77,940	97,462	114,567	131,807	151,734	176,001	205,265
justment for financial ervices	−1,410	1,586	−1,964	−2,712	−3,542	−3,707	−4,687	−5,390	−5,769	−7,338	−9,732
sidual error	−497	432	−724	−1,076	263	720	1,705	526	−661	−2,199	−2,045
ss domestic product at actor cost	43,574	49,490	55,347	64,347	74,661	94,475	111,585	126,943	145,304	166,464	193,488
t property income from broad	554	502	538	1,257	1,415	773	1,365	104	592	846	−38
oss national product	44,128	49,992	55,885	65,604	76,076	95,248	112,950	127,047	145,896	167,310	193,450
ess Capital consumption	−4,428	−5,109	−5,900	−7,011	−8,648	−11,112	−13,415	−15,869	−18,686	−22,144	−27,045
tional income	39,700	44,883	49,985	58,593	67,428	84,136	99,535	111,178	127,210	145,166	166,405

URCE: Adapted from *National Income and Expenditure*, 1981, CSO.

The majority of the information on which the income method is based comes from government organisations. The Inland Revenue provides 75 per cent of the information concerning incomes, the remainder coming from the Department of Employment, the Census of Population, and the Census of Distribution. The Inland Revenue also provides data concerning the gross trading profits of companies, which are based on its tax assessments. Government departments provide figures concerning the trading surpluses received by official agencies of one kind or another which carry on productive activities, such as the public corporations, nationalised industries, and trading branches of central and local government. An estimate of the total income from rent is built up by combining the estimated rent from the different types of property. The Census of Production provides the information on the changes in the value of stocks.

As with the expenditure method, there are a number of problems that may arise when computing national income by this method. First, care must be taken to ensure that transfer payments are not included as part of income otherwise they will have been counted twice. Secondly, false information given to the Inland Revenue may tend to understate national income.

The Output Method

This involves calculating the total value of goods and services produced during a one-year period. Table 2.7 illustrates how these calculations were made between 1970–80. The table shows how the various industries have been presented as far as possible in line with the Standard Industrial Classification 1968. The figures represent the contribution of each industry in the form of value added to total production. To arrive at GDP at factor cost, total output is adjusted for financial services and the residual error. The remainder of the table shows how this figure is adjusted in the same way as the expenditure and income method for net property income from abroad and capital consumption to arrive at a figure for national income.

The output figures are based mainly on the Census of Production with government sample surveys providing details of the output of industries not covered by the census, and government records providing details of public sector activities.

There are a number of problems associated with the calculation of national income by this method. The principal difficulty is that of trying to avoid double counting. There is an obvious danger of including both the final output of an industry and also the value of the raw materials used in its production. For example, if a freezer sells for £150, and it contains steel worth £40, the total final output should not be £190 but rather £150, as the £40 worth of steel is included in this final selling price.

This method tends to understate total production as it fails to include activities which do not appear on the market—for instance, the production of home-grown vegetables; all do-it-yourself

Fig. 2.1: The simple circular flow model

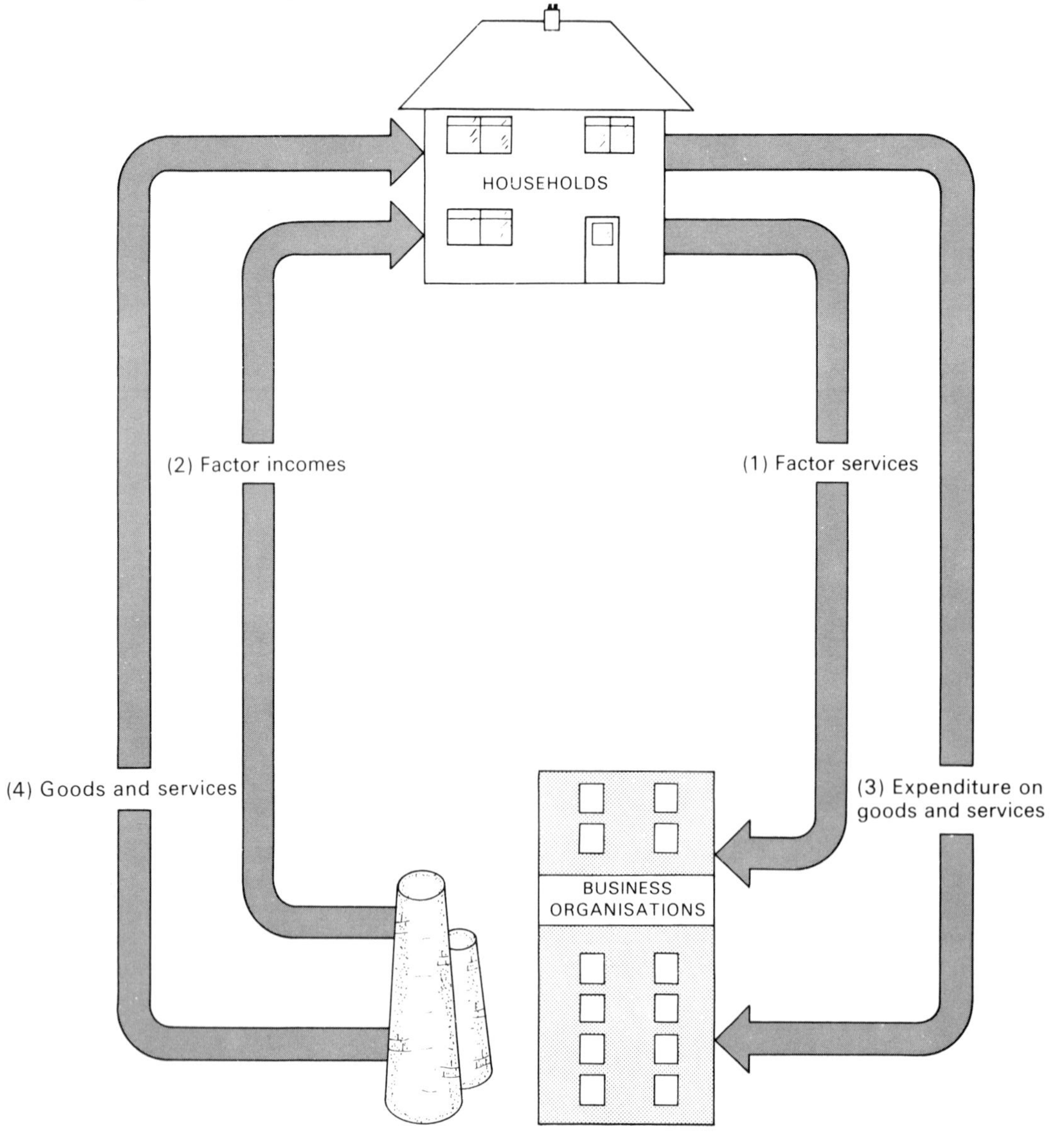

efforts; and the work of housewives and mothers, like washing, cleaning and child-minding. Finally, some industries, such as fishing and agriculture, actually consume some of their own output. In these cases efforts must be made to include this as part of the total output otherwise national income will be understated.

Theoretical analysis of national income by the circular flow approach
This section will concentrate on the development of a circular flow model of the economy. The model will help to explain the significance of the various components of national income, and how they interact with each other in the real world.

The **simple circular flow model** is shown in Fig. 2.1. The model is based on the flow of income between households and business organisations. Households provide business organisations with factor services, which are classified as labour, capital, land or enterprise; this is denoted by flow (1). In return for these factor services they receive payments in the form of wages, interest, rent and profit, which is shown by flow (2). Flows (3) and (4) illustrate how these incomes are used to purchase the goods and services produced by the business organisations. The flows are perfectly balanced, which means that the amount that households receive in the form of income (2) is exactly matched by the amount that they spend (3), which in turn is exactly balanced by the value of goods and services produced by the business organisations (4). Therefore, income equals expenditure which equals output. This state of balance is referred to as **equilibrium** and is a condition where there is no tendency for any of the flows of income, expenditure or output to change, and this would be the case in a situation where the demand for factor services and hence employment were stable.

In the real world there are other factors at work in the economy which either add to, or reduce, this flow of income; they are referred to as withdrawals and injections, and their effect is shown on the **full circular flow model** in Fig. 2.2 (p. 34).

1. **Withdrawals or leakages** are in the form of savings (S), taxation (T), and imports (M), all of which take income out of the system. The act of saving whether carried out by households or business organisations ultimately reduces the amount of income in the economy and hence the amount of expenditure undertaken by the households. Taxes imposed on business organisations or households have the effect of reducing the amount of factor incomes eventually received by the households. Expenditure on imports creates income for foreign business organisations and households and reduces that accruing to domestic business organisations and households. In the case of each withdrawal it will have the effect of reducing the level of income and expenditure in the flow, which will result in a fall in the demand for factor services, and hence in the level of factor incomes and the general level of activity and output in the economy.

2. **Injections** in the form of investment (I), government expenditure (G), and exports (X) represent an addition to the income of households that does not arise from the spending of domestic business organisations, or an addition to the income of business organisations that does not arise from the spending of households. The act of investing involves expenditure on capital goods which are used to aid further production. This investment expenditure will add to the total level of expenditure being undertaken in the economy. All forms of government expenditure whether on services, the nationalised industries or in the form of transfer payments will add to the total level of expenditure in the economy. Expenditure on exported goods will increase the total level of income in the economy, thereby creating income for domestic business organisations and households and reducing that accruing to foreign business organisations and households. In each case the increase in income created by the injection will have the effect of increasing the level of demand for factor services, and hence future levels of factor incomes and the general level of activity and output in the economy.

Initially, the combined effect of these withdrawals and injections is to upset the state of balance of the economy. However, equilibrium will be re-established when the amount of income which is withdrawn from the system is matched by the amount injected into the system, in other words, when withdrawals $(S+T+M)$ = injections $(I+G+X)$. This does not mean however that S must equal I, or G equal T, or M equal X; it merely means that the sum of the withdrawals must be equal to the sum of the injections. After these adjustments have occurred the level of expenditure in the economy will return to being equal with the level of income.

A new equilibrium position will be created by a change in any of the components of withdrawals and injections. An increase in *I*, *G* or *X*, or a reduction in *S*, *T* or *M* will have the effect of increasing the equilibrium level of national income and expenditure in the economy. This higher equilibrium point will be accompanied by an increased demand for factor services, and hence better employment prospects and a higher level of output and activity. For example, if a UK business organisation were to win a large contract for providing luxury cars to the Arab states this would have the effect of increasing export expenditure. This injection of expenditure would have to be met by an increase in the output of cars, therefore more factor services would be required and higher factor incomes would be paid out to households. Part of the extra income received by the households would be saved, part taxed and part spent on imports until eventually withdrawals would rise to the level of injections and a higher equilibrium level of national income and expenditure would have been established.

A fall in *I*, *G* or *X*, or an increase in *S*, *T* or *M* would have the opposite effect: it would reduce the equilibrium level of national income and expenditure in the economy. This lower equilibrium position would be accompanied by a reduction in

Fig. 2.2: The full circular flow model

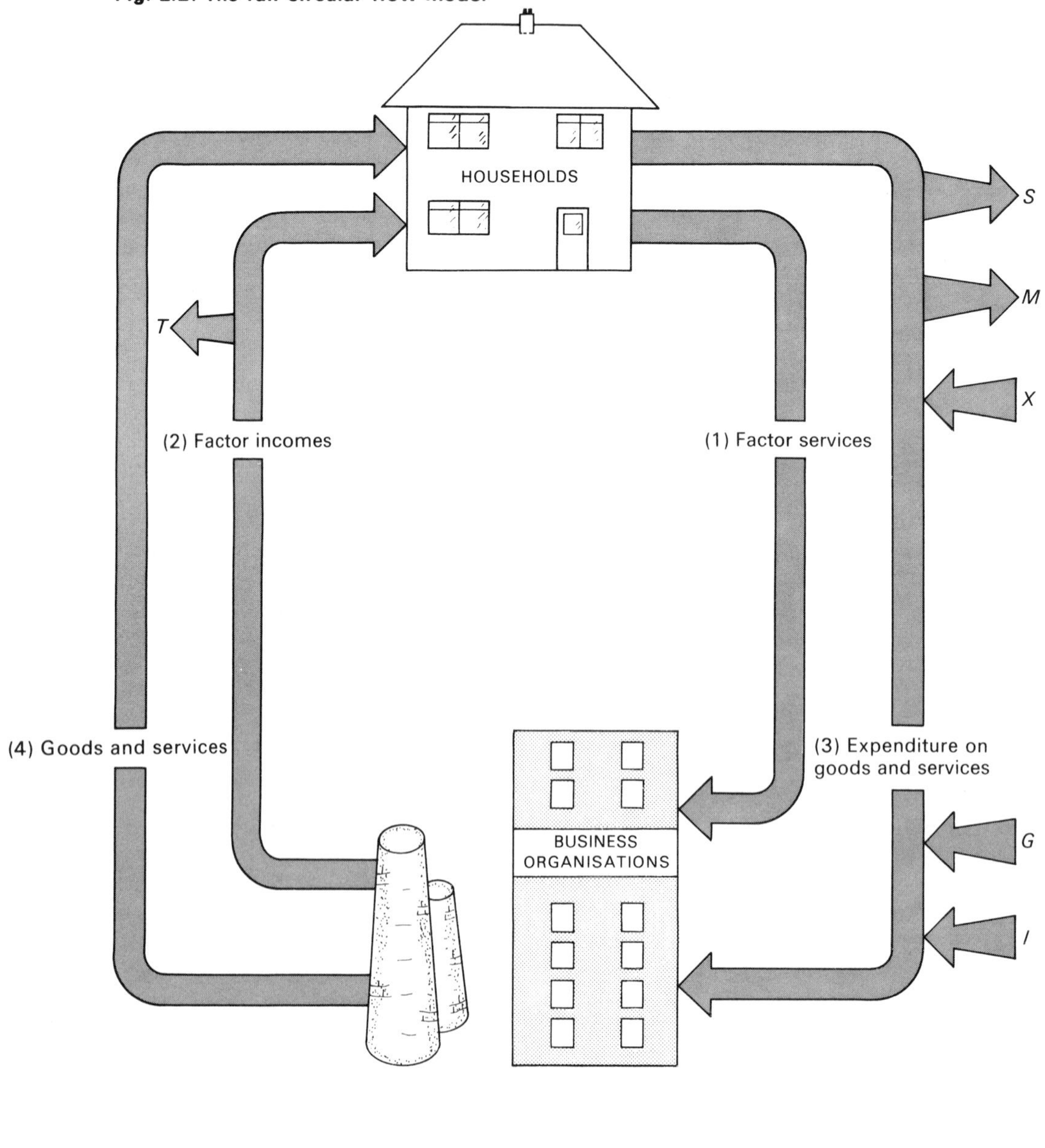

the demand for factor services, and a resultant danger of unemployment and a lower level of output and activity. For example, if the standard rate of income tax was increased by 5 per cent this would have the effect of withdrawing a larger proportion of income out of the economy. This would lead to a fall in household expenditure, which would mean that business organisations would need to cut back on output. Such reductions would result in a fall in the demand for factor services and a lower level of factor incomes. As income fell the volume of actual withdrawals would fall as well, because savings, taxation, and the level of imports are all obviously dependent upon the level of income. This would continue until withdrawals were equal to injections again and equilibrium was established at a lower level of national income and expenditure.

The equilibrium level of national income and expenditure may be illustrated diagrammatically as in Fig. 2.3. The axes are labelled as national income and expenditure so that the 45° line constructed from the origin shows a series of points at which the level of national income is always equal to the level of expenditure. Therefore, the line represents a series of equilibrium points between income and expenditure. To establish the point at which the economy is actually operating it is necessary to consider the aggregate level of expenditure in the economy. The circular flow model in Fig. 2.2 (page 34) shows that the total amount of expenditure undertaken in the economy is made up of domestic consumption by households, which may be represented by C, and then the three injections of investment I, government expenditure G, and exports X. This level of aggregate expenditure increases with the level of income until in Fig. 2.3 it intersects the 45° line at £8,000 million. This equilibrium level of national income and expenditure (£8,000 million) represents a point at which business organisations will be receiving back via expenditure an amount equal to the incomes they are paying out. Therefore it is a situation where there is no tendency for the level of national income, output and employment to change.

Fig. 2.3: Equilibrium

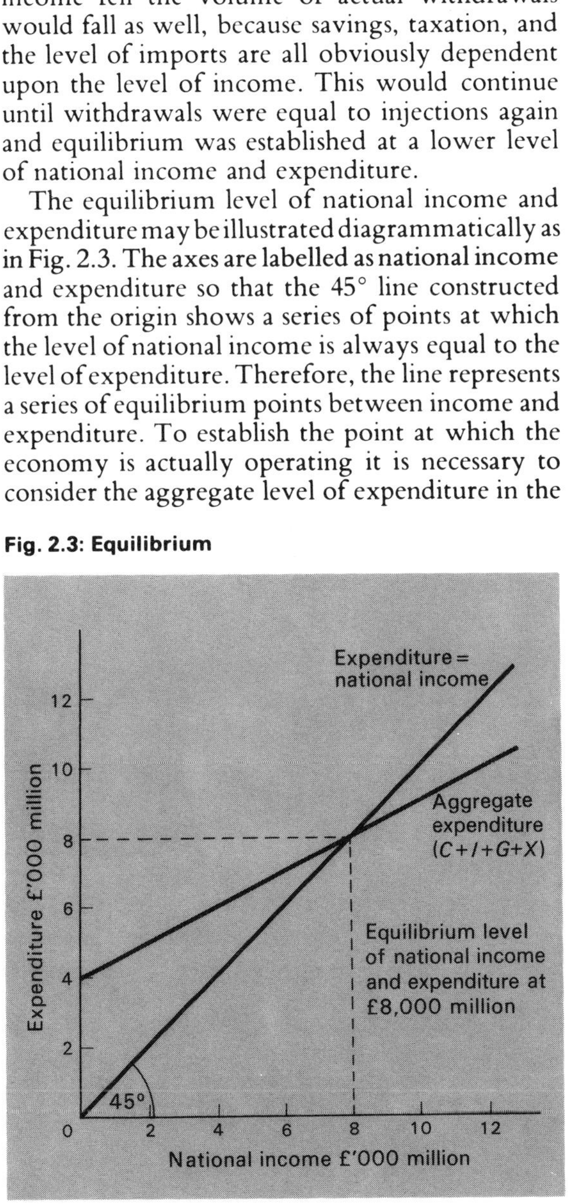

The value of national income measurement and analysis

National income statistics and analysis provide a useful basis for decision-making by both the government and business organisations. A comparison of national income statistics over a period of time helps to reveal whether the nation's standard of living is improving. To measure this in a meaningful fashion it would be necessary to express the figures in real terms. An even more realistic picture would be achieved if the figures were matched against population changes to give a *per capita* figure for national income.

The **output method** provides an indication as to how the economy is growing from year to year and which industries are contributing the most to that level of growth. This information is of great value to the government when planning an industrial strategy or to a business organisation which wishes to gauge its own performance in the context of a particular industry.

The **income method** shows the important distribution of national income between earned income in the form of wages and salaries, and unearned income in the form of profits, dividends, interest and rents. This information helps in the formation of government policies concerning the determination of what is considered to be an equitable distribution of income and wealth, and might be of interest to trade unions engaged in negotiations with business organisations or the government over wage claims.

Tables 2.5, 2.6 and 2.7 have all been taken from the summary tables of *National Income and Expenditure*, 1981 (CSO). This publication includes details concerning the *composition* of each one of the components of national income, national expenditure, and national product. This means that a deeper analysis of the significance of a particular component may be made by reference to this book. For example, consumers' expenditure is broken down into its main categories, so that it is possible to measure which items are of the greatest importance. By considering this information over a period of time trends may be established which are of considerable value for the future planning of government and business organisations.

Similar useful information may be derived from the analysis which is made of GDFCF according to the sector or industry undertaking it, and also according to the type of asset involved. The theoretical analysis involved in the circular flow model provides a means by which the implications of the national income statistics may be developed, the significance of the various components understood, and policy implications explored and developed. The fundamental point is that *the level of national income and expenditure determines the demand for factor services* and hence the level of employment and output in the economy.

3. How Government Policies are Formulated

In the UK mixed economy the type of business environment in which the organisation operates is determined by the interaction of government and free market forces. The extent of administrative and legislative intervention carried out by the government is dependent upon the kind of policies to which it is pledged and which it decides to follow. In formulating these policies the government is influenced by a variety of political, economic and social pressures. To appreciate their significance and effect it is necessary to consider the method and mechanism by which the policies are created, and how this mechanism may be influenced—and allows itself to be influenced—by these various pressures.

The UK mechanism for government policy-making

The constitution

The mechanism for forming policies influencing the organisation is based upon the constitution. This refers to the way in which the state is organised and governed according to a body of legal or traditional principles regulating the behaviour of different state authorities towards each other and those whom they govern. In the case of the UK there is no formal, written constitution but rather a set of accepted principles. This is felt to be an advantage as it means that the government is easily able to adapt its actions and institutions to changing circumstances and demands. Obviously this is something that a country like America with its written constitution is unable to do. The basis of the UK constitution is that the Queen and the two Houses of Parliament form the supreme legislative authority. This gives rise to a situation whereby the political leaders of the executive are members of the legislature and are responsible to Parliament. The government's term of office depends on support in the House of Commons, where it has to deal with criticism by the Opposition, which is always capable of taking over from it if the electorate should so decide. The main elements and institutions within the constitution are outlined in Fig. 3.1 (page 38). These will be discussed in detail in the following sections.

The Crown

The authority of the British Government is basically embodied in the Crown. In fact the Crown acts as the most important collective symbol for all the institutions of state. For example, government property is held in the name of the Crown. Legal actions against criminals are taken on behalf of the Crown. Officers of the law keep the King's or the Queen's peace, and service officers hold the King's or the Queen's commission. Finally, the government is often referred to as His or Her Majesty's. Apart from representing the country as the Head of State, the monarch also acts as the Head of the Church, thus combining the roles of representing secular and religious authority.

The actual monarch, as distinct from the Crown, is little more than a figurehead performing a ceremonial rather than a governmental role. As a constitutional monarch the present Queen has to act on the advice of her ministers. She has to give formal assent to laws passed by Parliament, and is responsible for naming the Prime Minister, and for dissolving Parliament in accordance with the Prime Minister's wishes. The Queen also opens Parliament, and formally appoints ministers, judges and bishops. She receives major government papers and has a consultation with the Prime Minister about once a week. With regard to these duties she has the right to discuss and even offer advice on governmental issues, although ultimately she is expected to accept the opinions and guidance of her ministers and of Parliament. Undoubtedly the most important aspect of the Queen's function revolves around her ceremonial role which involves, for example, her good will tours abroad, and her attendance at receptions given for visiting foreign dignitaries.

The Cabinet

British government is very often said to be

Cabinet government. This is because the real powers and rights of the Crown are vested in the Cabinet. The basic functions of the Cabinet are:

1. To frame government policies.
2. To formulate the legislation which is necessary to support those policies.
3. To control the civil service.
4. To co-ordinate the various activities of the departments of central government.

Due to the strength of party discipline within Parliament it is usually possible to ensure that policies instigated by the Cabinet will receive the approval of Parliament.

The **ministers** making up the Cabinet are drawn from the party which is in power in the House of Commons and are made up of members of both the Commons and the Lords. They also act as the executive heads of the major central government departments. A minister in charge of a particular department is held responsible for all the activities of that department and is answerable to Parliament for the execution of that responsibility. He also represents the interests of his department within the Cabinet, and tries to ensure that these are considered during the formation of any Cabinet policy. The Cabinet minister is helped in much of his departmental work by junior ministers, and also by the civil service. The latter is concerned with the bulk of departmental administration, and with assessing the implications of decisions taken by the minister on the work of the department. All Cabinet ministers take collective responsibility for all governmental decisions.

Fig. 3.1: The UK system of government

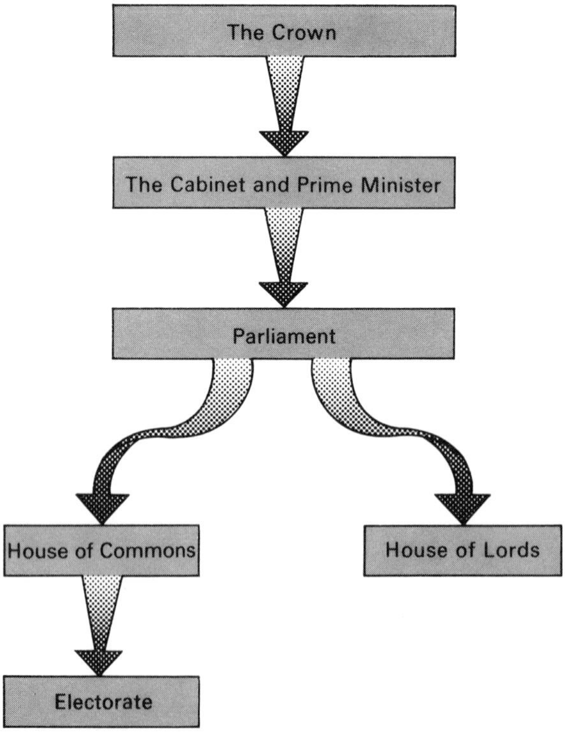

However, if a minister disagrees with his colleagues on a major issue he may feel it necessary to resign.

The **Prime Minister** stands at the head of the Cabinet and has the right to select its members. This power of patronage obviously gives the Prime Minister considerable authority over the members of the Cabinet. The Prime Minister's personal political authority is enhanced still further by party loyalty which exists between the members of the Cabinet, other ministers and the House of Commons. The Prime Minister takes over-all control for the direction of Cabinet business and policy, and generally does this by chairing the key Cabinet committees on defence, overseas policy and long-term economic policy. The Prime Minister may also choose to set up and chair *ad hoc* committees to deal with important matters of the moment. Ministers are unlikely to take serious policy steps without prior consultation with their leader.

Parliament

Parliament consists of two chambers: the House of Commons and the House of Lords. Between them these two chambers are responsible for making new laws for both local and national implementation, for acting as a watchdog on government actions, and offering criticism where it is felt to be necessary, and for providing by taxation the means of financing the work of the government and then scrutinising its expenditure.

The **House of Lords** consists of Spiritual Lords (including the archbishops of Canterbury and York and certain other bishops of the Church of England) and Temporal Lords, who are either hereditary peers or life peers. Potentially there are over 1,100 peers who could attend the House of Lords. However, in reality the number attending very rarely reaches anything like this figure as peers may apply for leave of absence during a parliamentary session. The average daily attendance tends to be around the 300 mark.

The government is usually represented by a number of ministers in the House of Lords who act as spokesmen for government policy. There are usually about three or four ministers of Cabinet rank in the Lords.

Apart from the general parliamentary functions that the House of Lords performs in conjunction with the House of Commons, it also acts as the final Court of Appeal for civil cases in the whole of the UK, and for criminal cases in England, Wales and Northern Ireland. By convention only the Lords of Appeal actually perform this function.

The **House of Commons** is composed of 650 elected MPs, who are required by law to contest their seats every five years in a General Election, although the Prime Minister may seek a dissolution of Parliament at an earlier date.

For **election** purposes the UK is divided into constituencies each of which returns one member to the House of Commons. The Representation of the People Act 1949, as amended by the Act of 1969, lays down the laws relating to parliamentary elections. Basically, election to the House of Commons has to be decided by secret ballot. All British subjects and citizens of the Irish Republic on the electoral register, who are eighteen years of age or over, and who are not subject to any legal incapability to do so, are allowed to vote. Anyone who is a British subject, twenty-one years of age or over, and not otherwise disqualified, may be elected to the House of Commons. Disqualification applies to members of the House of Lords, clergy of the Churches of England, Scotland and Ireland and of the Roman Catholic Church, undischarged bankrupts, and those ruled out by the 1957 House of Commons Disqualification Act. Elections are decided on a plurality system of voting, whereby the successful candidate is selected on the grounds that he has the largest number of votes, although not necessarily a majority over the sum of the other candidates' votes.

The majority of the Members of the House of Commons belong to organised **political parties.** The major parties represented in the House of Commons are Labour, Conservative, Liberal, Social Democrats, Scottish National, United Ulster Unionist, Plaid Cymru (Welsh Nationalist) and Social Democratic and Labour (Northern Ireland). At the time of an election each political party offers a group of rival policies to the electorate. The electorate, by voting for a particular candidate, indicate which parties they favour. The party which has the largest number of candidates elected, or which is able to command a majority of supporters in the House of Commons, forms the government. The party with the second largest following forms the official **Opposition,** whose major function is to question and criticise the actions of the government. The existence of this party system within Parliament ensures stable government, valuable and strong opposition, freedom of choice and democracy. At times of national emergency a coalition may be formed between the parties within the House of Commons in order to form a unified body for the solving of major problems.

New legislation
Parliament is responsible for passing new legislation. This is initially presented in the form of a Bill, which when it has gone through a number of stages of approval by Parliament is eventually passed and becomes an Act. There are two main types of Bills.

1. **Public Bills** These relate to matters of public policy and may be presented by a government minister or by a Private Member. The vast majority of public legislation is in fact drafted on behalf of ministers and has the support of the Cabinet before it is presented to Parliament by the appropriate minister. Generally, before the Bill is actually drafted, it is the normal practice for discussion to take place with various pressure groups, organisations and institutions who are interested in its contents. Sometimes the proposals of the Bill are set out in a **White Paper,** which has been approved by the Cabinet and is later discussed by Parliament. Occasionally a **Green Paper** may be published; this sets out for public discussion major ministerial proposals which are still at the formative stage. The purpose of allowing this public preview of future legislation is to enable the government to measure public support for and reaction towards their proposed policies, and also to determine the full implications of future legislation for particular groups. They then have the opportunity to take these points into consideration before actually drafting the Bill for parliamentary consideration and approval.

Private Members' Bills are introduced at a special allotted time on a Friday by back-bench Members of Parliament who have won the right to present their Bills in a special ballot. Due to the lack of parliamentary time very few of these Bills are debated and even fewer become law. However, some major legislation has been introduced in this way, for instance, the Abolition of Capital Punishment. Private Members' Bills can be introduced in the House of Lords at any time during the session.

Public Bills in general may be raised in either House. However, the more controversial Bills are normally started in the Commons, whereas those of a more technical nature, dealing with such problems as law reform, are generally started in the Lords. All Bills dealing with financial matters must be introduced in the Commons, and Bills concerned with government spending and revenue must be based on resolutions agreed by the House of Commons. The powers of the government are increased over financial legislation because if the main object of a Bill is to create a public charge it may be introduced only by a government minister.

2. **Private Bills** These are promoted by local councils, public corporations, private companies and private individuals who want to acquire certain additional powers or benefits. The Bills are very carefully scrutinised and if they are considered to be acceptable they may be started in either House. At the Committee Stage of parliamentary consideration a good deal of time may be given to an investigation of the main points of the Bill. Under certain circumstances, if outside groups object to any of the provisions of the Bill, they may put their objections as if they were in a court of law with the promoters of the Bill attempting to prove their case. In some instances both parties may be legally represented in these discussions.

All Bills have to go through a number of stages of **parliamentary consideration** before they become Acts. These various stages provide the opportunity for discussion, debate and improvement of the main proposals contained in the Bill.

In the House of Commons there are four stages for the Bill to pass through:

1. The **first reading** is the stage at which the Bill is formerly introduced and presented. It is then printed and published.

2. The **second reading** is concerned with a debate on the main principles of the Bill, which are usually outlined to the House by the minister responsible for it. If the Opposition agrees in principle with the Bill it will save criticisms of detail to a later stage. But if the Opposition objects totally to the Bill, it will vote against the motion for second reading. It may also put down an amendment for its rejection in order to give advance notice of its objections.

3. The **committee and report stage** provides the opportunity for alterations and amendments to be made to the details of the Bill. After the Bill has passed its second reading, if it is particularly important, it may be considered by a committee made up of the whole of the House of Commons; otherwise it will be sent to a specially formed Standing Committee. The Standing Committee

will be made up of about 20–50 Members of Parliament chosen in proportion to party strength. The Committee will study the Bill clause by clause, making alterations only where they are compatible with the main principles of the Bill. After the committee stage the Bill is reported to the House as it has been amended and the House is able to make any further amendments that it feels to be necessary. At this stage only the amendments and not the clauses are discussed.

4. The **third reading** of the Bill is the stage at which it is considered in its final amended form by the House. No debate is allowed unless there is a motion on the Order Paper in the name of at least six Members. If there is a debate it has to be confined to the contents of the Bill. Once the Bill has passed this stage it is sent to the House of Lords, and there it will pass through four similar stages.

The major differences in procedure between the Lords and Commons are, first, that any member of the Lords may introduce a Bill without notice or leave. Secondly, Bills other than those consolidating existing Acts are automatically committed to a Committee of the whole House after the second reading unless the House resolves to commit them to a Select Committee. Finally, although all Bills have to be passed by both Houses, financial legislation is not considered in detail by the Lords.

When a Bill has passed through its four stages in the Lords, the House of Commons and the House of Lords then have to agree on any amendments made by the Lords. If no agreement is reached the House of Commons may use the 1911 and 1949 Parliament Acts to get the Bill through. These Acts enable the House of Commons to present a Bill for Royal Assent without the agreement of the Lords so long as it originated in the House of Commons, and there has been a lapse of one year, and it is presented in a new session. According to the 1911 Act the consent of the House of Lords is not essential in the case of a money or financial Bill.

Once the Bill has been passed by the House of Commons it receives the Royal Assent and becomes an Act of Parliament. This means that its provisions become part of the law of the land.

Parliament as watchdog and critic of the government

One of the most important functions of Parliament is that of constantly assessing and re-assessing the actions of the government and offering constructive criticism where it is felt to be necessary. There are a number of different ways in which this assessment may be carried out.

Select Committees may be set up by either House to investigate a particular aspect of government activity and then to report back to the House. In the House of Commons the committees are set up in accordance with party strength and usually consist of 9–13 members, whereas in the Lords there is no restriction on numbers. Some committees are set up every session to deal with a particular issue during that session, for example the Public Accounts Committee or Expenditure Committee. Others are *ad hoc* and are set up to deal with important issues that require investigation, such as race relations or immigration. Select Committees in the House of Commons generally have the power to call upon individuals and institutions to provide necessary information. The House of Lords does not always give its committees these powers.

In 1966 a new type of Select Committee made up mainly of back-bench MPs was established to consider particular aspects of public affairs, like science and technology, agriculture, and education. Some of these committees have taken on a very special significance and importance; for example, the work of the Race Relations Committee has had a considerable influence on racial issues in the UK.

There are four main **parliamentary procedures** which enable the official Opposition party and even an individual back-bench MP to challenge the actions of the government:

1. During the passage of a Bill a strong objection may be made to its broad principles at the second reading, or amendments may be made at the committee stage.

2. The institution of parliamentary 'Question Time' provides an opportunity for asking ministers to justify the activities of their departments, and the Prime Minister to justify the direction of government policy.

3. The motion for the adjournment of the House may be used to start a discussion on a particular problem, which if it is felt by the House to be a very important matter may be given more time in the future.

4. 'Supply' days, which were originally used for the discussion of government estimates of expenditure, are very often used by the Opposition for the discussion of a particular department's general policies or administrative procedures.

The actions of the government may also be checked and assessed by the **Parliamentary Commissioner for Administration** (Ombudsman) whose main duty is to protect and safeguard the rights of citizens by looking into any complaints of maladministration made by the public, which may be referred to him by a Member of Parliament. The Commissioner has to report his findings to a special Select Committee, who will consider their implications.

Parliament's influence on finance and the Treasury
Parliament, and more especially the House of Commons, is able to influence government financial affairs. They are able to exercise this influence by authorising the different means of raising revenue, by giving consideration to the way in which money is to be spent and ensuring that it is spent as intended. In fact, no governmental financial changes may be made other than by Acts of Parliament.

The procedure for sanctioning government expenditure begins just before the end of the financial year when each department has to prepare an estimate for the House of Commons of the next year's expenditure. These estimates may be discussed during the twenty-nine allotted supply days, although the Opposition, as already noted, usually decides to spend these days considering the broader implications of policy. The estimates are embodied in the Appropriation Bill; to cover the period between the start of the financial year and the final passing of the Appropriation Act in July or August, votes on account for the civil service and defence departments are sanctioned in December or January. When the required resolutions have been passed a Consolidated Fund Act authorises the issue of the required money out of the Consolidated Fund.

The majority of government revenue, including lending from the National Loans Fund to the nationalised industries, is sanctioned by specific Acts which remain in force until they are repealed. The remainder comes from statutes such as the *Finance Act*. In March or April the Chancellor makes his Budget statement in which he reviews the nation's financial position and then lays down proposals for the raising of money by taxation to meet next year's expenditure. These proposals are embodied in the Finance Bill, which is debated and eventually passed as an Act. The House of Lords has very little chance to influence the Bill or government expenditure.

The House of Commons exercises further controls over government financial affairs through the work of two committees:

1. **The Public Accounts Committee** was set up in 1861 to ensure that expenditure goes on those purposes for which it was intended. It also acts as a powerful instrument for the exposure of waste and inefficiency. Its investigations are based on the annual reports of the Comptroller and Auditor-General, whose office audits the various departments' accounts, and draws attention to inefficiency and waste. The Public Accounts Committee reports its findings and recommendations to the House of Commons which regularly debates them. The Treasury gives consideration to the recommendations and discusses them with the departments involved. The Committee has had a number of notable successes, including the discovery in 1962 that Ferranti was making excessive profits from the development of guided missiles; as a result £$2\frac{1}{4}$ million was repaid to the government.

2. **The Expenditure Committee** was set up in 1971 to aid the House of Commons in achieving greater control over public expenditure. It attempts to do this by examining various government papers and plans on expenditure and those estimates it feels to be important. However, it is mainly concerned with broad policy and departmental organisation rather than with the very close scrutiny of particular estimates. It consists of forty-nine members and has the power to appoint sub-committees which are specifically concerned with such areas as defence and external affairs, trade and industry, education and the arts, employment and social services, environment and home affairs, and general expenditure. These sub-committees are able to give special attention to key areas, for example, the trade and industry sub-committee has been very critical in recent years of government financial assistance to both Chrysler and British Leyland.

The effect of political, economic and social pressures on policy-making

The first part of this chapter has broadly outlined the structure of government in the UK, and the procedures involved in the creation of any policy relating to the business organisation. It is now necessary to try to discover where the power really lies within the system and who is responsible for particular aspects of legislation relating to the business organisation. To achieve this objective it is important to identify where within the government mechanism the opportunity exists for influencing policy formation, and then to assess the extent to which it is affected by political, economic and social factors as reflected by public opinion and the actions of pressure groups.

The opportunity for influencing policy formation

The considerations of the mechanism for creating policies showed that policy formation is ultimately controlled by the government. This is because the government has the initiative in making policy: it decides which policies shall be implemented and which shall not. Due to its majority in the House of Commons it is able to get most of its policies implemented. The powers of parliamentary influence and of individual members are severely limited. The former really decides only on Private Members' Bills and on matters which the parties are prepared to leave to a free vote, and the latter is constrained to a large degree by the party machine. Therefore, most legislation and policy development emanates from the government, although it is prompted by a number of factors.

1. The government has to fulfil some of its election pledges and the promises made in its manifesto.
2. The government has to deal with current developments and problems, for example the Conservative Government had to introduce their statutory prices and incomes policy in 1972 in response to the deteriorating economic situation.
3. Various Royal Commissions and Committees of Enquiry provide information which requires legislation. Some of these Committees are of a permanent nature, like the Criminal Law Revision Committee and the Law Commission; and some are set up to deal with a particular issue, like the Roskill Commission on the Third London Airport.
4. Government departments may call for changes in legislation or for new legislation that influences their activities.

However, the opportunity directly to influence the mechanism of policy formation rests on two issues. First, the extent to which the government takes notice or even encourages any consultation with interested parties before the drafting of legislation. Secondly, the relative strength of the Opposition to influence the content of any Bill during its passage through Parliament. Various social, economic and political pressures will determine the degree to which these opportunities are taken up. These pressures are manifested in the form of public opinion and the activities of pressure groups. They also have a more subtle effect on policy by influencing the climate of opinion in which the government may be operating. This may force the government either consciously or unconsciously to acknowledge certain views or causes in future legislation.

The effect of public opinion on the formation of policies influencing the business organisation

Public opinion—or what the majority of people think about a particular issue or situation—varies according to age, race, religion, class, occupation, sex or membership of a particular organisation. Consequently, it is extremely difficult to measure or assess. The problem is aggravated by the fact that most of the UK's population forms the great so-called 'silent majority' which determines which party is in power, but whose opinions are very rarely heard. However, if their feelings are ignored the government may pay the price, as it takes only a uniform shift of 1 per cent from one party to another to cause a switch of eighteen seats, and hence a drop of thirty-six in the ruling party's majority.

There are a number of ways in which the government may attempt to gauge public opinion. These are illustrated in Fig. 3.2 (p. 44). First, the **public opinion polls,** which deal with a variety of different social, economic and political issues, provide a useful source of reference. The most significant types of polls have been the ones held just before a General Election in an attempt to forecast the possible result. Between 1945 and 1966 and in both 1979 and 1983 these were successful in their predictions, but in 1970 and the two elections of 1974 they were wrong. However, in defence of the polls it should be acknowledged that even when they failed to achieve the correct result their forecasts were generally within the statistical limits of their samples.

Secondly, a **study of the media,** such as an assessment of the types of letters being sent to the press, or the types of questions being asked on 'phone-in' programmes, may help to reveal some of the issues which concern the general public.

Thirdly, the results of **by-elections** may be

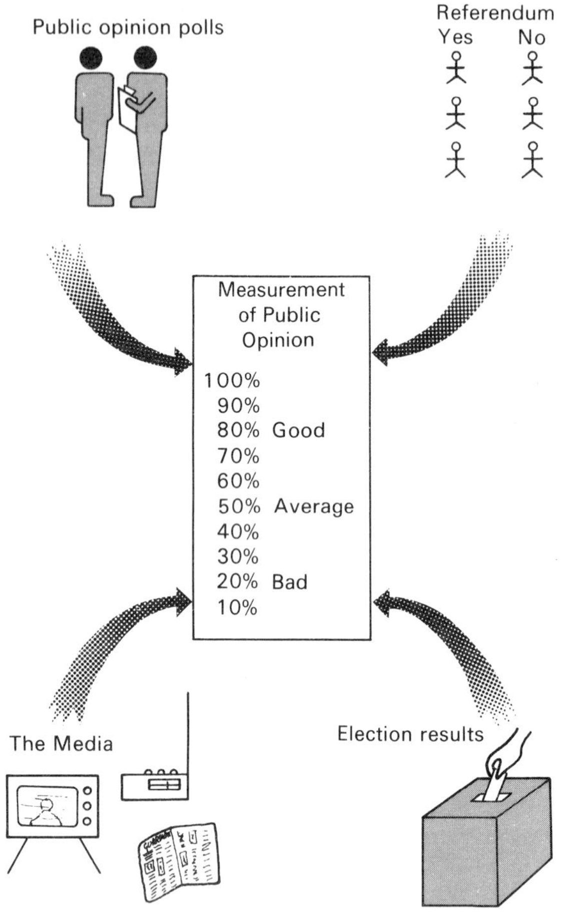

Fig. 3.2: The measurement of public opinion

considered as an indicator of public opinion. However, they are not as helpful as perhaps might at first be thought, because the results show the public's preference for a particular party without revealing the factors determining that preference. For example, public opinion polls have for many years indicated a general feeling against further nationalisation and yet this has not prevented a Labour Government intent upon such a policy from securing office. Does this mean that nationalisation is not a particularly important issue in determining party preference? The value of elections as a means of determining public opinion is down-graded still further when it is considered that 60 per cent of the electorate always vote the same way.

Finally a **referendum** may be used to measure public opinion on a particular issue. This was first tried in 1975 when a National Referendum was held on the question of EEC membership. It was tried again in 1979 to decide upon the question of devolution in Wales and Scotland. This is a fairly accurate method of measuring public opinion, although its accuracy ultimately depends upon the number of people who actually take part in the referendum. Problems also arise in determining whether an absolute or merely relative majority should be taken as a true reflection of public opinion.

Many policies influencing business organisations have been created on the basis of what is supposed to be a fair estimation of public opinion. Two typical examples have been the decisions concerning the siting of the Third London Airport and membership of the EEC. When the suggestion for a Third London Airport was first broached in the 1960s both the major political parties favoured its siting at Stansted. This met with considerable local opposition, although it was not until the Roskill Commission reported on the siting in 1971 that Stansted was dropped, and Cublington in Buckinghamshire adopted. Tremendous opposition was engendered in Cublington, which encouraged the Conservative Government to switch their attention to Maplin Sands in Essex. Again public opinion reacted there and the 1974 Labour Government turned its attention once more to Stansted. The question was then temporarily shelved, but was reopened in 1979 and Stansted still remains the most likely location.

In the case of the decision to join the EEC this seems to have been taken without much consideration being given to public opinion. In fact when Britain entered in 1973 the Gallup Poll revealed that 38 per cent of the population were in favour, 36 per cent were against and 26 per cent of the population were 'don't knows'. These results hardly suggest resounding support. The referendum in 1975 represented a rather belated attempt to include public opinion in a decision which would ultimately shape the future business environment. The fact that it attracted so much attention reflected how public opinion had largely been ignored when the decision was originally taken in 1973.

The effect of pressure groups

The *Guardian Directory of Pressure Groups* (Wilton House Publications) defines a pressure group as: 'an association of individuals joined together by a common interest, belief, activity or purpose that seeks to achieve its objectives, further its interests and enhance its status in relation to other groups, by gaining the approval and co-operation of authority in the form of favourable policies, legislation and conditions.' Potentially any group of individuals who feel sufficiently strongly about a particular issue are capable of acting as a pressure group. For example, a normally peaceful group of villagers might react very strongly if they were suddenly confronted by heavy lorries passing through their main street in order to get to a new motorway spur. They would probably form themselves into an action group, affiliate themselves to any relevant national organisation, and agitate for the building of a by-pass. There are three main types of pressure groups who are likely to try to influence the formation of policies relating to the business organisation. They may be broadly classified as interest, promotional and political groups.

1. *Interest groups* try to agitate and act as spokesmen for certain social or economic causes. Those which have had the greatest impact on the business environment are the employers' associations, like the Confederation of British Industry (CBI); the trade unions through the Trades' Union Congress (TUC) and the major unions, including the miners, railway workers, seamen, engineers and electricians; the professions, for instance, the Royal Institute of British Architects, the British Medical Association and the National Farmers' Union (NFU); and the various consumer groups.
2. *Promotional groups* are generally concerned with the achievement of one particular goal or the solution of one particular problem. A good example would be the pro- and anti-Common Market groups which attracted wide-ranging support, especially at the time of the referendum, or the National Society for the Prevention of Cruelty to Children.
3. *Political groups* generally seek power first and then the realisation of their objectives. Max Weber reflected this view when he described political parties as 'voluntary associations for propaganda and agitation seeking to acquire power in order to ... realise objectives, aims or personal advantages or both!'

Although the two major parties represent a wide group of interests they are still considered to stand for certain traditional special interests. The Labour Party stands for the interests of the trade union movement and in fact after the 1974 General Election 129 Labour Members were sponsored by trade unions. The Conservative Party is generally considered to represent the interests of the business world and normally has the sympathy and support of the professions, such as law and medicine, the various financial and commercial groups, the CBI and the NFU. After the 1974 General Election 72 Conservative MPs were company directors and 21 farmers and landowners. It receives a very large proportion of its finance from the business world.

There are a number of ways in which pressure groups may try to influence the formation of policy. They may attempt to get their views or their case put across in Parliament by enlisting the support of a Member of Parliament. This may be attempted either by adopting him as their spokesman, or giving him a position such as honorary vice-president of their society, or by trying to put one of their own supporters into Parliament by sponsoring his candidature. The final method is the one employed by the trade union movement which had 129 sponsored Labour Members of Parliament after the 1974 election. The only drawback to this method is that Members are generally expected to follow the party line even if it is in conflict with the particular interests of the pressure group that they represent.

Pressure groups may also try to influence the content of a Private Member's Bill by lobbying the Member of Parliament who is responsible for its launching. A very well-established pressure group, such as the CBI or the TUC, will probably make a direct approach to a minister or Cabinet minister. In certain cases a group spokesman may even be appointed to a government department's advisory committee. The NFU has always been able to exert pressure in this way. Finally, pressure groups will obviously try to employ the media to put their case across. For example, the major commercial banks spent a large amount of money on publicising their views on the question of nationalising all commercial banking activities. A great deal of the activity of pressure groups influences the business environment. The largest impact on policy formation undoubtedly comes from those groups representing workers, owners and consumers (these are represented in Fig. 3.3, page 46).

Individual trade unions, with the exception of perhaps some of the very large ones, are unable to exert very much pressure on policy. However, collectively, as part of the **TUC**, their power is

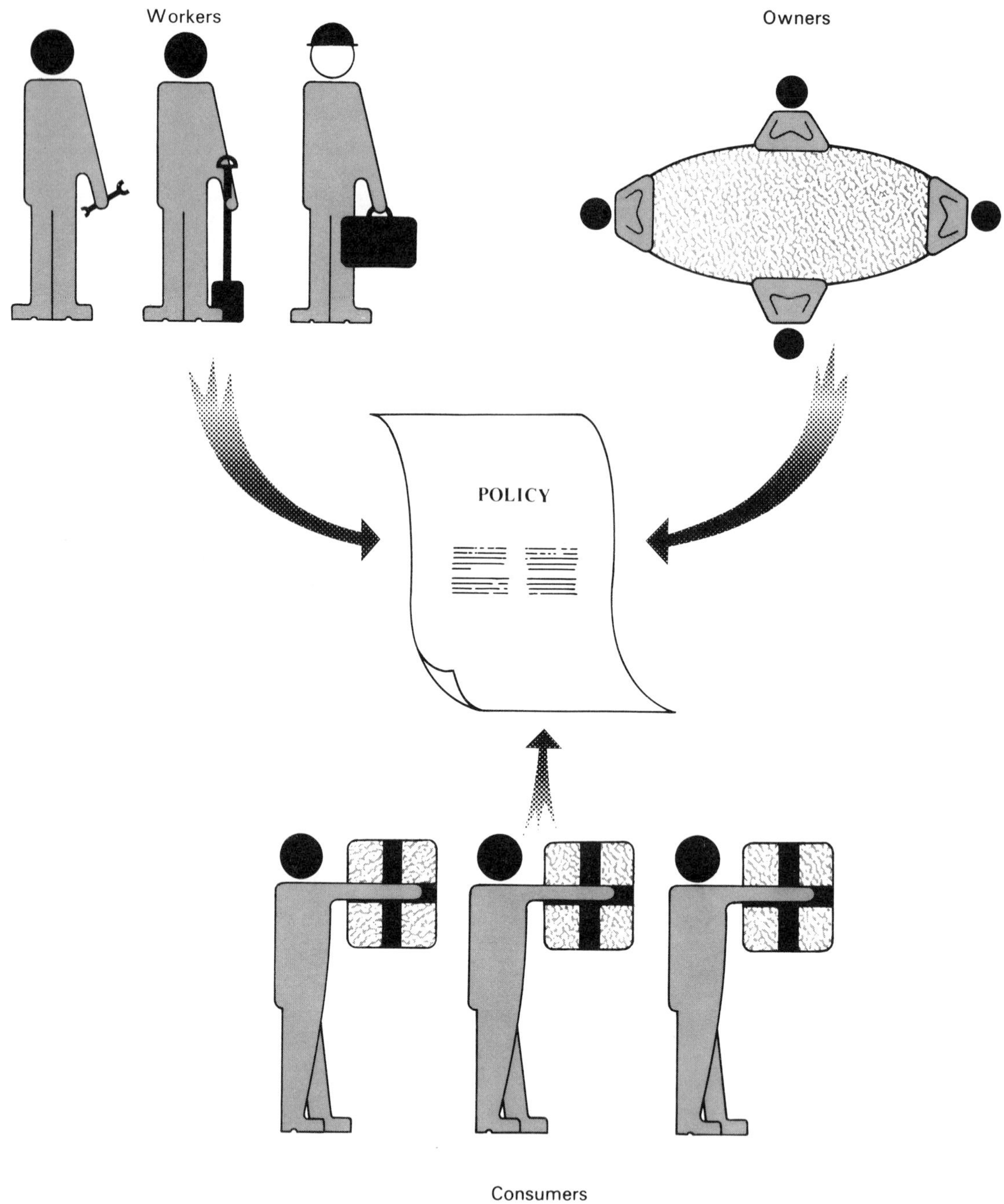

Fig. 3.3: The most important pressure groups influencing policy formation

considerable. The TUC was formed in 1868 as an association of trade unions. It now has over 11 million members in affiliated trade unions from a very wide spectrum of British industry, and it is accepted by government, industry and the labour force as the spokesman for workers' affairs.

The basic objective of the TUC is to improve the economic and social conditions of workers generally. It is also pledged to co-operate with other organisations with objectives similar to its own and to assist in solving industrial disputes. The TUC tries to achieve these objectives by acting as a pressure group in its own right—as it did when it strongly opposed the Conservative Government's Industrial Relations Act—or when it worked with the Labour Government to form a social contract and a series of voluntary incomes policies. It also acts as a pressure group by working on a number of advisory committees alongside the government. Finally, the TUC is represented on about 119 official and unofficial bodies concerned with matters of interest and importance to trade unions. Its representation ranges from the Economic and Social Committee of the EEC to the St John Ambulance Association.

As the TUC represents about half of the total work force its views are considered to be fairly authoritative and its powers are extensive. Its major weakness is that it has to represent extremely diverse interests which sometimes come into conflict. For example, if it was involved in the formulation of a policy for an integrated transport system which involved a shift from road to rail this would cause friction between the Transport and General Workers' Union representing the road haulage lorry drivers and the British Rail unions. Undoubtedly, the TUC's major contribution towards the formulation of policies relating to the business environment has been the important part it played in destroying the Industrial Relations Act, its contribution towards the creation of a series of voluntary incomes policies, and its efforts during the 1970s to extend the public sector and to redistribute income and wealth more equally.

By grouping together in the same way as trade unions, employers' associations within the **CBI** are able to have a considerable impact on policy formation in the business environment. The CBI was founded in July 1965 by the merger of the British Employers' Confederation, the Federation of British Industries, the National Association of British Manufacturers and the Industrial Association of Wales. Its membership is made up of approximately 12,000 firms and 200 employers' associations and trade associations. The basic objective of the CBI is to act as a spokesman for British business, support the free enterprise system and create the type of business environment in which industry may flourish.

To achieve these objectives it acts as a pressure group in its own right by negotiating with both the government and the trade unions and it is also represented on around 140 wide-ranging official and unofficial bodies. They include such government organisations as the National Economic Development Council and the Industrial Safety Advisory Council, and also independent groups such as the Business and Industry Committee of the OECD and the Union of Industries of the EEC. Its powers are fairly extensive especially as it is recognised by the government as the spokesman for business.

The CBI suffers from the same weaknesses as the TUC in trying to represent very diverse interests, ranging from the public to the private sectors and from multinational to small businesses. In fact, the case of the small businesses came to a head when they broke away from the CBI and formed the Society of Independent Manufacturers, which later became known as the Smaller Businesses Association with over 3,000 members. The CBI has made a major contribution towards the formation of policies relating to the business environment. It has achieved this by its co-operation with the government and TUC on the formation of a voluntary incomes policy, and also on such legislation as the 1974 Health and Safety at Work Act.

Finally, individual consumers are able to influence policy by forming pressure groups. Two of the most effective consumer groups are the **Consumers Association** and the **National Federation of Consumer Groups.** The former was started in 1957 when it published *Which?* and it has since grown to around 7,000 members. Its basic objective is to provide an impartial testing of consumer goods and services and to promote greater consumer protection. Although its membership is relatively small the results of its testing services are held in considerable regard. It has also successfully contributed to the lobby for the Consumers Credit Act and Unsolicited Goods Act.

The National Federation of Consumer Groups was established in 1961 with the backing of the Consumers Association. It has 60 groups with over 11,000 members. It is basically concerned with consumer protection and has lobbied for standard packaging, the banning of exclusion clauses in service contracts and the setting up of a Small Claims Court.

4. Contract and Consumer Protection

A contract as a voluntary bargain

A contract is a **legally binding agreement** between two parties. The contract is one of the essential ingredients of business life. It is the basis of all commercial agreements whether for sale of goods, credit transactions, the provision of services, insurance or the setting up of business. It is the basis of all agreements between employees and employers.

Contracts can range from the most simple—for example, the purchase of a cup of tea in a cafe—to the more complex, where a large construction contract may be entered into by a civil engineering company with a foreign government, which involves an outlay of millions of pounds over several years.

The law will recognise all varieties of contracts, even if bizarre or inadequate for one of the parties. For instance, if a businessman enters into a contract which eventually involves him in more expense than he envisaged, the courts will not intervene to repair this bad agreement. Parties are free to enter into any contractual agreement that they wish, subject only to the restrictions or constraints laid down by the courts in the form of contract law. The contractual agreement must contain the following features (the details of which will be dealt with later, pages 50–61):

1. The courts must be satisfied that the parties have intended that their agreement was to have legal effect and also that a firm and clear agreement has been reached and the parties are not still going through phases of negotiation.
2. The law also recognises that each agreement must contain some form of **consideration** to be given by each of the contracting parties, and not be merely an empty promise.
3. The agreement must be one from which the courts can ascertain the intention of the parties. Also, if there is no **genuine consent** between the parties, the courts will not recognise such an agreement.
4. The contract must comply with any laid-down formalities; contracts of hire purchase must be in writing, otherwise they are unenforceable.
5. The parties to an agreement must have the legal **capacity** to enter into a contract.
6. The agreement must not in any way be unlawful.

The concept of freedom of contract is further constrained by the influence of legislation in specialist areas. For example, the Sale of Goods Act 1979 provides a detailed framework of rules within which the buying and selling of goods is governed. The Consumer Credit Act 1974 regulates nearly all consumer credit agreements and lays down criminal sanctions to prevent undesirable practices. In the special area of employment, there is legislation (as we have seen in Book 1) that makes it difficult to dismiss an employee without a sound reason.

Therefore, although there is still much scope for parties to negotiate varied contracts, there are now many areas of contract where the parties no longer have the licence enjoyed by contracting parties in the past.

Unequal bargaining situations

In the private sector

An early principle of contract, particularly in the field of sale of goods, was *caveat emptor* ('let the buyer beware'). Parties to an agreement were regarded as of equal standing and consequently it was thought that if a person entered into a contract that he later regretted then he must pay the price of his own foolish actions.

This particular belief is no longer completely tenable today. Of course it is right that the law does not intervene to remedy pure errors of judgement, or carelessness in entering into bad bargains, but the law has increasingly sought to protect those who are obviously the weaker party in a contractual situation, in particular the non-specialist consumer.

For instance, in the private sector products have become increasingly technical and sophisticated to an extent beyond the understanding of the average consumer. The growth of industry this century has seen the expansion of the corporation and the impersonal institution replacing a more identifiable master. Large companies have organisational resources, including legal and financial backing, which would make them the dominant party in any negotiations with consumers.

The growth of business power has caused the increasing use of the **standard form contract.** These contracts are uniform agreements containing a collection of rules which have been constructed and preconsidered by the organisation's legal advisers, with the aim not only of simplifying business procedure within the organisation but also often of reducing the businessman's risks in a contract and giving him maximum protection from liability.

There may be a danger for the consumer who must accept the terms of a standard form contract or not enter into the contract. Many consumers do not have the knowledge to analyse such a written document or are simply apathetic when faced with it. They sign without challenging the terms it contains and, unless there is something unlawful about the agreement, they are bound to terms that have not been comprehended and in many cases not even read. Even if the consumer had the knowledge or even the desire to challenge the contractual terms included in a standard form it would be rare for any renegotiation to be accepted. The choice would be either to accept the standard form contract in its entirety or to take one's custom elsewhere. Competition between firms does mean that there is a choice of products and services, but if all the firms in the market use a similar standard form the choice is the unenviable one of accepting this type of contract or going without.

Irrespective of whether a contract is in standard form, the average consumer, and to a large extent the small businessman, could be at a disadvantage when negotiating contracts with large organisations. They will have the expertise, the powers of persuasion through advertisements and trained salesmen, they can offer inducements through gifts and discounts and easy terms. Often the sale is cloaked in slick presentation and an aura of goodwill which evaporates once the sale has been made. The other contracting party may not possess the education or aptitude to rebut any of the claims made by the seller. Therefore the law must protect those who do not have the abilities to protect their own interests, and prevent their exploitation.

Parliament and the courts have done much in recent years to redress the inequalities in contractual bargaining due to the different economic strengths of parties to a contract. As we shall see in more detail later statutes such as the Sale of Goods Act 1979, the Consumer Credit Act 1974, the Unfair Contract Terms Act 1977, the Fair Trading Act 1973, and the Trade Descriptions Act 1968 have improved the position of the weaker party and prevented much continued exploitation.

Once the rules of any contractual situation have been clearly formulated, it is up to the individual to ensure that they are obeyed. Enforcement is theoretically equal in the courts—no distinction is made between the powerful and the weak, subject to the stamina required to pursue the process of litigation through the courts, with the attendant financial burden, plus the risk of costs if the action fails. Everyone has a duty to keep his contractual promise, otherwise there would be a breakdown of activity and trade.

In the public sector

The public sector is complicated by a variety of institutions created either by individual Acts of Parliament as part of the process of nationalisation, for example, of the coal, gas and electricity industries, or as a result of the government purchasing a stake in an organisation such as British Petroleum, or alternatively as an acquisition under the powers given in the Industry Act 1975, for example, Rolls-Royce.

Many of these organisations have absolute monopoly powers: a consumer has no alternative but to contract for electricity from the Regional Board. Also the extent of each corporation's powers varies according to what is laid down in the enabling Act. Each public corporation is subject to the principle of *ultra vires* but there have been few cases before the courts because their powers have usually been drawn widely enough to make it difficult for them to act unlawfully.

The contracting individual is confronted with a large, powerful organisation and is therefore in the same potentially weak position as the consumer dealing in the private sector. In some cases his position is even more inadequate. For instance, the Post Office Act 1969, which established the Post Office as a separate corporation, continued its wide **immunity** from all actions in contract and tort when dealing with the post and telecommunication.

However, the other public corporations are subject to the same laws of the land as any other body. The problem is again one of power. There are safeguards and administrative procedures (which will be considered later—see page 65). Perhaps the most effective control on their actions is their political responsibility to their assigned minister and to Parliament in general. The fact that there exists little administrative case law in these areas is perhaps a testimony to their sense of responsibility. Also the Competition Act 1980 has provisions to refer to the Monopolies and Mergers Commission any public undertakings which abuse their monopoly position.

The essentials of a valid contract

It is necessary to appreciate in a little more depth the basic constituents of *any* contract, whether simple or complex. It is interesting to note that the majority of the fundamental contractual rules have been developed by the courts themselves as the need arose, with little assistance as yet from Parliament. We shall, however, be concentrating only on those major principles which affect relations between organisations and organisations and between organisations and members of the public.

Before examining the essentials of a valid contract it is necessary to consider some terms that frequently occur.

Defective contracts

Contracts that contain some legal defect may be void, voidable or unenforceable; **void** means basically without any legal validity. A **voidable** contract is binding unless one party exercises his right to have it set aside. An **unenforceable** contract (for example, an unwritten hire purchase agreement) is binding in law but neither party will be able to enforce its obligation in a court of law.

The contractual agreement

A contract will come into existence when the two parties involved make an agreement which is enforceable by law. In simple terms, this comes about when one party (the offeror) makes a firm offer to the other (the offeree) who accepts. In the commercial world the parties do not of course have to be individuals—they may be consumers, or identifiable businessmen such as sole traders, but they may also be partnerships, limited companies, local authorities, even governments. There are very few restrictions on the number, or identity of, the people comprising a contracting party, and it is essential as part of this country's economic way of life that contracts are formed with foreign institutions and organisations so that trade can take place. Although in the majority of cases an offer is made to a clearly defined party, an offer can be made to the world at large (*Carlill v. Carbolic Smoke Ball Co.* (1893)). This would occur, for instance, where an organisation makes an offer perhaps as a promotion gimmick to provide to the general public some good or service substantially reduced in price, in return for their performance of some task such as the return of an appropriate number of product wrappers.

The courts will want to be certain that in fact an offer has been made which is capable of being accepted to form a binding contract. A legal offer will be distinguished from what is known as an **invitation to treat.** A good example of this occurred in the case of *Fisher v. Bell* (1961) where a shopkeeper was prosecuted for offering a flick-knife for sale in his shop window contrary to existing statutory law. He was acquitted because he was not offering for sale, he was merely inviting offers. This particular problem has been avoided for the future by many statutes including a section covering this eventuality, for instance, in the Trade Descriptions Act 1968 which says that 'persons exposing goods for supply or having goods in his possession for supply shall be deemed to offer to supply them'.

The following, therefore, are regarded as examples of invitations to treat: prices marked on goods on display; advertisements (apart from the circumstances raised in *Carlill v. Carbolic Smoke Ball Co.* (1893) where the defendants promised in an advertisement £100 to anyone who contracted influenza after subscribing to their cause of treatment—this was regarded as a firm offer); requests for information; invitations to tender for a contract; and the issuing of a company prospectus inviting applications for shares.

Therefore if a retailer inadvertently misprices an article, there is no legal obligation for him to sell the good at this incorrect price because the potential contract is still at the negotiating stage. However, many organisations would sell at this lower price as a way of maintaining their reputation with the customer. Also the *Trade Descriptions Act 1968* makes it a criminal offence under Section 11 to mislead consumers over prices. There are allowed defences, but a firm constantly stating incorrect prices would be liable for prosecution.

Acceptance

In the event of a disputed contract where complex business negotiations are taking place the courts will want to be satisfied that the offer has been *accepted*. It may be difficult to state exactly when a contract is formed. Offer and acceptance can be orally made, and if businessmen do not want to be contractually bound until a written agreement has been prepared, they must clearly say so. The phrase 'subject to contract' is usually accepted as meaning that the parties do not yet wish to be bound. The care required can be seen in the case of *Branca v. Cobarro* (1947) where a contract to sell some property contained the words 'this is a provisional agreement until a full legalised agreement drawn up by a solicitor and embodying all the conditions herewith stated and is signed . . .' The Court of Appeal held that this was a binding agreement, not a conditional assent.

It is worth stressing there must be a **firm offer** and a **clear unconditional acceptance** before a contract will occur. There are occasions when it is not quite certain whether parties have reached agreement. Every person has the right within the law to negotiate any term he wishes. This freedom of contract is, however, not always properly supported by care in expressing terms. Phrases and words used by a businessman are not always those a lawyer would use. Hence, ambiguities, uncertainty and vagueness sometimes appear in agreements. The courts will not attempt to rewrite and enforce a contract if it is without meaning or definition. For instance, in *Scammell v. Ouston* (1941) an agreement for the acquisition of a motor van had as its central phrase 'this order is given on the understanding that the balance of the purchase price can be had on hire purchase terms over a period of two years'. The court held that there was no binding agreement as the hire purchase terms had not been determined. This agreement was too vague, but if the court knew that the parties were aware or should have been aware that there were such details—because of a trade custom or *previous regular dealings between the two parties*—the agreement would have been enforced.

The courts recognise that laymen sometimes use a more imprecise language than that expected from a lawyer, and that this does occasionally lead to inaccuracies and ambiguity in agreements. Therefore there is not an inflexible application of the rule developed in the above if the courts can see that the parties *intended* to be legally bound. Statements are carefully considered in the context of their express and implied meaning and particular attention is paid, as stated above, to any previous dealings between the parties, trade custom and any other relevant factor.

Thus in *Foley v. Classique Coaches* (1934) a contract entered into by the defendants to buy land from Foley on condition that they purchased all their petrol from him 'at a price to be agreed by the parties from time to time', was held to be a binding agreement because the contract stated that any disputes over the price could be settled by arbitration. Another example is the case of *Brown v. Gould* (1972) where an option to renew a lease was determined according to the 'market value' of the premises. This apparently vague assessment of the price could be fairly easily determined.

In business negotiations where the parties are under some pressure to complete a contract within a limited time, further problems on agreement can arise. Whereas many contractual situations allow for a certain amount of bargaining, this is not always the case. In such circumstances acceptance of an offer must be **unconditional.** A conditional acceptance is known as a counter-offer and this effectively counts as a rejection of the offer. Therefore in *Northland Airlines Ltd v. Ferranti Motors Ltd.* (1970) an agreement was negotiated to sell aircraft. The telegraphed terms requested an initial deposit of £5,000 but instead the offeree held the £5,000 in trust pending delivery which he expected in 30 days. The defendants disposed of the aircraft elsewhere. In an action for damages it was held that they were justified in doing this because the plaintiff, by withholding the deposit and quoting a delivery date, had rejected the original offer.

Generally, the acceptance of an offer must be communicated to the offeror, otherwise a contract could be made with an offeree without his consent. The decision laid down in *Felthouse v. Bindley* (1862) was that silence cannot be called an acceptance. For instance, business could not involve a casual message which claimed 'if I hear no more . . .' resulting in a binding contract.

This common law principle was given further support by the passing of the Unsolicited Goods and Services Act 1971 (amended 1975). The objective of this legislation is to protect the consumer from inertia selling—the unsavoury practice of sending unsuspecting people unsolicited goods through the post and relying on ignorance or apathy to extract unwarranted payment. The Act states that any unsolicited goods can be treated as unconditional gifts if the sender has not collected them after 30 days' notice. Alternatively, the recipient can do nothing at all and the goods become his after six months. The legislation also provides for fines for those who request payment for unsolicited goods (higher fines can be imposed if this is accompanied by threats).

Communication of acceptance can be dispensed with. For instance, many commercial contracts involve a customer simply ordering goods from a supplier by means of a written communication. In many cases the contract is completed by the physical delivery of the goods and a formal acceptance is deemed to be unnecessary.

However, if a formal acceptance by post is required, the offeror should give careful thought to the means of acceptance because it was established in *Adams v. Lindsell* (1818) that the posting of a properly addressed acceptance constitutes a binding contract. This precedent has been allowed to run to its logical conclusion and in *Household Fire Insurance Co. Ltd. v. Grant* (1879) it was said that there is a binding contract even if the posted acceptance never reaches its destination. But if business organisations do not wish to suffer from the vagaries of the post it is simply a matter of stating that the contract is not formed until the offeror has received communication of the offeree's intention (*Holwell Securities Ltd v. Hughes* (1974)).

The revocation of an offer

If businessmen are involved in lengthy negotiations there is always the probability that the offer may be revoked before it has been accepted. If the offeror has a change of mind concerning the business deal, he need only communicate this fact to the other party, either personally or by way of an agent (*Dickinson v. Dodds* (1870)), and acceptance can no longer be made. It should be noted that the postal rule discussed above does not apply in the same way to an offeror's revocation. Once an offer has been made it is up to the offeror to **communicate** any revocation to the offeree before it becomes effective (*Henthorn v. Fraser* (1892)). Even if the offeror has promised to keep the offer open for a number of days, the offeree can rely only on the businessman's integrity to do so. If a party is really concerned to keep the offer open, he must propose some form of payment which will then secure the option for him. Often business negotiations can be expected to meet certain deadlines. If the offeree is given a fixed number of days in which to consider an offer then acceptance must be within this period of time or the offer will lapse. A problem may arise when the offer contains no specified time for acceptance. Each case is then judged on its merits, but the test is that the offer will lapse after a reasonable period of time. Obviously, if the offer implies haste, unnecessary delay will lose the contract.

It is worth considering in general terms at this stage that not all agreements are contracts. This is because the parties have *no intention of entering into legal relations*. Much of the law on this subject is centred around domestic and social agreements, which are not usually recognised by the courts as binding agreements.

In business, commercial agreements are presumed to be binding in law. The only rare exception is where there is strong evidence to the contrary, such as a clause stating that it is 'binding in honour only'; this would seem to be a bar to any legal jurisdiction.

Collective agreements between an employer and employee are also not recognised in common law as creating legal relations (*Ford Motor Co. v. Amalgamated Union of Engineering and Foundry Workers*, 1969). Recognising the instability in industrial relations that could arise if such agreements were enforced, the Trade Union and Labour Relations Act 1974 (Section 18) states that collective agreements are not enforceable unless in a written agreement there is an express intention to be bound.

The 'battle of the forms'

As has been seen, forming the initial contractual agreement is not without its difficulties. The rules laid down in the cases are capable of exact legal precision and meaning. However, in the business world contractual performance is not always carefully planned in accordance with such principles. Indeed, many contracts are of a relatively routine nature, and each party to the agreement merely seeks to include his own terms and conditions by attaching to the various order and acknowledgement slips standard terms and conditions—offer is succeeded by counter-offer, and so on ... In the event of a dispute which cannot be resolved amicably, it is often a question of the courts examining the total number of documents and adopting the approach of 'last past the post'.

> In some cases the battle is won by the man who fires the last shot. He is the man who puts forward the latest terms and conditions, and, if they are not objected to by the other party, he may be taken to have agreed to them.
>
> *Lord Denning—Butler Machine Tool Co. Ltd. v. Ex-Cell-o Co. Ltd. (1979)*

A clear example can be seen in *British Road Services v. Arthur Crutchley & Co. Ltd.* (1968). One of the issues in this case was the liability of the defendants to the loss of a consignment of whisky. The plaintiffs had delivered the load and their driver had handed over a delivery note containing the plaintiffs' terms and conditions. However, the delivery note was stamped by the defendants' employee 'Received on AC's conditions'. This action amounted to a counter-offer, with the acceptance coming with the actual delivery of the consignment of whisky.

Having examined the basic rules governing agreement in a contractual situation, we must now consider one other essential ingredient in any contract—consideration.

Consideration

The rules relating to consideration are complex, but generally every contract must be supported by consideration. Consideration can be defined in simple terms as 'that which is actually given or accepted in return for a promise'—therefore the courts are concerned with what the parties bargained to do, and are not concerned with empty promises. Any contract for the sale of goods gives a good example of consideration in a contract: the goods are given on one side in return for cash or a credit payment on the other. It must be remembered that a contract is still binding if the consideration is **executory**—where the promise is to be carried out at some future time as opposed to being executed when the consideration is completed (most contracts start off with an agreement binding the parties to do something in the future).

The courts will not enquire into the adequacy or otherwise of a contract. The parties must use their own judgement and make the best possible bargain. Therefore if a company miscalculates on a contract and underestimates the cost of its overheads, it will not be able to obtain the help of any court in rewriting the contract. Organisations that are involved in long-term contracts normally protect themselves from the ravages of inflation by building into the agreement a price-variation clause. Similarly, if a consumer pays a high price for a good which could have been obtained cheaper elsewhere, the courts will give him no redress. If, however, contracts are priced unusually high or low, the courts will examine any suggestion of duress, undue influence or fraud.

There are perhaps two notable exceptions to the general rule from the area of Consumer Protection.

The Consumer Credit Act 1974 introduced the concept of the **extortionate agreement.** Any credit agreement may be examined and amended and altered by the County Court if the agreement appears to be grossly exorbitant, or in the circumstances is contrary to fair dealing—in particular the rate of interest charged will be the subject of scrutiny.

The Act also includes sections to combat the more offensive aspects of door-to-door selling by allowing a customer who has signed a document *away from trade premises* after *oral persuasion* to cancel the agreement within five days commencing usually after signing or after receiving the second statutory copy. This is the important exception to the rule that a party cannot back out of a contract once it is made.

A number of difficulties have arisen over promises to perform existing obligations. An employee is contractually bound to perform duties which are reasonably incidental to the terms of his contract, for example, to work a few minutes later than normal to complete an important task, or to cover temporarily for an absentee. A promise by an employer to pay for these duties would not be enforceable.

No consideration exists in such situations. For example, if a debtor owes a creditor £1,000 which he is finding it difficult to raise and the creditor agrees to accept a smaller sum, he can always renege on his promise and sue for the balance as this offer is insufficient in discharging the full debt. In the case of *Foakes v. Beer* (1884), for instance, a judgement was obtained by Mrs. Beer against Dr. Foakes for a large debt. He asked and was given the time to pay and it was agreed that no further action would be taken. He paid off the debt and was subsequently sued for judgement interest. Mrs. Beer's claim was successful because her promise not to take further proceedings was not supported by sufficient consideration.

Some criticism has been levelled at this particular rule of consideration, and a number of exceptions have been developed. One of the most notable is the defence of **equitable estoppel** which may be raised if a promise not to enforce normal contractual rights has been relied upon. For example in *Central London Property Trust v. High Trees House* (1947) the plaintiffs leased a block of flats to the defendants at an annual rental of £2,500. The landlord agreed in writing to a reduction in the rent to £1,250 in 1940, as the wartime conditions had considerably increased vacancies. At the end of the war, rent was still being paid at the reduced rate despite the flats being fully let, and the plaintiffs sought to have the rent restored to its correct level, and claimed arrears for the duration of the war as there had been insufficient consideration to allow a reduction in rent. The Court allowed the plaintiffs to claim the full rent again now that the adverse conditions affecting the lease had ended, but they would be estopped from claiming any arrears.

This particular doctrine is only applied when it is obviously fair to do so. In *D and C Builders v. Rees* (1966) the defendants offered the plaintiffs a smaller sum than was owed for work done by the builders, stating that unless this was accepted as full settlement for the debt nothing would be paid. The debtor was relying on this pressure succeeding because of the precarious financial state of the builders. The builders had reluctantly accepted this smaller sum, but subsequently sued for the balance and were entitled to succeed. Certainly the doctrine of estoppel could not be applied justly where there had been evidence of intimidation.

One particular point of note is that there is a possibility for businessmen to negotiate payment of a smaller sum in advance of the due date (often, of course, this is actively encouraged with the common practice of offering discounts for early payment). The advantage of early payment is always appreciated in a business as it becomes part of the working capital and can be used to pay off existing debts, pay wages or perhaps be invested in materials and made to work for the betterment of the organisation.

Let us now consider two final rules which may affect the construction and implementation of a business contract:

1. Consideration must not be *past.* If one party makes a promise (i.e. of payment) after the other party has performed some act or service, the subsequent promise is not supported by any consideration. For example in *Roscorla v. Thomas* (1842) after the plaintiff had purchased a horse the defendant made certain claims regarding its character which were groundless. But the court decided that these added comments were not part of the original contract. This means that a businessman's light conversation after a contract has been formed is to be treated as empty promises, but if any contract fails to achieve its expectation—for instance, if a good sold is unmerchantable—remedies quickly present themselves for breach of contract.

This particular principle must not be confused with an implied promise to pay for work performed upon request. Unless the agreement is inchoate, payment will have to be made for any commercial proposition. Indeed, the Sale of Goods Act 1979 states that in the event of parties being unable to agree on a price for work, the courts will assess a reasonable sum.

2. A further and final rule concerning consideration is that only those party to a contract can involve themselves in litigation. This rule is based on the doctrine of **privity of contract.** Strangers to a contract cannot sue on it (even if they are receiving some benefit) because they have provided no consideration in return for the promise. For example, if a consumer purchased a gift from a shop, the recipient of that gift would not be able to take action in contract—only the purchaser, if an article was subsequently found to be defective.

As with many legal principles there are some major exceptions. For instance, those insured under the Road Traffic Act 1972 can claim compensation though they are not parties to the insurance contract. Also, in those few occasions where goods are lawfully sold under a price maintenance condition (Resale Prices Act 1976), for example under the Net Book Agreement (1974), the supplier can enforce the price maintenance against any retailer whether or not he is a party to the contract of sale. Privity of contract, a principle evolved in the courts over many years, makes a great deal of sense, for it narrows the scope of litigation down to the true contracting parties—those who are obliged by law to see that the agreement is performed according to its terms and conditions. Statutes such as the Sale of Goods Act 1979 give added responsiblity to the parties by introducing the concept of strict liability with its sections dealing with implied terms.

Recent developments have seen attempts to remove some of the constraints imposed by the principle. In *Jackson v. Horizon Holidays Ltd.* (1975), the plaintiff contracted for a holiday for himself and his family. The holiday failed to match up to the contract description and he claimed damages. Lord Denning, Master of the Rolls, in his judgement felt that there were occasions where if A makes a contract on behalf of and for the benefit of B, then A can recover damages for himself and others. This judgement should, however, be treated with some caution as it was disapproved in the House of Lords in *Woodrow Investment Development Ltd. v. Wimpey Construction Ltd.* (1980).

The validity of agreements

Many agreements are not binding in law because they contain some defect which effectively removes any consensus between the parties. One common type of alleged defect is a mistake.

Mistake in a contract

There are always likely to be mistakes in agreements because of human error or simply of bad judgement. The courts do not recognise those mistakes which are errors of judgement. Subject to any misrepresentation, these contracts remain binding and are another example of the application of the *caveat emptor* principle. Therefore if a company gives its customers delivery schedules which are too ambitious, failure to meet them may lead to civil sanctions against the organisation for breach of contract.

A mistake is likely to affect the validity of a contract only if it is a fundamental one (known legally as an **operative mistake**). Let us examine some of the areas in business and commercial life where mistakes will have an effect on the outcome of a contract.

One particular problem occurs when a document is **mistakenly signed.** If the document is not read then of course any lawful term contained in the contractual document is binding. If the document signed is of a different nature (for example, a busy manager signing without bothering to check the contents), it *may* be possible to raise the plea of *non est factum* (a defence which means it is not my act). Obviously, if there has been some fraud the contract may be easily avoided on these grounds, but if innocent third parties have become involved in the agreement it will be more difficult to avoid since the decision made in *Saunders v. Anglia Building Society* (1971). In this case an old lady lost the title deeds to her house after assigning her property to a rogue who used it to raise finance for his business. She had intended to transfer the property to her nephew but was fooled by the rogue's fraud. She did not read the document (her glasses were broken) but nonetheless her plea of mistake failed. It seems that signers of full capacity must prove that they have not been negligent in signing or liability cannot be denied.

The **mistaken identity** of a contracting party may constitute a fundamental mistake if personal identity is a *material element* in a contract. Therefore, if the plaintiff contracts with the defendant thinking he is someone else, and the defendant knows this but relies on the fraudulent deception, the contract is void for mistake. However, proving that the identity of a party is material to a contract has turned out to be somewhat difficult. In most cases it is a question of a business deal being induced by fraud. Therefore the mistake that is made is one of creditworthiness which makes the contract voidable as long as innocent third parties have not intervened.

For example, in the case of *Kings Norton Metal Co. v. Edridge Merrett and Co. Ltd.* (1897) the plaintiffs received an order from a firm called 'Hallam & Co.' on suitably embellished paper. This firm was a deception and the idea of a rogue to make money. The order was processed and the goods were eventually sold by the rogue to the defendants. It was held that the goods could not be recovered from the innocent defendants—there was no mistaken identity by the vendors, merely an unwise willingness to enter into a contract without checking the credit standing of the rogue company.

However, when the contracting parties are not in face-to-face contact with each other, the parties' identity may be significant. For instance, in *Archer v. Stone* (1895) the defendant was inviting offers for his property (a leasehold shop), yet for personal reasons he had no intention of selling it to a party named Smith. Smith wished to purchase the lease and appointed Archer to carry out the purchase. Archer told the defendant that he was not buying on behalf of Smith and the sale proceeded. On discovering the truth of the situation, the defendant refused to proceed any further and a decree of specific performance was sought. This was refused by the court because the defendant would not have gone on with the sale if he had known the true identity of the contracting party.

Thus businessmen and consumers alike must not rely on a contract being set aside because of human error. The courts do appear to examine each case on its merits, but when there is a real lack of agreement—where the parties make a **mutual mistake** (each party making a different mistake)—the courts will usually declare the contract void.

This occurred in *Raffles v Wichelhaus* (1864) where both parties were contracting for the delivery of some cotton from Bombay but were referring to two different ships of the same name. Consequently there were two different delivery dates and a void contract. Such a decision by the courts usually holds when the contract is obviously completely defective. But businessmen and consumers alike will find contracts containing mutual mistakes enforced if *some intention* is found (and certainly if the mistake reflects real carelessness by one party). For instance in *Wood v. Scarth* (1858) the plaintiff sued the defendant for not conveying property after a lease agreement had been made. The defendant had intended a premium of £500 to be paid as well as an annual rent, but the defendant's agent had not made this clear, and an agreement had been negotiated and completed by the agent on terms which did not include the premium payment. The plaintiff sued for specific performance and although the court felt it would not be equitable to grant specific performance, damages were awarded for breach of contract, as the plaintiff could not have been aware of the premium payment.

However, where the parties make the same or, as it is known, a **common mistake,** the common law will not generally allow this to have any effect on the contract in the absence of fraud or misrepresentation. For instance, in the case of *Amalgamated Investment and Property Co. Ltd. v. John Walker and Son Ltd.* (1976), the defendants sold some industrial property to the plaintiffs for £1·7 million. Both parties were aware that the property was being purchased with a view to redevelopment, and that planning permission would be needed. However, just one day after the property was in fact purchased, the Department of the Environment informed the defendants that planning permission would not be given as the property was to be listed as being of special architectural and historic interest. The plaintiffs claimed rescission of the contract, as the property in its existing state would only be worth about £200,000. The court held that the common mistake that the property was suitable for and capable of development did *not* upset the contract. The loss was part of the normal risks of business.

An exception to this principle is where the parties are contracting in the mistaken belief that the subject matter of the agreement is in existence. For example in *Couturier v. Hastie* (1856), an agreement was made to supply a quantity of corn, but at the time the agreement was made the master of the ship bringing the corn to its destination had already sold it as it had begun to deteriorate in the ship's hold.

The harshness of the common law rule is sometimes tempered by the law of equity which may make such contracts voidable in order to redress any serious imbalance and injustice in the contract. Also where parties have fully agreed and orally negotiated the terms of a contract, and desire to have these terms set down in a written record, but this does not reflect the true intention of the parties, the courts will rectify (i.e. rewrite) the agreement. But strong evidence must be shown to the court that the written evidence does not show the true intention of the parties.

A **unilateral mistake**—where one party makes a mistake as to some aspect of the subject matter of the contract—is one that can easily occur in business. An example of such carelessness was in *Higgins v. Northampton Corporation* (1927), where a building contractor made an error on his calculations in submitting a tender for the construction of some houses for the defendants. The defendants accepted the tender which was priced lower than it should have been. The court, however, held that the contract was nonetheless binding because the error was not one which the defendants were aware of or should have been aware of—the error not being particularly noticeable. This case can be compared with *Webster v. Cecil* (1861), where the defendant made an offer by letter to sell his property for £1,250. The plaintiff knew this must be a mistake, because previous negotiations had resulted in a refusal at £2,000. The intended offer was in fact £2,250, and the courts refused the plaintiff's request for a decree of specific performance.

Even if the mistake is one which the other party ought to have appreciated, then equitable principles developed in cases such as *Central London Property Trust v. High Trees House* (1947) can be used by the courts to redress inequalities. For example, in *Avon County Council v. Howlett* (1983) an employee was overpaid salary and sickness benefits to the sum of £1,000 over a period of two years. The employer's attempt to recover the overpayment failed because of the principle of estoppel by representation. The representation was that the employee was in fact entitled to the said payments. The employer owed the defendant a duty not to misrepresent the sum of money to which he was entitled.

As well as mistake, the validity of a contract can be upset by a misrepresentation.

Misrepresentation

Contracts do not usually materialise without some pre-contractual negotiation. Any statements of fact which induce a contract are known as **representations.** If these statements are untrue they are regarded as misrepresentations. Before a remedy is sought it must be established that the misrepresentation was believed and relied upon by the party alleging resultant harm. The courts will disregard alleged statements which are no more than opinions or 'trader's puffs', such as vague advertisements.

With the aid of the Misrepresentation Act 1967 the courts are now in a position to protect victims of all types of false inducement. Actionable misrepresentation is divided into three main types:

1. *Innocent misrepresentation*
This is where the maker of the false statement (the **representor**) had reasonable grounds to believe his statement was true. Nonetheless the injured party can claim the equitable doctrine of rescission (or cancelling) of the contract and the parties are restored to their pre-contractual position. However, the courts may not always decide to allow such a remedy if they feel that it may cause unreasonable injustice to one party. It may be felt that an award of damages is a more adequate means of compensation.
2. *Negligent misrepresentation*
This category of misrepresentation was recognised by Section 2(1) of the Misrepresentation Act 1967 and is a false statement (which may have been made honestly) made by a party who had *no reasonable grounds for believing the statement to be true*. The courts can grant rescission to the injured party and may also make an award of damages based on the principles of negligence. The introduction of this extra category of misrepresentation makes it easier for a more satisfactory remedy to be achieved, because a representor now has to prove that his remarks were innocently made.

Damages were awarded in the case of *Jarvis v. Swan Tours Ltd.* (1973) when the defendant holiday company misled the plaintiff in its brochure as to the entertainment and facilities available. The holiday had cost the plaintiff just over £63, but the Court of Appeal awarded £125 as a true estimate of the actual loss, including in the compensation a figure for distress and disappointment.

3. *Fraudulent misrepresentation*
This is perhaps difficult to prove (and hence an action under Section 2(1) is the more probable). Fraud is committed where the statement is made *knowing* it to be false or where it is made *completely recklessly*. Rescission is again the obvious reward, and also damages can be obtained under the tort of deceit.

For example, in the case of *Doyle v. Olby* (1969) where the appellant was induced to purchase an ailing business on the basis of a number of fraudulent misrepresentations, the damages awarded were such as to compensate not only the loss on resale of the business, but also included a figure for anxiety and stress in trying to keep the business solvent. Lord Denning said on this point: 'All such damages can be recovered. It does not lie in the mouth of the fraudulent person to say that they could not reasonably have been foreseen'.

An action for misrepresentation must be brought before the courts fairly quickly. A contract is voidable for misrepresentation, but the right to equitable rescission is lost if there is any delay or if the parties cannot be restored to their original position. Consequently many business negotiations remain very cautious, because the parties are reluctant to make statements which could be construed as representations. Complete silence does not constitute a representation. But the terms of a contract must still be performed satisfactorily, for otherwise there will be alternative actions for breach of contract.

It must be noted that the law on misrepresentation has its counterpart in criminal legislation—the Trade Descriptions Act 1968, which will be examined in detail later (see page 64).

The capacity of the contracting parties
The parties to an agreement must have the capacity to enter into a contract, and as a general rule *everyone has the capacity*. There is a quantity of law, however, based on the contractual capacity of *infants*, but since the Law Reform Act 1969 reduced the age of majority to eighteen, the problems surrounding infants' capacity have diminished as their youth prevents them making or being allowed to make contracts of consequence.

It should, however, be said that as a form of specialised consumer protection, the Infants Relief Act 1874 effectively removes the liability of infants to all contractual situations. Infants can themselves sue on a contract through a next friend, for instance, in *Godley v. Perry* (1961) an infant was successful in his suit against a retailer who sold him a defective catapult which broke and blinded him in one eye. But in return an infant cannot be sued for contractual debts, outstanding accounts or loans. (There is nothing to prevent infants from entering into cash transactions, but at least their exploitation in credit deals is effectively curtailed.)

The major exception to infants' lack of contractual capacity is that they are bound to pay a reasonable price for *necessaries*—namely, those goods and services without which an infant could not reasonably exist. Infants can also enter into contracts of a more permanent nature, such as leases, partnerships and the purchasing of shares in a company. These are known as *voidable* contracts, which means that the infant can avoid liability within his infancy or within a short period of obtaining adulthood.

It is improbable that many infants will engage in contracts of substantial monetary value, but if they do attempt to become entrepreneurs in their own right, they are prevented from engaging in any contracts involving trade, such as paying off hire purchase instalments.

Corporations

Corporations do, of course, have a contractual capacity. In the case of the nationalised industries, this is determined by the particular statutes or charters which set up the organisations and which control their powers. Any contract made outside their statutory provisions is *ultra vires* but it would be very difficult to veto any of their operations in this way because the legislation governing their operations usually gives them wide powers. Thus there is possibly a threat from public corporations but by ministerial and parliamentary control of these monopolistic organisations their actions have been kept effectively under review. The small amount of case history concerning these bodies is perhaps a reflection of a job well done.

The contractual capacity of companies registered under the Companies Acts 1948–81 is determined by what is known as the **objects clause** in their Memorandum of Association—an essential document submitted at their registration. This effectively details what the company is legally permitted to do, and any company acting outside its objects clause is acting *ultra vires*. However, under the European Communities Act 1972, S9(1), those dealing with a company in good faith, who have no knowledge of its objects clause, but whose business is based on a contract *approved by the directors*, will still be able to sue on the contracts made. The influence of this European Law is likely to be diminished because in reality corporations contract through any of their employee agents. Directors do not of course get involved in the approval of all the company's contracts. Furthermore, most objects clauses are usually drafted widely to cover most business eventualities.

The terms of a contract

It is now necessary to consider the actual contents of a contract. If a dispute arises and in the event of litigation, the court will need to examine the terms upon which the contract was based. Initially, most attention will centre around the **express terms.** Most business contracts will be in writing and this makes the task of the court easier, leaving only questions of interpretation. Oral evidence is perfectly admissible if the contract is an oral one—the judicial judgement is simply required to work harder. But if the contract is a written one oral evidence is rarely admissible unless it can be established that the oral terms are clearly part of the written agreement.

In order to assess liability, the courts examining an alleged breach of a contractual term will classify it as either a **condition** (a major term), or a **warranty** (a minor term). This classification is necessary because the remedies available to the injured party are dependent upon it. A breach of condition allows the injured party to repudiate the contract, or continue with the contract and claim compensation for the loss incurred, whereas a breach of warranty enables a claim to be made for damages only.

Distinguishing between a condition and a warranty is not always an easy matter for the courts. They rely of course on the obvious intentions of the parties, but there is a developing tendency to consider just how serious the alleged breach turns out to be in fact before deciding whether it is a breach of condition or of warranty (see *Hongkong Fir Shipping Co. Ltd. v. Kawasaki Kisen Kaisha Ltd.* (1962)).

The implied terms—what is known as an 'innominate' term until identified

Terms can be implied into a contractual situation by the judges themselves as we have already seen in the field of employment in Book 1. The courts will always seek to honour the intentions of the contracting parties, particularly when on the surface the agreements appear inchoate.

However, Parliament is increasingly introducing terms **implied by statute.** As an example we can examine the implied terms of the Sale of Goods Act 1979, which make a major contribution to the field of **consumer protection.**

1. *The right to sell goods*
The seller must have the right to transfer ownership of the goods to the buyer at the time the contract is entered into and at the time of delivery. This is mainly used today to catch those contractual disputes which involve undischarged hire purchase commitments.

A breach of any of the implied terms is a breach of an implied condition and entitles the buyer either to repudiate the contract and recover the full purchase price, and/or claim damages irrespective of the use the goods have been put to. So in *Rowland v. Divall* (1923) the plaintiff who had to return a stolen car was entitled to the full contract price, despite having used the car for four months, because the courts adjudged that there had been a total failure of consideration.

Most businesses will not, of course, be engaged in selling stolen goods, but another way that this section of the statute can be violated is by the seller infringing trade marks or patents.

2. *Goods must correspond to their description*
Many sales, particularly those by mail order, take place with a reference describing the goods in some way. If the goods fail to comply with the description the buyer has a right to reject the goods or claim damages. The courts will not necessarily be concerned with trifling breaches, but the obligation to match the description exactly can be an exacting one. In *Re Moore and Landauer* (1921) the buyer was able to reject a large order of peaches because his specification indicated he wanted the tins packed in boxes of thirty but some of the delivered consignment was packed in boxes of twenty-four.

The courts have said that this section also covers not only mail order but situations where the buyer has seen the goods, as in *Beale v. Taylor* (1967) where the buyer thought he was purchasing a 1961 Triumph Herald. But an older car had been welded to the front of the 1961 version—allowing the plaintiff to recover the purchase price. An amendment in the Act clarifies this situation by stating 'a sale of goods shall not be prevented from being a sale by description by reason only that, being exposed for sale or hire, they are selected by the buyer'; thus a sale in a self-selection supermarket is covered as the goods being generally labelled describe themselves.

3. *Goods must be of merchantable quality and fitness of purpose*
If a person is buying goods from a business organisation they must be of *merchantable quality*—that is 'reasonably fit for the purpose for which the goods are commonly bought'. The courts will gauge merchantable quality by the price and age of the goods and by assessing how long the goods should remain in a state of merchantable quality (*Bartlett v. Sydney Marcus Ltd* (1965)). Goods failing to meet this standard can be rejected. Rejection is not possible if the defects in the goods have been specifically pointed out to the buyer (such as where a retailer sells off slightly shop-soiled goods). Nor will there be any protection under the Act for defects in the goods which the buyer, after examining the goods, should have discovered. There is added protection for buyers who make known to the seller the purpose for which they are buying the goods. Goods may be perfectly merchantable, but if they fail to conform with the buyer's stated purpose the contract is in breach of condition.

The standard of fitness is, however, a *reasonable* one. There is no such responsibility placed on the seller if the buyer does not make known the purpose for which he desires the goods, or if it is apparent that he has relied on his own skill and judgement in making the purchase. The test for merchantable quality and fitness for purpose is indeed a reasonable one but once proved by the plaintiff the defendant is not allowed to rely on the defence that he took all known precautions to avoid defective goods. Liability is strict (*Frost v. Aylesbury Dairy Co. Ltd* (1905)).

Despite the substantial protection given by this implied term, there are still considerable difficulties in defining merchantable quality—particularly with complex consumer durables such as motor cars. Future legislation may seek to define such principles more clearly to avoid unnecessary and sometimes fruitless litigation.

4. *Sale by sample*
On those occasions when the sale is agreed to be by sample there is an implied condition that the bulk must correspond with the sample in quality. The standard of this point has been seen in the case of *E. and S. Ruben v. Faire Bros.* (1949), where the seller delivered a quantity of vulcanised rubber material based on a sample. The sample had been smooth and soft whereas the bulk was creased and crinkly. It was held that there was a breach of condition, even though a simple process of warming would have put the defect to rights. 'It is not in compliance with the contractual obligation if an article is delivered which is not in accordance with the sample.'—Hilbery J. There is a further implied condition that the buyer must be given a reason-

able opportunity of being able to make comparison of the bulk with the sample. It is also an implied condition that the goods are free from any defect which a reasonable examination of the sample would not reveal. (Where the goods are sold by sample as well as by description the goods must correspond with both the sample and the description.) The Supply of Goods (Implied Terms) Act 1973 and the Supply of Goods and Services Act 1982, have incorporated similar terms into contracts of hire purchase, work and materials, and hire.

Exclusion of the implied terms

The Unfair Contract Terms Act 1977 amends the right given under the Sale of Goods Act 1979 for parties to contract out of the implied terms by mutual agreement. This right has been removed because of the weaker bargaining position of consumers, and the growth of carefully constructed, small-print standard form contracts which consumers, because of ignorance or apathy, rarely read.

In the case of consumer sales, any clause exempting the seller from liability from the implied terms discussed above is *void*. As far as business (non-consumer) sales are concerned the liability for title cannot be restricted or removed, and any such attempt on the other implied terms is also void unless it satisfies the test of reasonableness.

A further measure to improve the protection offered to consumers is the Consumer Transactions (Restriction on Statements) Order 1976, made under the Fair Trading Act 1973, which now makes it a criminal offence for traders to attempt to mislead consumers by notice of their rights to the statutory protection of the implied terms. Penalties include a £1,000 maximum fine upon summary conviction. More persistent or serious offenders may be charged on indictment where a much larger fine can be levied, and as an ultimate sanction, a prison sentence of up to two years can be given.

This piece of subordinate legislation passed in conjunction with its parent Act is a further example of Parliament's interest in consumer protection and the establishment of fair trading standards. This Act created the independent office of Director-General of Fair Trading, with over-all responsibility for keeping under review commercial trading standards. In the event of gathering satisfactory information on unsavoury trading practices, the Director may recommend legislative action to the Secretary of State, via the Consumer Protection Advisory Committee.

As far as business contracts are concerned, Parliament has considered that there are circumstances in which it is reasonable to include an exclusion clause—particularly where the bargaining position of the parties is not so unequal as is the case with the majority of consumers. For example, large, powerful buyers have legal resources to analyse in detail any contract they may enter to, but sellers with a monopolistic hold on the market are less likely to be able to rely on an exclusion clause.

Exclusion clauses in general

As mentioned earlier in this chapter, the doctrine of *caveat emptor* is no longer fully appreciated by the courts and Parliament where the contractual bargaining position of the parties is unequal. Exclusion clauses in particular have been viewed with suspicion and occasionally hostility. The courts have evolved a number of common law principles which have hardened their resolve against unfair clauses.

For instance, each clause must be clearly communicated. Contracts which are signed are binding on the signee—if they are lawful—irrespective of whether the document has been read or understood. If, however, the courts find a clause which is in any way ambiguous, the construction adopted is always that which is against the party relying on the clause. Obviously any clause introduced after the contract has been negotiated will not be effective. For instance, in *Thornton v. Shoe Lane Parking* (1971), the plaintiff suffered personal injuries after taking his car from the defendants' car park. The owners attempted to rely on an exclusion clause printed on a ticket issued from an automatic machine. This was defeated in the courts because it was adjudged that the ticket came too late in the contract to be enforceable.

Those involved in contractual negotiations are expected to spend some time examining any contractual document that forms part of the agreement. The only real assistance given by the courts is that if the document is not regarded as a contractual document—for example, a mere deck-chair ticket—any terms contained within it will not be binding (*Chapelton v. Barry UDC* (1940)).

The courts have also devoted some time (and some argument) to developing what is known as the **doctrine of fundamental breach.** Basically, the theory behind this is that no exclusion clause will protect a party from actions which are fundamentally different from what he was contracted to do, unless it is reasonable to do so (*Photo Production v. Securicor* (1980)).

However, the Unfair Contract Terms Act 1977 should remove from most contracts any unreasonable exclusion clause.

The Unfair Contract Terms Act 1977

The Act has made a comprehensive attack on those who attempt unreasonably to exclude or restrict liability. The Act mainly concerns itself with breaches of duty arising in the course of business, and reflects much of the resentment the judiciary have shown towards exclusion clauses in recent years. Virtually the whole range of contracts are covered by this statute. Section 2 (which covers non-contractual as well as contractual notices) provides that liability for the death or personal injury of another person resulting from negligence cannot be excluded or restricted. Furthermore, such liability for other loss or damage cannot be excluded unless it satisfies the requirement of *reasonableness*.

This means that the courts will examine any term to see if it is fair and reasonable 'having regard to the circumstances which were or ought reasonably to have been in contemplation of the parties when the contract was made'.

Negligent liability is defined as a breach of the recognised obligations of skill or care expected under contract and common law, plus the duty imposed by the Occupiers Liability Act 1957. The standard of skill or care is no higher than previously recognised.

Section 2 also appreciates that many are ignorant of the law and of their specific rights, by clearly stating that the defence of *volenti non fit injuria* (the voluntary assumption of risk) is not necessarily available because the injured party has agreed to or is aware of the exclusion clause.

We have already discussed the problem of standard form contracts and Section 3 of the Act tackles the unequal bargaining strengths that often result between parties by declaring that where a person contracts as a consumer or on other written standard terms, the other party cannot exclude liability for breach of contract or claim to render the contract substantially different than is expected—including no performance at all—unless the requirement of reasonableness is satisfied.

A further provision seeks to control manufacturers or distributors making use of 'phoney guarantees'. Consumers suffering loss or damage because of defective goods cannot be prevented from suing in negligence.

The Act also substantially repeats the protection given in the Misrepresentation Act 1967, Section 3, preventing the exclusion of liability for misrepresentation unless it satisfies the test of reasonableness. It would probably never be reasonable to exclude fraudulent misrepresentation, but in other areas it may be possible—notably with agents—*Overbrook Estate Ltd. v. Glencombe Properties Ltd.* (1974).

Illegal contracts

With the assistance of Parliament the courts have evolved a large number of contractual situations affecting organisations which are regarded as illegal and void. Obviously any contract which is based on the basis of a crime or a tort is illegal. The most important aspect of illegality with regard to commercial organisations are restraints of trade.

Any attempt to restrict a person from wholly or partially carrying on this trade or business is void unless it satisfies the court's test of reasonableness in that it protects commercial interests and is generally in the interests of the public at large (*Herbert Morris Ltd. v. Saxelby* (1916)).

It is reasonable to expect a businessman to seek to protect his goodwill when purchasing a business. He will want to prevent the vendor from competing against him to the extent that it will damage the interests which he has purchased. The courts will not, however, enforce any agreement which is wider than necessary to protect those interests, nor will it uphold any agreement which creates a monopolistic situation which is detrimental to consumers.

With regard to employees, the firm will not be able to prevent pure skill and knowledge being exercised by an employee against a former employer. But protection of confidential information, trade secrets or business connections is permitted as long as the restraint is not wider than necessary. (In the majority of cases the courts recognise this as a basic implied duty of any employee's contract, and a formal restraint of trade is not required, unless it is merely to formalise the duty.) A good example is seen in *Forster & Sons v. Suggett* (1918), where the works manager of a glass-blowing company was prevented for a period of five years from working in a similar capacity with a rival company, because of his knowledge of secret manufacturing processes.

Statutory restraints which regulate trading conditions between parties are laid down in the Restrictive Trade Practices Act 1976 and the Resale Prices Act 1976 which are mentioned later in more detail (page 66).

Discharge of contracts

The discharge of a contract—which means that the contract is at an end—can cause difficulties. If the parties perform their obligations completely and satisfactorily, the contract is discharged. However, if one of the parties does not fully perform his obligations, the contract is *not* discharged and the party failing in his obligations cannot recover any payment for work done.

This does not include divisible contracts where the parties agree to payment even if one party has not yet performed his obligations. Difficulties occur when there has been what is termed **substantial performance.** The degree of substantiality is for the courts to decide, but if a party completes a contract apart from some unimportant matter, payment is possible subject to a deduction for the incomplete performance.

Discharge by frustration is where an event may occur which destroys the basis of the contract. The courts will allow such a discharge only under a number of limited headings, as follows: statutory interference; where the subject matter of the contract has perished; or if, although no fault of either party, there is a fundamental change in circumstances. The courts will not allow this doctrine to be applied if any of the alleged frustrating events could have been foreseen, controlled or provided for. For example, in *Tsakiroglau v. Noblee and Thorl* (1962), the closure of the Suez Canal in 1956 did not frustrate a contract to deliver ground-nuts to the plaintiff. The Cape route made the contract more difficult but not impossible to perform.

If frustration is allowed, the contract ceases at that point and any monies are recoverable, subject to an award of compensation if one of the parties had received some benefit prior to frustration (Law Reform (Frustrated Contracts) Act 1943). A *force majeure* clause is a common inclusion in commercial contracts—avoiding by predetermination the difficulties and expense of proving frustration.

Breach of contract

Perhaps the most common form of dispute in a contract is a breach (see 'The terms of a contract', page 57). If this occurs then the injured party can treat the contract as discharged and sue for damages (as far as his own performance is concerned). If the breach is an important term of a contract and goes to the very root of the agreement (a breach of condition), then the whole contract can be treated as discharged as well as a claim for damages being lodged.

The remedies available in a civil action were noted in Book 1, damages being the most common remedy. The amount of damages for breach of contract normally reflects the actual loss suffered by the plaintiff—a true compensation. Thus in *Vacwell Engineering v. B.D.H. Chemicals* (1969), the sellers supplied the plaintiff with a chemical, contained in glass ampoules, which exploded on contact with water. The sellers were unaware of this. The resultant explosion was greater than it might have been because a number of the glass ampoules were being washed together. Nonetheless damages were payable for the breach of the implied term that the goods should have been of merchantable quality.

However, defendants do not have to pay compensation for all losses that occur. Some losses are **too remote.** This principle was established in *Hadley v. Baxendale* (1854) which stated that damages are only payable for losses that are reasonably predictable. For example, if a supplier is late in making a delivery it is reasonably predictable that loss of profits may occur, although exceptional losses would not be recoverable if, for instance, one particularly valuable contract was lost.

In all contractual breaches the parties are expected to take reasonable steps to minimise the loss, therefore mitigating any claim that may eventually be made.

Consumer credit

In the essentials of a valid contract, we have dealt with the protection given to a consumer by way of the implied terms, and related legislation. The Consumer Credit Act 1974 is another example of consumer protection worth mentioning in the highly complex field of credit transactions.

The Consumer Credit Act 1974

The Consumer Credit Act 1974 rationalised and improved the law relating to credit, with the intention of replacing much of the existing legislation (e.g. Hire Purchase Act 1965) and nearly every credit trader was affected. With some notable transactions, such as the credit attached to the conveyance of land or small financial loans below £30, the statute applies to virtually all types of credit agreement, where the debtor (or hirer) is an *individual*, rather than a corporation, and the amount of credit advanced does not exceed £5,000. The oversight of this new legislation is in the hands of the Director-General of Fair Trading. This Act is very technical and we shall give an overview of the most important provisions of the legislation which are as follows:

1. The requirement of every credit agency to obtain a licence from the Director-General presumably will not be granted if the applicant has a record of dishonesty, deceitfulness, or any similar unfair trading practice.

2. A control (with criminal sanctions if necessary) over advertisements about credit which may be construed as misleading; the prevention of canvassing for credit business off trade premises.

3. A properly drawn up agreement of the credit transaction must contain terms laid down in regulations by the Secretary of State. Before entering into an agreement, it is required that the debtor is given information about the credit provided and the rate of charge for the credit. The agreement itself must contain a statement of the debtor's principal rights and duties and the protection and remedies available. It must be signed by both parties and be legible.

The debtor is also entitled to a copy of the agreement at the time of the contract, and a second copy within seven days if the agreement is accepted at a later date. An improperly executed agreement will be unenforceable except by court order.

4. Provision is made under the legislation for the cancellation of agreements made away from trade premises (that is, door-to-door selling) provided there are sufficient oral negotiations prior to the sale. There is a 'cooling off' period of five days from receipt of the statutory copy or a notice of his cancellation rights during which the debtor can cancel.

5. Perhaps the most important protection for the consumer under the Act concerns the procedure for the termination of the agreement by the creditor, for instance, because the debtor has fallen into arrears. Before terminating the agreement or enforcing any other terms, such as repossession of the goods or the enforcement of security, a **default notice** must be served on the debtor specifying the nature of the breach and the remedy to be taken (not less than seven days). This gives the debtor time to remedy any defect in the agreement which he had perhaps not realised. If the debtor complies with instructions set out in the default notice, the breach is regarded as not having occurred. Failure to comply with the default notice means that the creditor can take action on any term of the agreement. But there is also a category of goods known as 'protected goods' where the debtor is faced with termination by the creditor after one-third of the total agreement price has been paid. Goods which are protected can only be recovered by a court order. This does not, of course, prevent the creditor from persuading the debtor to part voluntarily with goods, or to take out an action for any arrears of payment.

Having to seek a return order in the County Court enables the debtor to make a defence about his financial difficulties. The courts are usually sympathetic to debtors who have genuine financial problems, and they can grant a time order allowing the debtor to repay the arrears by instalments. The application also enables the debtor to claim that the credit agreement is extortionate, for example, if the repayments are grossly exorbitant or contrary to standards of fair trading. The court has the power to have the whole or part of the obligation set aside.

The Act allows the debtor or hirer the right to terminate the agreement himself if he feels unable to continue with his obligations. If a debtor terminates, his liability ceases when:

1. Any arrears have been paid.

2. Half of the total price of the agreement has been paid, or the amount in the minimum payments clause, or the creditor's actual loss—whichever is the smallest sum.

3. Any sum has been paid to the creditor as compensation for not taking reasonable care of the goods in his possession.

Hirers too have the right to terminate by giving notice equal to the length of the payment intervals if less than three months. Termination is not possible unless the agreement has been in operation for at least eighteen months (nor does it apply to agreements over £300 p.a. or those made within the course of business).

Consumer protection by criminal sanctions

The Trade Descriptions Act 1968

Legislation such as this reinforces the civil legislation aimed at protecting the consumer in unequal bargaining situations. Organisations are punished by criminal sanctions if they are convicted of making false trade descriptions in contractual situations. Fines up to £1,000 can be levied if, as is usual, the conviction is before the magistrates at a summary level. But upon indictment at the Crown Court an unlimited fine can be imposed for persistent or more serious offenders. Although unlikely, it is possible for the culprit to be imprisoned for up to two years. The extent of the fines can be seen in *R. v. Hammerton's Cars Ltd.* (1976) where two offences of supplying cars with false odometer readings were committed and fines of £1,000 and £500 were given. The real punishment, of course, is the damage to the organisation's reputation in the community.

The responsibility for **enforcement** lies with officers of the local Trading Standards Department. Their powers under the Act are extensive and businessmen must be prepared for these officers at all times. They have the right to make test purchases and, when it is in the interests of a possible conviction, to seize goods and documents (any wilful obstruction of their duties is in itself an offence).

Criminal liability

The **areas of offence** are covered by Section 1(1) of the Act which states:

> 'Any person who, in the course of a trade or business
> (a) applies a false trade description to goods; or
> (b) supplies, or offers to supply, any goods to which a false trade description is applied;
> shall, subject to the provisions of the Act, be guilty of an offence.'

Section 6 of the Act avoids the problem of an **invitation to treat** by stating that it is an offence to have the goods in possession with a false trade description attached.

What actually constitutes a trade description is defined in Section 2, as any indication direct or indirect of:

(a) quantity, size or gauge
(b) method of manufacture or production
(c) composition
(d) fitness for purpose, strength, performance, behaviour or accuracy
(e) any other physical characteristics
(f) testing by any person and the results thereof
(g) approval by any person or conformity with an approved type
(h) place or date of manufacture, production etc.
(i) person by whom manufactured or processed
(j) other history, including previous ownership or use.

But a trade description is only false when it is false **to a material degree.** The Act mentions other areas of specific misdescription or misleading circumstances, which may constitute an offence: **advertisements** must not be misleading, and it is an offence to make misleading statements about **prices,** for example, that a good is sold at less than the recommended price. If a price reduction is proclaimed, the good must have been offered at a higher price for a continuous period of not less than twenty-eight days in the previous six months, unless it is clearly stated to the contrary.

An example of a misleading price occurred in *Richards v. Westminster Motors Ltd.* (1975), where a mini-bus was offered for sale at a price 'usually £1,900–£1,395'. When a buyer made an offer he was told that VAT was to be added making a total price of £1,530·50. This constituted an offence because the average man would have regarded the actual price as being £1,395.

An offence is also committed if in the course of trade or business a false statement is made knowingly or recklessly about the provision of **services.**

Although offences under the Trade Descriptions Act are regarded as strict liability, it is possible for defences to be raised. Section 24 states that it is a defence to prove:

(a) that the commission of the offence was due to a mistake or reliance on information supplied to the defendant, or to the act or default of another person, an accident or some other cause beyond his control, and

(b) that he took all reasonable precautions and exercised all due diligence to avoid the commission of such offence by himself or any person under his control.

Thus in *Tesco Supermarkets v. Nattrass* (1972) the organisation advertised a special price reduction on packets of washing powder. The shop had run out of these packets carrying the offer, and the company was summonsed after a shopper's complaint. The action failed because the manager, who had been properly trained, had not noticed the situation. This was not the fault of the company who had taken 'reasonable precaution' and acted with 'due diligence', to make sure that the law was complied with. (A successful action could have been taken out against the manager himself.)

It is worth noting that although this Act is enforced on behalf of the consumer, the Powers of the Criminal Courts Act 1973 do allow for compensation to be given to the victim at the same time that punishment is meted out. This saves the consumer the trouble and expense of taking a civil action.

Other consumer protection legislation

The Trade Descriptions Act 1968 is just one example of legislation imposing criminal sanctions in the field of consumer protection. There are several other complex pieces of legislation giving substantial protection in specialist consumer areas.

The Weights and Measures Acts 1963, 1976 and 1979 control and standardise the sizes and dimensions of packages and call for weights, quantities and constituents to be clearly marked.

The Food and Drugs Act 1955 controls the regulations relating to food hygiene, and how it is presented and sold.

The Prices Act 1974 requires the marking of prices on selected goods, including the unit price so that customers can accurately work out the true cost.

The Consumer Safety Act 1978 gives the Secretary of State over-all responsibility for the control of any product which is commercially unsafe. It allows for ministerial regulations to be initiated outlawing individual practices. For example, a statutory instrument was passed in 1969 stating that domestic electrical wiring should conform to a new standard colour code, and an order made in 1974 controls the toxic and poisonous substances in writing implements.

Product liability

A possible future development in the area of consumer protection may be legislation to strengthen product liability, which means basically to increase manufacturers' liability to the consumer if defective products are produced. The **Royal Commission on Civil Liability and Personal Injury** (the Pearson Report 1978) made recommendations on this subject reflecting steps already taken by the EEC to introduce product liability.

The major proposal is that manufacturers should be *strictly* liable for death and injury caused by their defective products. If such a proposal becomes law, this will also be in line with existing legislation in the United States. But the major criticism is that manufacturers might be forced to raise prices to cover the increased insurance costs and extra quality control necessary, making it a high price to pay for consumer protection.

Monopolies, mergers and restrictive practices

A further measure of protection of the consumer's interest is the legislation controlling monopolies, mergers and restrictive practices contained in the **Fair Trading Act 1973.** The Act established a new independent post of Director-General of Fair Trading, who has been given responsibility to examine all commercial activities relating to the supply of goods and services to the public. His responsibilities include fact-finding and the monitoring of monopolies and mergers.

With regard to monopolies he may make recommendations to the Monopolies and Mergers Commission to investigate monopolistic practices. A situation where a single firm or group of firms controls one-quarter of the market may be put forward for investigation. The Office of Fair Trading gathers information concerning the monopoly and it is a criminal offence under the Fair Trading Act 1973 wilfully to obstruct them in a fact-finding mission, or to give false replies. If necessary a public hearing will be held at which the organisation under investigation can be legally represented to answer any questions. After investigation, the Monopolies and Mergers Commission can lay a published report before Parliament which may wish to take legislative action to correct any mischief. The action may include the transfer of property and shares.

The Director-General is also chairman of the Merger Panel, which investigates mergers whose combined asset value is above £5 million or the resultant merger would create a monopoly (a quarter of the market controlled). The Secretary of State for Trade and Industry may make a recommendation to the Commission for further investigation and for a report to be made to Parliament. Usually legislative action is unnecessary, for the mere threat of it is usually sufficient to dissuade firms from continuing any activity which the Commission believes to be against the public interest. It is not assumed that monopolistic organisational activity is against the public interest *per se*.

However, with regard to restrictive practices

there is an assumption that they are against the public interest unless refuted by the organisation accused. A restrictive practice occurs when organisations collectively agree to restrict the production, supply and distribution of goods.

The Restrictive Trade Practices Act 1976

Much of the legislation relating to restrictive practices is now contained in the Restrictive Trade Practices Act 1976. The principal points are that it requires a register to be kept of all restrictive agreements. The Director-General is responsible for the register and organisations must notify all agreements which attempt, for example, to restrict the quantities of goods to be produced, or to fix the prices charged or paid for goods, or to have a collective agreement on the terms of the contracts, or to restrict the supply of goods to persons or areas.

Unless disbanded these agreements will be brought before the Restrictive Practices Court, which is staffed by judges and specialist laymen, who have the duty to examine the agreements to see if the claim that they are against the public interest can be rebutted. It may be possible to prove this by selecting one of the recommended 'gateways', for example:

(a) that the restriction is reasonably necessary having regard to the character of the goods, to protect the public against injury;

(b) that the removal of the restriction would deny to the public, as purchasers, consumers or users, other specific and substantial benefits or advantages;

(c) that the restriction is reasonably necessary to counteract measures taken by a person not party to the agreement;

(d) that the restriction is reasonably necessary to enable the persons party to the agreement to negotiate fair terms with a person not party to it who controls a preponderant part of the trade, business or market in the goods concerned;

(e) that the removal of the restriction would be likely to have a serious and persistent adverse effect on the general level of unemployment;

(f) that the removal of the restriction would be likely to cause a reduction in the volume of earnings of the export business, which is substantial either in relation to the whole export business of the UK, or in relation to the whole business (including export business) of the trade or industry;

(g) that the restriction is reasonably required for purposes connected with the maintenance of any restriction accepted by the parties;

(h) that the restriction does not directly or indirectly restrict or discourage competition to any material degree in any relevant trade or industry and is not likely to do so.

Despite the large number of 'gateways', in the majority of cases the court finds that agreements are contrary to the public interest and order that they cease, e.g. re the Yarn Spinners Agreement (1959). An injunction can be issued to enforce the decision which, if disobeyed, constitutes a contempt of court, and heavy fines can be imposed.

The Restrictive Trade Practices Act 1976 contains provisions which further strengthen restrictive practices legislation by bringing services into its jurisdiction. The practice whereby firms exchange information is also made illegal. This legislation reflects and takes into account the influence of the Treaty of Rome (Articles 85 and 86) which generally prohibits restrictive competition.

The Resale Prices Act 1976 prevents manufacturers and suppliers from imposing conditions for the maintenance of minimum prices for which goods are sold. An individual supplier can, however, *recommend* a minimum price. The enforcement of the Act is by the Director-General through the Restrictive Practices Court.

For instance, in *R. v. Chocolate and Sugar Confectionery Reference* (1967), the suppliers were unable to prove that the lifting of resale price maintenance would have a serious and detrimental effect on customers. Their claim that there would be a large closure of small retail establishments was rejected by the Restrictive Practices Court, who found it hard to believe that people would travel long distances just for a bar of chocolate.

The Competition Act 1980 attempted to cover 'anti-competitive' practices not covered by existing legislation. A **course of conduct** is anti-competitive if it has the effect of 'restricting, preventing or distorting' competition, for example, a firm using its monopolistic position in the market to prevent sales of its commodity through discount stores.

Responsibility for the implementation of these provisions lies with the Director-General who can make a **competitive reference** to the Monopolies and Mergers Commission, if it is felt such a practice exists. This he will do if he fails to obtain an undertaking from the trader to cease or modify his trading practice. An adverse report by the commission may result in an order by the Secretary of State requiring the trader to show how he is going to remedy his practice.

5. Government Policies and Control of the Economy

The circular flow of income and demand management

The circular flow of income analysis in Chapter 2 demonstrated how an equilibrium level of national income, output and employment is established in a simplified model of how an economy works. One method employed in that analysis was based upon determining a position where total income in the economy was equal to total expenditure. When this situation existed there would be no tendency for the level of output in the economy to change and thus an equilibrium level of national income would have been reached. This would be the case as the money being paid out by firms in the form of incomes to households providing factor services was being matched by the money flowing back into firms via the various types of expenditure. There would be no reason therefore why total output should be changed and so national income and employment would also be in equilibrium. In short, the level of output in the economy was justified in that it was being absorbed by the total expenditure in the economy.

The other method employed used the injections/withdrawals approach in that equilibrium would be established when the total injections into the circular flow were equal to the total withdrawals from the circular flow. This would produce the same equilibrium position, as this also implied that the money being paid out by firms was matched by the money being returned to them. Both methods must produce the same result, since if national income was equal to aggregate expenditure, then at the same time injections must equal withdrawals.

Fig. 5.1 uses the expenditure/income method to determine equilibrium and depicts an economy which has reached an equilibrium level of national income of £8,000 million, since this is the position where the aggregate expenditure schedule ($C+I+G+X$) cuts the 45° line, and thus the level of national income, where expenditure equals income.

The unpredictable nature of an unregulated economy

There is however no automatic mechanism whereby an economy will reach an equilibrium level of national income and output which also reflects a fully employed economy. Indeed the economy in Fig. 5.1 has reached an equilibrium which has left spare capacity, as the level of national income and output which could be produced if full employment were reached is £10,000 million. There is no reason why this economy will move towards this full employment situation as aggregate expenditure is not sufficient to warrant the level of national income and output which full employment would produce. It would be a complete coincidence if the millions of independent decisions concerning spending plans in this economy added up to an amount that would produce full employment. Aggregate expenditure in this example is only £8,000 million and so the

Fig. 5.1

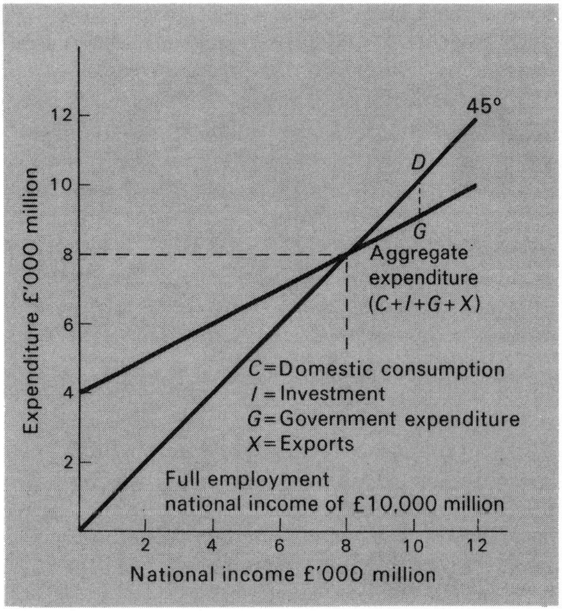

amount of money being paid out by firms in the form of incomes is in excess of the money flowing back into firms via expenditure. Thus this level of output and employment is not justified in terms of demand, and full employment would only be attained if aggregate expenditure was £10,000 million. This economy is suffering from what is termed a **deflationary gap,** and this can be defined as the amount of additional expenditure required to produce full employment; in Fig. 5.1 this is equivalent to *DG*. If the aggregate expenditure schedule was at a higher level, the deflationary gap would have been removed.

This was the sort of situation which existed in the UK economy during the inter-war years when unemployment reached 22 per cent at times, and rarely fell below 10 per cent. This severe and prolonged recession, however, was not in accordance with the traditional theories which formed the basis of the most popular economic thinking during those years, as it was generally held that an economy would always show a tendency to move towards a full employment level of national income. Any unemployment that arose would be a purely temporary phenomenon, as accepted economic theory was centred around economic mechanisms operating in a free market economy that would soon overcome any tendency for the economy to move away from the full employment position.

If, for example, unemployment did exist, the resulting excess supply of labour was expected to produce the same result as anticipated in a product market where excess supply existed, namely, a fall in price or—where labour was concerned—a fall in the general level of wages. Lower wage rates would then induce firms to employ more labour. This downward flexibility in wages played an important part in the classical school of economic thought which relied very heavily upon automatic corrective mechanisms so that full employment would be the general rule. A further example of such an adjustment would be if, at full employment, there was an increase in savings. According to our circular flow of income analysis, this would cause a fall in the equilibrium level of national income and a rise in unemployment. The classical school, however, believed that an increase in savings would cause interest rates to fall, and the lower cost of borrowing money would stimulate investment expenditure, and this would compensate for the fall in consumer expenditure and help preserve full employment.

Traditional economists therefore attributed the prolonged and severe unemployment in the inter-war period to the growth of activities in the economy which led to imperfections in the working of the economic system. Such imperfections were said to be largely the fault of trade unions, which attempted to resist a fall in wage rates, and of government absorbing funds which should have been left in the economy for the purpose of increased private investment expenditure. Following this line of thought led the government to pursue policies which sought to cut wage rates and reduce government expenditure, including plans to cut unemployment benefits. Again according to our earlier analysis, this would lead to even lower levels of demand and worsen the situation, hardly creating an economic climate that would stimulate private investment expenditure.

The recognition of the need for government intervention

It was the work of John Maynard Keynes, and in particular his book *The General Theory of Employment, Interest and Money*, published in 1936, which showed that the workings of an unregulated economy could persistently produce an equilibrium level of national income and output which fell short of a full employment position, and that full employment equilibrium would be the exception rather than the general rule. Keynes recognised that government policies were aggravating the situation and the correct approach required the government to stimulate the level of demand by cutting taxes and increasing government expenditure. This would have involved the government in running a budget deficit, but this was a complete break from the long-standing obligation of the government to balance its expenditure with its tax revenues. The proposals which Keynes put forward were not fully accepted and it was the arms build-up as the threat of war increased which helped reduce unemployment.

It was not until the post-war period that serious attention was paid to Keynesian techniques of influencing the overall level of economic activity by managing total demand. The importance attached to the breakthrough in economic thinking which Keynes made was reflected in a White Paper produced in 1944 expressing the government's intention to avoid the return of mass unemployment. The government's confidence in the new measures available led to a commitment to secure 'a high and stable level of employment'. This it sought to achieve by the use of appropriate fiscal and monetary measures designed to ensure that total demand in the economy was always sufficient to produce full employment.

Although the development of demand management policies was essentially promoted to avoid the possibility of large-scale unemployment, they also helped to deal with another situation which Keynes recognised could arise if the economy were left to its own devices. The situation could arise where the level of aggregate expenditure was such that it was running in excess of the productive capabilities of the economy. The threat always existed in an unregulated economy that the total demand for the output of firms could more than outweigh the ability of firms to meet this demand. This position would arise if the economy had already attained a state of full employment because total spending had actually reached a level sufficient to provide employment for all those seeking work. Keynes of course demonstrated that there were a virtually infinite number of less than full employment equilibrium positions, but also investigated the likely repercussions on the economy of this full employment ceiling being reached.

Fig. 5.2 illustrates an economy that has reached a full employment equilibrium and has given rise to a national income of £10,000 million. Until this

Fig. 5.2

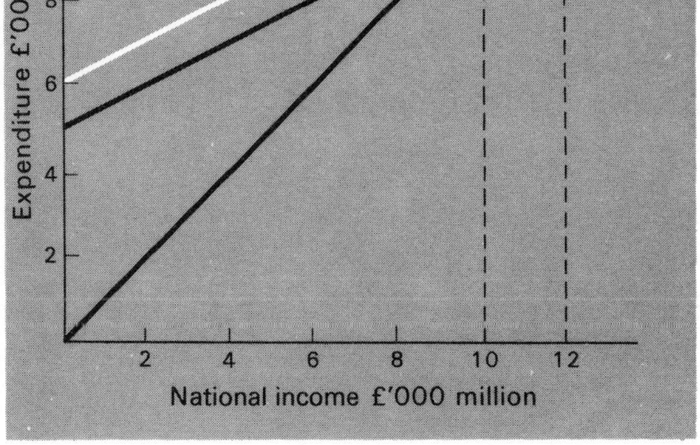

full employment position was reached any increase in aggregate expenditure could be met by an increase in output, as use could be made of existing unemployed labour to meet any such increase in demand, without any significant impact upon the general level of prices. Thus increases in national income and output up to £10,000 million would be in real terms, in that such movements did represent an actual increase in the output of goods and services, and a corresponding rise in real income for the economy as a whole. More output was being produced, and the incomes were being generated to allow this output to be purchased by households providing the factor services to firms expanding their output.

It is now assumed that the aggregate expenditure schedule in Fig. 5.2 shifts upwards because of an increase in one of its components, or a combination of them. If, for example, private investment expenditure increases, a condition of **excess demand** will be produced as there is no automatic and immediate means by which this increased injection will be balanced by an increase in withdrawals. The classical school of economists claimed that an increase in the demand for investment funds would raise interest rates, and thus lead to an increase in savings to make room for the additional investment demand. This assumed that savings were very sensitive to changes in interest rates, but this proved an unreliable assumption.

Our analysis shows, however, that the result of the increase in investment expenditure is to increase total demand and add to the competitive demand for labour. Firms wish to take advantage of the increase in demand for final output and seek to attract labour from each other by offering higher wages, while being obliged to pay higher wages in order to retain their existing work force. This excess demand in the economy has worked its way through to the labour market and also provides labour with a stronger bargaining position when negotiating wage rates. Thus the absence of unemployed labour will lead to a pulling up of the general level of wages and a rise in the costs of production. Because of the existence of excess demand in the economy firms are confident that they can raise their prices to cover these increased costs without experiencing a decline in sales. This will produce an increase in the cost of living which labour seeks to overcome by claiming higher wages. The continued existence of excess demand means that firms yield to such demands and leads to the creation of an **inflationary spiral** as prices and wages continue to rise. Thus the increased level of national income of £2,000 million in Fig. 5.2 is solely a movement in money terms, in that it is the same total output of goods and services as occurred at full employment, but now expressed at higher prices. Similarly, the money value of national income has increased, but since this does not reflect an increase in actual output, real incomes have remained unchanged.

This chain of events was due to the creation of an **inflationary gap** in the economy which can be defined as the extent to which aggregate expenditure at full employment exceeds the full employment level of national income and output. This is equivalent to *IG* in Fig. 5.2. This inflationary condition is potentially unstable, as the rate of inflation could gather momentum and lead to very substantial price increases. It will have a damaging effect upon those who depend upon fixed incomes, have little bargaining power or live on past savings. The economy's competitive position will deteriorate, exports will suffer, and at the same time imports will become more attractive, leading to an unfavourable balance of payments. Such, however, is the unpredictable nature of an unregulated economy that the internal position could be rapidly reversed if total demand were suddenly to slacken, perhaps because of a review of investment plans by firms that leads to a cut in their expenditure programmes. Prices in general, and wages in particular, are not very flexible in a downward direction, so the reduction in total demand in this economy will produce unemployment rather than a significant fall in prices.

Wages and prices tend to operate with a ratchet effect in that they are very sticky in a downward direction. The end result of a sudden fall in demand is unemployment, accompanied by prices and incomes at the inflated levels for remaining output and employment. We then have a level of national income higher than the original £10,000 million, but a situation of less than full employment. In Fig. 5.2 the rise in national income to £12,000 million was due to 20 per cent inflation. A fall in demand will remove inflation (as inflation is the *process* of rising prices, not simply high prices), and the aggregate expenditure schedule will shift downwards. The intersection of this new aggregate expenditure schedule and the 45° line may produce an equilibrium level of national income of £10,500 million, and this fall will give a fair indication of the amount of unemployment that has been produced. As far as this economy is concerned, the full employment level of national income is £12,000 million, as this is now the value associated with full employment output. This sequence of events is illustrated in Fig. 5.3, where the parcel represents the actual output of the economy, the price tag gives the money

Fig. 5.3

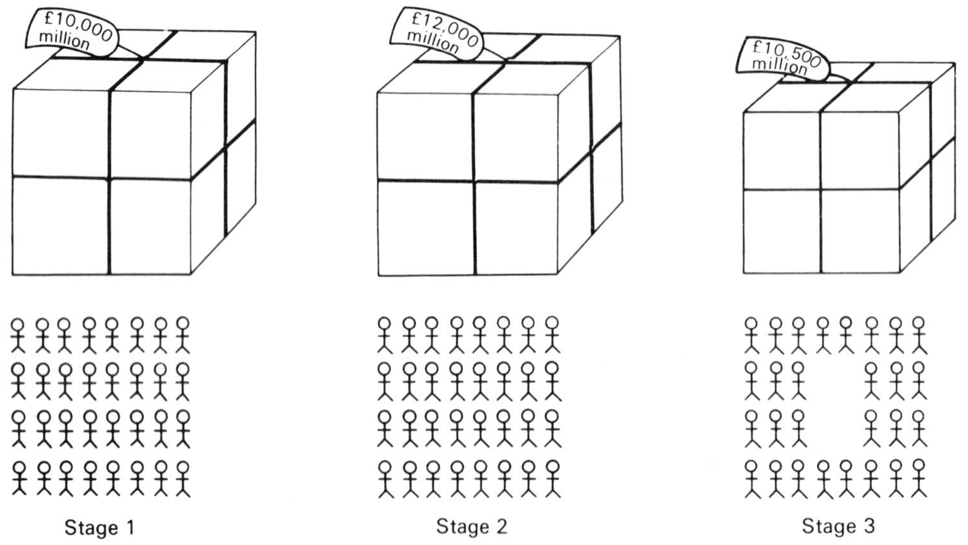

value of this output and the money value of national income, while each figure represents the employment of 100,000 workers.

Full employment exists at both stages 1 and 2; note that the physical size of the parcels remains the same, but the parcel in stage 2 has a higher price tag. At stage 3 the parcel has got smaller (by 12½ per cent) when compared with the parcel in stages 1 and 2, although the price tag on parcel 3 is still higher than the price tag on parcel 1. Note that fewer workers will be required to produce the parcel at stage 3. Keynesian economics provided the key for maintaining full employment, but this did increase the risk of spilling over into an inflationary situation. Nevertheless, the same basic principles which indicated how a *deflationary* gap should be closed, could be used to tackle a situation that was leading to the development of an *inflationary* gap.

To counter the fluctuations in the economy that would otherwise produce unemployment or inflation, the principles of **demand management** were embodied in fiscal and monetary measures that for much of the post-war period acted as the main tools for regulating the economy.

Fiscal policy in theory

This is the use of the government's powers in the fields of expenditure and taxation to influence the over-all level of economic activity in the economy. Annual and interim budgets are now constructed only after careful consideration has been given to the existing and predicted state of the economy as a whole. Economic data are collected and analysed to discover what is happening to key factors in the economy, and then forecasts are made concerning the direction in which these factors are moving the economy, and the likely pace of these movements. If, for example, the diagnosis and forecasts provide evidence that the future level of demand in the economy was likely to be excessive and produce an unacceptable rate of inflation, the government will budget to achieve a surplus. A budget surplus means that the net effect of its taxation and expenditure programmes is to produce a withdrawal of purchasing power from the economy. This will help to produce a level of total demand which is more in line with the productive capacity of the economy and avoid the inflationary pressures exerted by a condition of excess demand. Similarly, the budget can be used to deal with a situation which forecasts suggest is likely to produce a level of demand in the economy that will leave an unacceptable level of unemployment. In this event the government will aim for a budget deficit so that the net effect is to increase total demand in the economy and promote greater employment.

Taxation

Direct taxes

The manipulation of direct taxes is a means of altering the spending power of both individuals and firms and are those taxes levied on various types of incomes.

(a) **Income tax** is levied upon the income of individuals according to the band within which their income falls. In October 1977 it ranged from a basic rate of 33p in the pound to an effective rate of 98p in the pound for those on exceptionally high incomes. The top rate of income tax was 83p in the pound, but in addition there was a surcharge on the higher levels of investment income of 10–15 per cent. In 1979 these were lowered to 30p and 60p respectively.

Table 5.1 shows that income tax accounted for over £28,000 million in 1981–82 and thus changes in this tax, to the basic rate in particular, are likely to have a significant impact upon total spending in the economy. If, for example, the government wishes to stimulate demand, a cut in the basic rate—at which the bulk of those paying tax con-

Table 5.1: Net Receipts of the Board of Inland Revenue

£ million

Financial year	*Total**	*Income tax*	*Corporation tax*	*Development land tax*	*Capital gains tax*	*Capital transfer tax*	*Petroleum† revenue tax*	*Stamp duties*
1981–82	40,282	28,725	4,925	38	526	480	4,605	797

* Including various duties not shown under separate headings. † Including supplementary petroleum tax.
SOURCE: *Financial Statistics.*

tribute—will have a more significant effect than if a reduction was made in the higher rates of tax. Moreover, those paying tax at the basic rate will tend to spend a much larger proportion of this increase in their net income compared with those on higher incomes. The latter group will display a much higher **marginal propensity to save** (that is, the proportion of an increase in income which is *saved* will be higher). If, however, the government wishes to cut consumer expenditure, they would need to increase the basic rates of income tax, as this income group will have a higher **marginal propensity to consume** (that is, the part of an increase in income which is *spent* will be higher), and thus a reduction in net income will produce a significant fall in consumer expenditure.

(b) **Corporation tax** is levied on a company's profits. A reduction in the rate of corporation tax will raise post-tax profits and may permit the payment of an increased dividend to shareholders if the company so desires. But perhaps of greater importance is the resulting increase in the funds available to the company for investment from its internal sources. The extent to which firms will increase their investment plans does, however, depend very heavily on the ability of the government to raise the general level of business confidence. Such investment will not be undertaken if those responsible for private investment expenditure are not optimistic about the strength and duration of their future markets. Investment expenditure will not only lead to an immediate increase in employment in the capital goods industries, but also raise the future productive potential of the economy and full employment will then be associated with a higher level of real output and income.

(c) **Taxes on capital** account for about 3 per cent of the revenue derived from direct taxes, and thus changes in them are not likely to have any marked and immediate impact upon total demand. The **Capital Gains Tax** is levied on the increase in the value of certain types of capital assets and was basically conceived as a means of effecting a redistribution of income at the expense of those who made capital gains via transactions on the Stock Exchange. It was aimed at those whose income was essentially derived from the sale of assets such as land, and the speculative purchase of property and shares which had appreciated in value by the time of the sale.

Capital Transfer Tax covers gifts made during the taxpayer's lifetime as well as those made at death. It is another tax that seeks to achieve a redistribution of income and wealth. Changes in these taxes may have an effect upon such activities as savings and investment, and in particular Capital Transfer Tax has been adjusted to reduce the impact upon the welfare of small firms where a strong family interest exists.

A more specific **Development Land Tax** was introduced in 1976 to tax the profits derived from the sale of land which has gained development rights. As yet it is difficult to predict the repercussions which this tax will have upon particular types of economic activity.

(d) The net income of both individuals and firms can also be affected by changes in the **allowances** which they are granted, as this will raise that part of income which is free of tax. For example, each individual is allowed to claim certain allowances according to personal circumstances such as marital status and dependent relatives. The tax burden of firms can be influenced, for example, by changes in initial allowances, which is the amount a business is allowed to deduct in respect of the cost of a new capital asset. In addition firms can make a deduction for depreciation before its taxable profit is assessed. By altering these allowances the government seeks to encourage investment expenditure on additional or improved productive capacity.

Indirect taxes

Total demand in the economy can also be influenced by changes in indirect taxes which are those not levied directly upon individuals but upon the activities of individuals and in particular those activities associated with expenditure of various kinds. Table 5.2 (page 72) gives an indication of the revenue derived from the different types of indirect taxes in 1981–82.

(a) **Value Added Tax** (VAT) is a tax levied at each stage of processing where value is added, and a wide range of output is liable to this tax. It is broadly based and is less concentrated than other indirect taxes. In 1978 the rate of VAT was 8 per cent, although a higher rate of 12½ per cent was payable on a wide range of consumer durables. In 1979 a standard rate of 15 per cent was introduced.

Changes in the level of VAT can alter the amount of money which a consumer has left after making a purchase. If, for example, the basic rate was reduced, this would release more money for additional expenditure as a fall in total withdrawals from the economy will stimulate total

Table 5.2: Net receipts by HM Customs and Excise *£ million*

Year	*Total*	*Alcohol*	*Tobacco*	*Betting and gaming*	*Hydro-carbon oils*	*Protective duties*	*VAT*	*Car tax*	*Other*
1981–82	25,237	4,100	3,415	512	4,644	957	11,848	507	244

SOURCE: *Financial Statistics.*

demand. Similarly, an increase in this tax would withdraw purchasing power and deflate the level of demand. The government could also use VAT to achieve a reduction in demand, which was concentrated primarily upon certain classes of goods and services, by applying a higher rate to specific items. For example, excess demand may be particularly severe in the market for certain consumer durables or export demand may be encouraged by giving goods or services sold overseas a preferential or zero rating.

(b) **Excise duties** are taxes on home-produced goods as distinct from customs duties which are levied on imports and are not primarily imposed with a view to raising revenue. As Table 5.2 indicates the main sources of excise revenue are alcohol, tobacco and fuel oils. The demand for these items tends to be very insensitive to price increases (i.e. demand is price inelastic) and increases in the duties can have a very significant impact upon the amount of spending power withdrawn from the economy.

(c) **Import duties** do make a contribution to revenue but are primarily intended to discourage the purchase of imported items. In Table 5.2 they are referred to as 'protective duties'. An increase in such duties can help stimulate the demand for domestic output, as imported items will become relatively less competitive and this will reduce the withdrawal from the economy in the form of expenditure on imports. One of the effects of such action is to contribute towards the closing of a deflationary gap and promote employment in domestic firms.

(d) Other sources of revenue and therefore potential areas for adjustment include betting and gaming taxes, stamp duties on certain documents and motor vehicle road fund licences. The latter in particular has been used to tax spending power away from consumers and is received by the Department of Transport.

These then are the main areas where taxes can be adjusted to regulate total spending power within the economy and assist the government in pursuing its economic objectives. To varying degrees the taxes and allowances described can be altered in order to shift the aggregate expenditure schedule by the desired amount by operating on the components represented by domestic consumption, investment and export expenditure. This leaves government expenditure as the only component of total demand which has not as yet been described from the point of view of fiscal policy.

Government expenditure

In the financial year 1981–82 the ratio of total public expenditure to GDP was estimated at approximately 42 per cent. Table 5.3 shows the scale and variety of this expenditure and the ability of the government to exert a major influence upon total demand by altering the level of its expenditure in various areas.

If it is the aim of the government to reflate the level of demand, this can be achieved by a combination of tax cuts and an increase in its own expenditure. The subsequent budget deficit will be financed by borrowing which involves the sale of government securities. This operation will be conducted on behalf of the government by the Bank of England and the Treasury. This budget deficit will add to the **National Debt** and interest must be paid to those who have loaned money to the government. The cost of servicing the National Debt amounted to £9,854 million in 1980–81.

Increased expenditure can be injected into the economy via investment in the social services, such as health and education, or by helping local authorities to extend the scale of these services by raising the level of employment to staff these services. The government can further stimulate demand by encouraging the nationalised industries to bring forward their investment programmes, and by increasing such items as unemployment benefits, child benefits and pensions. These increases, along

Table 5.3: Total public expenditure by programme, 1981–82

	£ million
Defence	12,606
Overseas aid	960
Net payment to EC institutions	153
Other overseas services	573
Agriculture, fisheries, food and forestry	1,372
Industry, energy, trade and employment	5,319
Transport	3,898
Housing	3,137
Other environmental services	3,244
Law, order and protective services	3,774
Education and science, arts and libraries	12,348
Health and personal social services	12,751
Social security	28,510
Other public services	1,556
Common services	1,453
Scotland	5,772
Wales	2,243
Northern Ireland	3,218
Government lending to nationalised industries	1,457
Adjustments	
Nationalised industries net overseas and market borrowing	260
Special sales of assets	79
Total	104,684

SOURCE: *Economic Progress Report, February 1983.*

with improved personal allowances, will be a means of raising the spending power of those who do not benefit from cuts in direct taxes because they are currently unemployed, retired from work or have not yet reached an income level at which they become liable to any significant amount of income tax. There is also scope to concentrate part of the expenditure upon those geographical areas where unemployment is much higher than the national average, by raising the financial incentives for firms to locate or expand in the Assisted Areas. Thus, by using such measures, the government can help to compensate for the deficiency of demand in the private sector of the economy.

If, however, the government's economic advisers believed that future demand was likely to prove excessive, the government would have to consider what total level of demand was permissible and what the make-up of this demand should be. The main choice would be between consumer expenditure and government expenditure, since the government would not wish to endanger the long-term prosperity of the economy and the balance of payments by action which would directly inhibit private investment and exports. Thus the budget's necessary surplus could be achieved by an increase in personal and indirect tax in conjunction with some cuts in the government's own expenditure in areas which it did not regard as priorities. Nevertheless, the deflation of markets which would result from this reduction in total expenditure might depress business confidence and so ultimately lead to a fall in investment by the private sector.

Fiscal policies and the multiplier effect

Whether the net effect of the budgetary changes is to withdraw purchasing power or increase it, the Chancellor will be required to take account of the multiplier effect of any such initial changes upon the level of national income. For example, if the government leaves taxes unchanged and at the same time raises its annual expenditure on road-building by £300 million, the eventual rise in national incomes as a result of the initial increase in injections will be a multiple of the original £300 million. This results from the following chain of events. The expenditure on roads will become the income of the firms and their employees and suppliers contracted to build the roads, such as civil engineering and construction companies. The initial rise in national income in the economy is thus £300 million, but this will give rise to further expenditure and create income elsewhere in the economy.

The circular flow of income analysis in Chapter 2 recognised that not all the income of £300 million received by those supplying factor services involved in the road-building programme will be passed on in the form of expenditure to domestic firms. This arises as withdrawals occur in the form of savings, taxation and expenditure on imports. Thus only a part of the original income of £300 million will be passed on in the form of expenditure and remain within the circular flow of income.

The amount withdrawn will depend upon the summation of the marginal propensity to save (*MPS*), the marginal tax rate (*MTR*), and the marginal propensity to import (*MPM*). For the sake of simplicity it is assumed that the $MPS = 0{\cdot}10$, the $MTR = 0{\cdot}30$ and the $MPM = 0{\cdot}20$, so that the fraction of each additional unit of income withdrawn is three-fifths (0·60). If this is the case, only £120 million will be passed on by those who originally received the income derived from the £300 million spent on roads. This £120 million has, however, created income elsewhere in the economy for those supplying the goods and services upon which the £120 million was spent. The process of income creation will continue, as £48 million of this £120 million will be returned to the circular flow and generate yet another rise in incomes. Thus the level of national income has already increased by £468 million (i.e. £300 million + 120 million + £48 million).

The rise in national income and the rise in employment will come to an end when a new equilibrium has been reached. The condition for equilibrium is of course where aggregate expenditure is equal to national income, or where total injections are matched by total withdrawals. Assuming that the economy was already in a state of equilibrium before the budgetary changes, the result of the increases in the road-building programme was that total injections exceeded total withdrawals by £300 million. This then gives rise to an increase in national income which continues until additional withdrawals have been generated in the form of savings, taxes and imports which total £300 million. Only then will total injections again equal total withdrawals, and to generate additional withdrawals of £300 million national income must rise by £500 million. Thus the Chancellor would have been aiming to achieve a rise in national income of £500 million and, taking account of the **multiplier,** this involved increased government expenditure of £300 million. The value of the multiplier (M) was $1\frac{2}{3}$ and can be determined by the following formula:

$$M=\frac{1}{MPS+MTR+MPM}=\frac{1}{0{\cdot}10+0{\cdot}30+0{\cdot}20}=\frac{1}{0{\cdot}60}=1\tfrac{2}{3}$$

This concept of the multiplier can also be seen in Fig. 5.1 which initially displayed an economy with a deflationary gap (*DG*). To close this gap it would be necessary to shift the aggregate expenditure upwards and again an increase in government expenditure (*G*) could achieve this objective.

Note, however, that in this particular case the desired increase in national income of £2,000 million will require an increase in government expenditure of £1,000 million. In this economy the propensity to 'withdraw' must have produced a multiplier with a value of 2.

So far the importance of the multiplier for fiscal policy has been described only within the context of examples in which the aim of such policies was to *increase* the level of economic activity. Of equal importance, however, is that the multiplier will exaggerate the impact upon national income and employment of a reduction in injections. If the government had *cut* its spending on roads by £300 million, this would have produced a fall in national income that would have continued until a corresponding reduction in withdrawals had occurred. In this case a fall in national income of £500 million would result, as this will mean that national income has fallen by an amount sufficient to reduce savings, taxes and imports by £300 million, and so match the lower level of injections caused by the reduction in government expenditure. This multiplier effect in a downward direction will be of particular importance to a government taking action to remove a prospective inflationary gap.

It should also be stressed that a multiplier effect can be set in motion by a change in any other component(s) of aggregate expenditure. It has already been described how alterations in direct and indirect taxes and allowances can influence total demand because of their effects upon domestic consumption, private investment expenditure and export sales. For example, improved investment allowances may raise investment expenditure, while cuts in income tax will promote increased consumer expenditure. Both changes will combine to produce a multiplier effect within the economy in much the same way as did the earlier examples using an increase in government expenditure. The student should now refer back to the section describing the changes in direct and indirect taxes on pages 71–2 and attempt to trace the repercussions of these changes on the aggregate expenditure schedule, as this exercise will again illustrate the existence of a multiplier effect which can be set in motion by such changes.

Fiscal policy in practice

(a) Time lags

The success of the changes designed to regulate the economy will depend heavily upon the scope and accuracy of economic data that attempt to discover what is currently happening in key sectors of the economy, the current levels of important categories of expenditure and the amount of spare capacity that exists in the economy. Particular reference will be made to movements in the general price level and employment. There is then the problem of forecasting in which direction these key indicators are moving and their respective rates of change. Successful stabilisation means that inflationary or recessionary conditions or other potential economic problems must be identified as early as possible in order that preventative action can be taken. The position is further complicated by the existence of time lags not only between the collection of data, their interpretation and the production of economic forecasts, but also between constructing the budget itself, the implementation of budgetary changes and the eventual impact of these changes upon the economy.

In particular some items of government spending have proved very difficult to cut until a relatively long period of time has elapsed. Capital projects have often borne the brunt of government cuts, despite strong recommendations that for short-term changes in the economy public expenditure should be 'a tool of the last resort' because of its sudden disruptive impact on certain sectors of the economy.

Between the diagnosis of the problem and the impact of fiscal measures, the economy may now not only be moving at a different pace, but may even be changing direction. For example, the budget may have been designed to reflate demand to counteract a prospective recession, but such is the difficulty in predicting the behaviour of such groups as consumers, investors, employers, trade unions and employees, that the economy may be recovering under its own momentum. The position may also have been influenced by a change in the external economic situation, such as a sudden upturn in the level of world trade. By the time the budgetary measures start to have an effect they may no longer prove appropriate, and instead of being a stabilising influence upon the economy they may prove to be destabilising. Because of these problems, efforts are continually being made to achieve more accurate up-to-date information upon which to base forecasts and these, in turn, can be improved by the development of more sophisticated models of how the economy operates and what influences its behaviour.

(b) Inflexibility

Since budgets were traditionally introduced once a year, fiscal measures lacked any real degree of flexibility. To deal with any unforeseen changes in the economy that required more immediate corrective action, and to allow adjustments between annual budgets, the **regulator** was introduced in 1962 which gave the Chancellor the power to alter indirect taxes by up to 10 per cent during the current financial year. This was increased to 25 per cent in 1977 so that an indirect tax of 10 per cent can be lowered to $7\frac{1}{2}$ per cent or raised to $12\frac{1}{2}$ per cent between annual budgets. Greater flexibility in fiscal policy has led to the use of interim or 'mini' budgets, but this practice does have certain disadvantages if used too frequently.

(c) Conflicting economic objectives and fine tuning

Demand management as conducted by fiscal policy was advocated when the major objective was to overcome mass unemployment which Keynes recognised was the result of a deficiency of demand. If the main objective is to promote full employment and a large adjustment is needed, then a directional change of this sort can be achieved by fiscal measures. In the post-war period, however, governments may have been too confident in their newly acquired economic weapons and, as a consequence, perhaps became too ambitious in their objectives. They sought to achieve several objectives apart from full employment. These were price stability, a satisfactory balance of payments and a strong currency, and a reasonable rate of economic growth. Events have generally proved, however, that these objectives cannot be achieved simultaneously and this is partly due to the inherent weaknesses associated with fiscal measures. They have been described as 'blunt weapons' or likened to 'heavy artillery' in that they are 'slow to manœuvre and cumbersome in effect'. The result is that some of the government's objectives may be achieved but others may have to be sacrificed along the way.

Some examples will illustrate the nature of the problem:

(i) Assume that the government is concerned about growing unemployment and deals with the situation via a budget deficit to reflate demand. It may wish to reduce unemployment from, say, 4 per cent to below 3 per cent. If this is the case, there is not much room for error as the economy could easily spill over into an inflationary situation once full employment is reached. The lack of accurate up-to-date information, forecasting problems and the time lags may hasten this eventuality of excess demand. Inflationary pressures develop as the economy suffers shortages and bottlenecks and this will lead to a deterioration in the balance of payments. Exports become less competitive and some exports will be redirected to the home market to satisfy demand. At the same time the initial growth in industrial output would have led to an increase in the import of stocks of raw materials and semi-processed goods. Domestic inflation will also make imported goods more attractive both from the point of view of price and delivery dates.

For these reasons, then, the balance of payments will deteriorate and the country's gold and foreign currency reserves will fall, as they will be used to finance the growing deficit. The position will be further aggravated by speculative activities against the currency as rumours strengthen concerning the prospect of the currency being devalued. The speculative selling of the currency will result in a further loss of reserves if the value of the currency is to be defended.

A further major problem is that the sudden stimulation of demand at home will not necessarily have led to a significant increase in private investment as companies may not believe that this 'go' phase will last long enough to make long-term investment worth while. Thus when full employment is reached, resources may have shifted in favour of consumption at the expense of investment goods, and economic growth will suffer as a consequence. The end result of the increase in demand is therefore that full employment *is* achieved, but only at the price of inflation, a rapid deterioration in the balance of payments, a weakening of the currency, and a loss of gold and foreign currency reserves. It is also doubtful whether any long-term improvement can be obtained in the over-all rate of economic growth.

(ii) Now assume that the government tackles this new inflationary situation by deflating the

Fig. 5.4

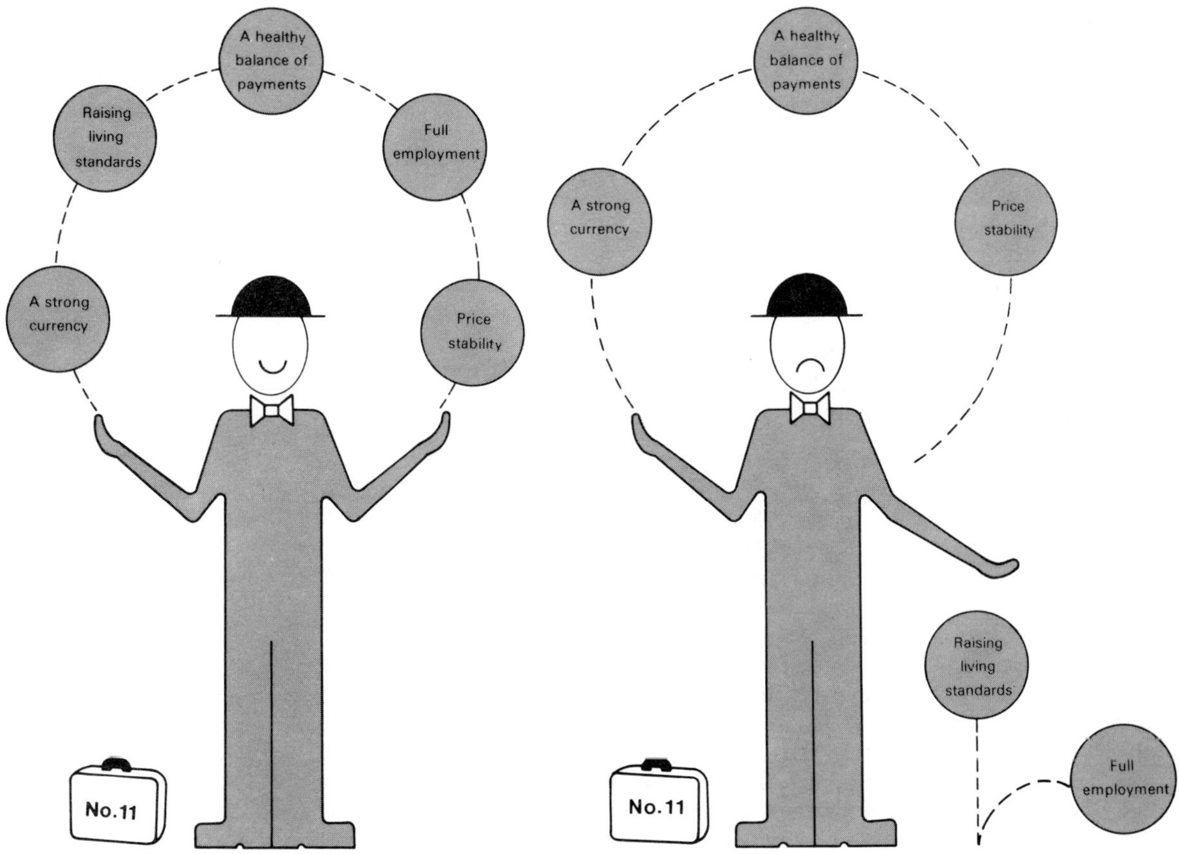

level of demand by introducing a budget surplus. This will cause a fall in output and a rise in unemployment. During this 'stop' phase the balance of payments may eventually start to improve as inflation falls to a level below that ruling in the economies of the main competitors abroad. Exports may therefore regain their competitive position and the depressed home market may finally oblige firms to seek an increase in their overseas sales. At the same time, the fall in national income and output will slow down the import of both manufactures and imports required by industry. The depressed home market, however, will not have produced an economic climate in which firms will invest in additional or improved productive capacity, and so the rate of economic growth will suffer. Once again the major economic objectives have proved incompatible, as success on prices, the balance of payments and the currency has been achieved at the expense of higher unemployment and a lower growth rate. The problem of conflicting economic objectives is shown in Fig. 5.4.

These are some of the limitations associated with fiscal measures and, when combined with the complexity of government objectives, they have contributed to the **'stop–go'** nature of the UK economy in the post-war period. Fiscal policy was being asked to achieve objectives for which it was never originally intended and which were far removed from the first simple and single objective of preventing mass unemployment.

(d) Minibudgets

It is increasingly recognised that the position has been further aggravated by the use of minibudgets which have meant too frequent interventions with the level of demand. Because of the unreliability of economic forecasts it may prove more advantageous to wait in order to determine what action is needed rather than deal with a situation that may be clouded by time lags. Sudden fiscal changes may result only in a confused situation at a later date. Frequent and perhaps unpredictable changes may have increased the problem of uncertainty in the economy and led to a low level of business confidence and an increasing reluctance to undertake investment expenditure. Thus the 'stop–go' cycle can in itself become a factor that inhibits economic growth, as the situation may demand policies that can operate with greater precision and help to improve business expectations by reducing the need suddenly to deflate demand. The cumulative effect of 'stop–go' is shown in Fig. 5.5 (page 78).

(e) Supply

A major problem facing the UK economy is one of supply as the economy can readily be pushed towards full employment, but then the need is to raise the productive capacity of the economy. If living standards are to be measured in material terms, improvements can only be achieved if real output can be raised, and this requires an increase in productivity. Unfortunately, fiscal policy does not at the moment readily lend itself to dealing with those issues which are concerned with raising productivity.

(f) Inflation

The deflation of demand is a means of tackling inflation which is caused by excess demand but has definite limitations if the inflation is caused by other factors. Serious inflation has existed in the UK economy since the end of the 1960s, despite periods of exceptionally high unemployment. At times this has largely been due to prices being pushed up by wage and salary increases in excess of productivity. Inflation under these circumstances will create additional unemployment as higher prices, in the absence of excess demand, will result in a fall in demand and this will be further depressed by exports becoming less competitive and imports more attractive. The rise in the cost of living then provokes additional wage claims and as inflation continues so unemployment will increase (see Fig. 5.6, p. 79). Until the budget of 1972 the government refused to stimulate demand to soak up the resulting unemployment and similarly refused to alter the exchange rate to assist the UK's international trading position. Since, however, growing unemployment did not lead to more moderate wage increases, the government finally produced an expansionary budget in March 1972 and allowed the currency to **float** to ease the strain on the balance of payments. It was hoped that this reflation would reduce unemployment and the expansions of output would in particular be directed towards exports, as world trade was growing rapidly and a competitive advantage would be given to exports by any depreciation of sterling. This decision to float the currency was a further indication that maintaining the value of sterling was not compatible with attempts to achieve a rapid expansion of the general level of economic activity in the economy.

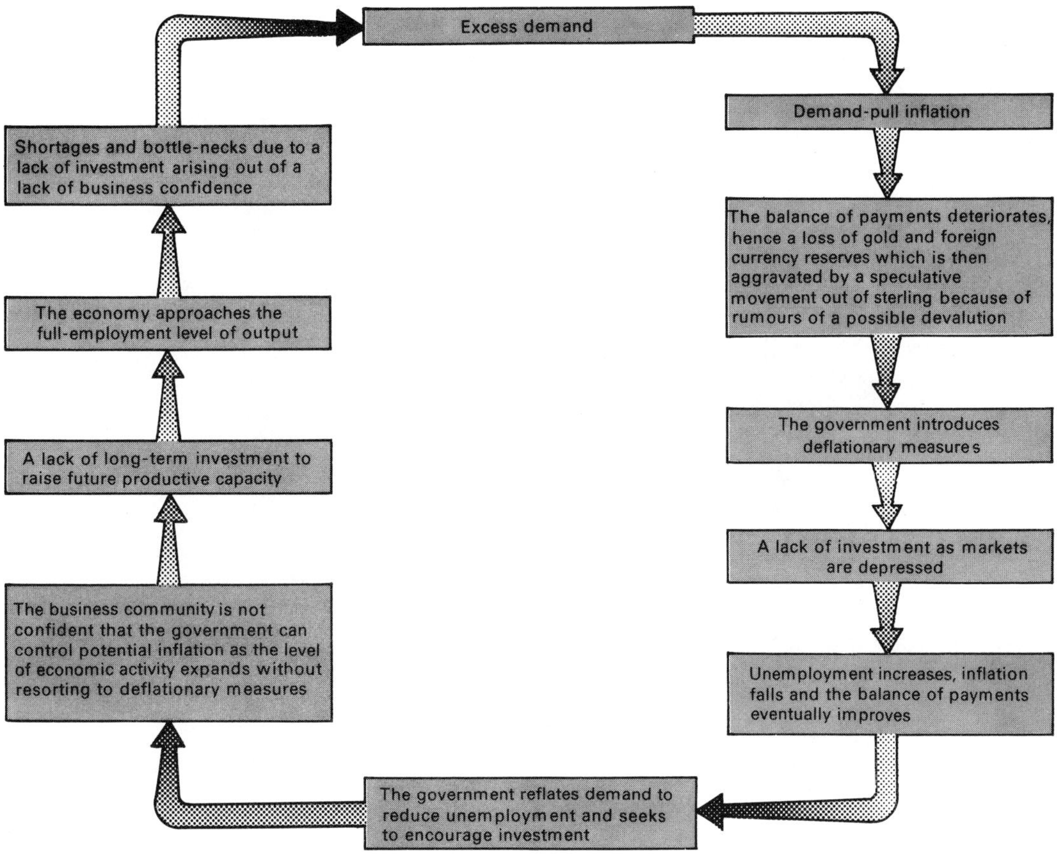

Fig. 5.5: The 'stop–go' cycle

Strong inflationary pressures were then exerted by the increase in the world price of oil from the end of 1973 onwards, and the substantial rise in the world price of some essential commodities in 1973–4, followed by an increase in import costs as sterling rapidly depreciated from 1975 onwards. Thus inflation was given added momentum and unemployment was further aggravated by the massive withdrawal of purchasing power from the economy in the form of very high import prices. It was difficult to see how the traditional use of fiscal policies operating on demand could alleviate the inflationary situation. Indeed in 1974 the government was faced with the reality of failing to achieve any of its post-war objectives as there was rapid inflation, a large balance of payments deficit, a depreciating currency, rising unemployment and an actual fall in industrial output.

(g) Public sector borrowing

The budgetary policies of governments from 1972 onwards tended to increase the amount of money which the public sector was obliged to borrow. This not only increased interest rates, but such was the scale of public sector expenditure that both investment and labour were increasingly denied to the private sector of the economy. This contributed to a reduction in the relative size of the private manufacturing sector in particular, as the wealth which this sector was producing was increasingly being absorbed by government spending at the expense of private investment and exports. The increase in the public sector borrowing requirement (PSBR) contributed to a substantial increase in the **money supply.** This gave added support to those economists who saw the root cause of inflation as being an increase in the money supply in excess of the anticipated increase

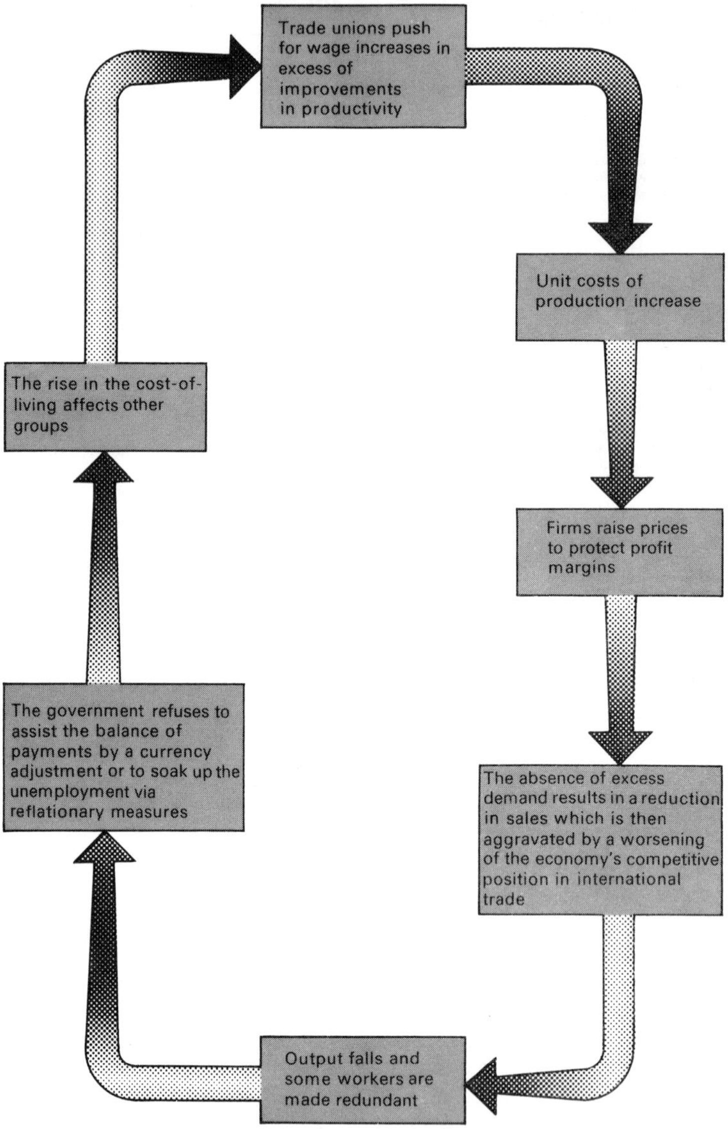

Fig. 5.6: The 'cost–push' cycle

in the economy's real output during a particular period. A further explanation of this money supply issue is given in the section dealing with monetary policy.

(h) Wage claims

The problem has also arisen that increases in indirect taxes in particular have played their part in determining the size of wage claims because of their impact upon the cost-of-living index. Indirect taxes aimed at deflating demand to reduce inflation, or the size of the PSBR, can therefore themselves contribute to inflationary wage increases.

The basis for demand management via monetary policy

The level of total spending in the economy can also be influenced by economic measures designed

Table 5.4: Analysis of advances to UK residents by banks in the UK

Amounts outstanding £ million

	Total	*Financial*	*Manufacturing*	*Other production*	*Personal*	*Services*
February 1981	60,163	8,777	15,949	6,959	9,534	18,944
Amount in sterling	49,924	6,140	12,195	6,106	9,500	15,074
February 1982	79,929	12,670	17,524	8,837	15,582	25,318
Amount in sterling	63,967	6,471	13,926	7,370	15,532	20,667

SOURCE: Central Statistical Office.

to establish what is considered to be an acceptable increase in the availability of credit. Just as fiscal measures can seek to control certain key macro variables in the economy so also can the monetary measures outlined in the following sections. Monetary policy does, however, tend to be less selective in its impact upon total spending when compared with the scope afforded by fiscal policy.

A large part of total expenditure in an advanced economy is financed through the provision of credit, and changes in both the rate of interest charged to those using credit, and its general availability, can influence total demand in the economy. Monetary measures can be used to raise or lower the price of credit and also to institute a period of 'tight' or 'easy' credit. If the government believes that the economy is heading towards a period of excess demand, then to avoid possible inflation the level of demand can be deflated by measures which seek to raise interest rates. The cost of borrowing money may lead to a reduction in that part of consumer and investment expenditure which is financed by credit. These measures can be reinforced by action which aims at making credit more difficult to obtain even though the potentital borrower may be prepared to pay a higher rate of interest. A fall in interest rates and a greater availability of credit can be resorted to if the government wishes to reflate demand to help deal with growing unemployment. The importance of credit can be seen in Table 5.4 which deals with credit in the form of advances made by banks in the UK. There are, of course, other sources of credit, such as hire purchase and other instalment credit business, and at the same time in 1982 the total amount outstanding to finance houses and retailers was over £6,000m.

The following description of monetary policy concentrates primarily upon how such measures influenced the lending activities of commercial banks between 1971 and 1981. The scope of monetary policy, however, also embraced other financial institutions that received deposits and made loans, and made up the 'fringe' or 'secondary' banks.

The process of credit creation has already been described in Chapter 2, and in order to help understand how monetary measures operated, it is now necessary to take a closer look at the outlets which the banks seek for their customers' deposits. This will help to illustrate the constraints within which this process of credit creation operates, and how the government brought pressure to bear upon the process in the period before 1981.

The previous analysis in Chapter 2 dealt with an example in which the banks were solely concerned with maintaining a cash reserve against their liabilities while the remaining cash was turned into interest-bearing assets. The actual distribution of these assets between various alternatives must work within the constraint of keeping an acceptable balance between **liquidity** and **profitability**. These two factors, however, pull in separate directions. In order to be able to meet the possible withdrawal of cash by clients who have placed deposits with it, the bank must follow sound banking principles whereby some assets must be kept in cash and others in a form which is regarded as liquid.

The degree of liquidity associated with an asset depends upon the relative ease with which it can be turned into cash and the extent to which a capital loss may be incurred on any transactions involved. Generally speaking, the more liquid an asset the less profitable it proves in terms of yielding a rate of interest. Thus an asset, secured from a sound organisation, which both matures in a very

Table 5.5: Liabilities and assets of London Clearing Banks, July 1980

£ million

Liabilities		*Assets*		
Sterling deposits	39,649	1. Notes and coins	925	
Other currency deposits	10,095	2. Balances with the Bank of England	343	Reserve assets
Total, including capital and other liabilities	59,504	3. Money at call and short notice	2,212	Reserve assets
Eligible liabilities	33,761	4. UK and Northern Ireland Treasury bills	523	Reserve assets
		5. Other bills	969	Reserve assets
		6. British Government stocks 0–1 year	276	Reserve assets
		7. Special and supplementary deposits	422	
		8. Market loans and bills (other than Reserve Assets)	4,296	
		9. Investments	2,083	
		10. Advances	29,191	
		Assets in other currencies and miscellaneous sterling assets	17,577	

* Other currency figures are affected by changes in exchange rates.
SOURCE: Central Statistical Office.

short period of time and where the risk of a capital loss if sold before maturity is negligible, will be regarded as an extremely liquid asset and virtually as good as cash itself. Because of the nature of such assets the market for them will produce a relatively low rate of interest. After all, the individual or institution receiving the funds as a loan is committed to repayment in a short period of time and will be prepared to pay only a relatively low rate of interest when compared with raising funds on a longer-term basis. An asset will be considered much less liquid if it has a much longer period to run before maturity. At the same time, the longer this period is the greater the possibility of having to sell the asset to obtain cash before its maturity date.

Such a sale at an inopportune time may result in a capital loss on the transaction if the current price has fallen below the original purchase price. The holders of such assets must, therefore, be paid a much higher rate of interest if they are to be induced to part with their cash.

Some assets may be exceptionally illiquid if there is no ready market for them, and profitability will depend very heavily upon the creditworthiness of the borrowers and their ability to meet their financial commitments at the agreed time. Such risks will be associated with an even higher rate of interest, as the possibility of default of payment is combined with the absence of a ready market where the asset can be sold. There is, therefore, a whole spectrum of interest rates produced by the forces of demand and supply for different assets, and the interest rate differentials that arise will reflect the nature of such assets from the point of view of liquidity and risk.

Although sound banking principles suggest that an acceptable balance is kept between liquidity and profitability, the banks had to adhere to certain directions from the government as to what was the minimum relationship that had to be maintained between their liabilities and their liquid assets. Between 1971 and 1981 the UK banks were obliged to maintain a certain ratio between **'eligible liabilities'** and **'reserve assets'**. This is shown in Table 5.5 which gives the liabilities and some of the principal assets which concern us from the point of view of monetary policy, as it was implemented during that period.

Eligible liabilities comprised, in broad terms, sterling deposit liabilities (excluding deposits having an original maturity of over two years), plus any sterling resources obtained by switching currencies into sterling. In Table 5.5 the total eligible liabilities amounted to £33,761 million. Reserve assets included the following:

(a) Balances with the Bank of England (other than special and supplementary deposits).

(b) Money at call and short notice (with listed discount market institutions).

(c) British Government and Northern Ireland Treasury bills.

(d) UK local authority bills eligible for rediscount at the Bank of England.

(e) Commercial bills eligible for rediscount at the Bank of England (up to a maximum of 2 per cent of eligible liabilities) and accepted as first-class bills of exchange by the clearing banks and other important areas of the banking system.

(f) British Government stocks.

(g) Stocks of the nationalised industries guaranteed by the government with one year left to maturity.

These are the assets which the government recognised as reserve assets in that they met the criteria decided upon in terms of defining liquidity. The **reserve ratio** was the total of these reserve assets as a percentage of the total eligible liabilities. Each bank was required by the government to maintain reserve assets amounting to at least *12½ per cent of its eligible liabilities* and this provided the government with the means of influencing the level of bank credit. Arrangements also existed for other institutions, such as discount houses and finance houses, although the formulae differed.

Item 1 in Table 5.5 refers to cash but it was already functioning by meeting the demands by customers for cash during everyday banking activities, and hence was not regarded as a 'reserve'. Items 2–6 qualified as reserve assets and between them totalled £4,323 million. They constituted 12.8 per cent of eligible liabilities, indicating that these banks were operating well within their minimum reserve ratio.

Balances held on a current account basis at the Bank of England are in Item 2 and are obviously balances available to the banks. Item 3 are interest-yielding assets, in that they refer to loans made to the London discount houses on a very short-term basis as the description implies. They constitute very liquid assets as repayment can be on demand or very short notice and are a convenient means of meeting a cash shortage. This will be reflected in a relatively low rate of interest.

Treasury bills under Item 4 are issued by the government to raise money to cover those periods when it is incurring expenditure in excess of its current revenue. They are very short-term securities as they mature after only 90 days. They are bought by the discount houses with funds deposited with them but as they approach maturity they are bought by the banks themselves. A Treasury bill may have a maturity value of £100 and the discount market may be prepared to pay £98 for it, which means that the bill has been discounted. If a discount house holds the bill to maturity then the bill would have produced a yield equivalent to approximately 8·2 per cent per annum (i.e. $\frac{2}{98} \times 100 \times 4$). Since they are bought by the discount houses and then sold at a later date to the banks, the yield will be shared between the two institutions. They thus constitute a highly liquid asset for the banks and a ready market also exists for them.

Item 5 includes the other bills which could be classified as reserve assets in the form of UK local authority bills and first-class commercial bills, which the Bank of England was prepared to accept and therefore rediscount. These bills refer to the raising of short-term loans by local authorities and those commercial transactions in the private sector which require short-term finance for the purposes of trade. Again these bills may have originally been purchased by the discount market before being obtained by the banks themselves.

Item 6 deals with British Government stock and such securities are the means by which the government can raise funds on a longer-term basis and the holder receives a rate of interest at intervals before maturity. As these securities approach their maturity date the more liquid they become and when less than one year remains before maturity they could be regarded as reserve assets. The same classification was also given to loans raised by the nationalised industries since they have the guaranteed support of the government. These securities in Item 6 are **'gilt-edged'** in that they will be repaid in full on the agreed date and the previous lack of liquidity would have been due to the possibility of an enforced sale that could have produced a capital loss if their current market price was depressed. This risk of a capital loss is lessened as they approach maturity.

Item 7 will be dealt with when pre-1981 monetary policies are discussed (page 87). Market loans and bills (other than reserve assets) are those assets which, for such reasons as their duration, could not be counted as sufficiently liquid to permit their use as reserve assets. Item 8 represents some of the most profitable assets for the banks. The majority of such investments are in British Government stocks, and stocks issued by the nationalised industries which are guaranteed by the government. They will have various maturity dates in excess of one year or may be undated. As such they carry a relatively high rate of interest to compensate the holder for a greater loss of liquidity and the banks would prefer to keep them until maturity rather than sell them on the Stock Exchange. When one year is left to maturity they could be transferred to Item 6. Advances in Item 10 constitute the most profitable outlet for the banks' funds and this reflects their illiquid nature. Advances cannot readily be recalled and there is a risk, depending upon the banks' judgement, that the arrangements for repayment cannot be adhered to by the customer to whom the advance was made.

Monetary policy in theory

Although monetary policy can be used to influence the lending activities of a wide range of financial institutions, the following sections will concentrate upon those measures that were directed at the commercial banks in the UK. The measures described are those that were used by the authorities (the Treasury and the Bank of England) at various times during the 1970s. They will be dealt with in the context of a decision by the government to deflate demand in the economy.

It was the need to maintain a reserve asset ratio that provided the authorities with a means of influencing the provision of credit by the banks and the demand for such credit. It was generally accepted that a formal change in the reserve asset ratio would not be used, but rather the practice was generally to put the existing ratio under a degree of pressure in order to bring about the required contraction of credit facilities.

1. Special and supplementary deposits

Item 7 in Table 5.5 shows that the London clearing banks were holding £422 million under this heading and they represent another form of balances with the Bank of England. They were not included as reserve assets as they amounted to 'frozen' assets, because they would only be released to the banks when the Bank of England agreed to do so. They did, however, earn a short-term rate of interest. Special deposits were a means of removing cash from the banks when the authorities believed that some restraint should be placed upon expenditure financed by credit. A call for special deposits to be placed with the Bank of England could have obliged the banks to sell some government securities on the Stock Exchange. This was one of the ways by which the banks could fill the gap in their reserve assets which would have fallen because of the need to provide the Bank of England with the special deposits. Had the banks not sold some of their assets in order to maintain their total of reserve assets, then these reserve assets might have comprised less than $12\frac{1}{2}$ per cent of their eligible liabilities.

As a result of sales of securities from Item 8 in Table 5.5 the market for them will be depressed, as buyers will only be willing to absorb larger quantities at a lower price. A fall in the price of a security will, however, result in a rise in interest rates. This is demonstrated by the following example, which assumes that a particular type of security pays a fixed sum of money in interest each year, and also has a maturity value at some specified future date. The security may be paying a fixed sum of £100 each year and be currently priced at £800 with a maturity value of £1,000. In this case the £100 represents a rate of interest of $12\frac{1}{2}$ per cent per annum, but if the market price falls due to sudden selling pressure and settles at £700, then the fixed payment of £100 is now equivalent to an annual rate of interest of approximately 14·3 per cent ($\frac{100}{700} \times \frac{100}{1}$ per cent). If, of course, the new holder retains the security to the redemption date, then the interest earned over the remaining life of the security will be much higher. Account must be then taken of the difference between the price at which it was purchased and its £1,000 maturity value. The essential point is that a fall in the price of a particular type of security must mean a rise in the current rate of interest associated with it. Since, however, different types of securities reflect different degrees of liquidity, this will cause a sympathetic upward movement throughout the whole spectrum of interest rates. This movement comes to an end when, once again, interest rate differentials are a close reflection of the various degrees of liquidity which the market attaches to them.

This general rise in interest rates will affect institutions that lend, and banks will be obliged to charge a higher rate of interest on advances, for example. This is because banks will be forced to raise the interest which they in turn pay on money deposited with them in order to attract funds that may move elsewhere seeking to take advantage of what would otherwise be more attractive rates of interest. In short, the banks are forced to compete for deposits by offering at least an equally attractive rate of interest after taking account of relative degrees of liquidity. The banks will then be obliged to raise the interest rate charged on advances in order to maintain their profit margins. The government hopes that this will reduce the demand for bank credit and consequently a fall in that part of total expenditure financed by loans.

Alternatively the banks could have reduced the level of their advances by not re-lending some of the money when it was repaid and using it to top up their reserve assets. This avoids the need to sell government securities which the banks prefer to hold to maturity in order to maximise their return on such assets. The reduction in advances would then have the effect welcomed by the government of reducing total demand in the economy.

Supplementary deposits were an additional lever which could be used to slow down an increase in bank advances which, if left unchecked, could create inflationary pressures. These were used to moderate the growth of eligible liabilities. The bank may have felt that there was scope to raise the rate of interest payable on deposit accounts to attract more cash into the banks. In Table 5.5 this would have meant that both liabilities and assets had increased by the same amount. The result was that reserve assets would have been boosted by the increase in cash received from customers and their reserve assets would now have formed a higher percentage of eligible liabilities. Banks needed to maintain only 12½ per cent of this increased cash in reserve assets and the remainder could be used for other outlets which would have included additional advances. This would initiate a multiple expansion of credit along the same lines as was described in the process of credit creation in Chapter 2. This is because money lent by the bank will help increase deposits in the banking system as a whole, as the money is spent and becomes income elsewhere, part of which may be deposited in the recipient's account. The government may, therefore, have instituted supplementary deposits which had to be placed with the Bank of England and which became 'frozen' assets, and in this case it refused to pay a rate of interest.

The expansion of bank credit was made possible by the increase in interest-bearing deposits as this raised eligible liabilities. The authorities, therefore, established a guideline for the growth of that part of eligible liabilities that were interest-bearing.

For example, up to August 1977 a growth in interest-bearing deposits in excess of 3 per cent of a guideline meant that 5 per cent of such funds were withdrawn as supplementary deposits, 25 per cent of funds resulting from a 3–5 per cent excess growth were withdrawn, while further excesses beyond the guideline meant that 50 per cent of such new funds were removed by a call for supplementary deposits. Apart from slowing down the expansion of credit it meant that banks would be paying interest on such deposits made with them by clients but the 'frozen' part would not earn a rate of interest. This acted as a means of deterring banks from attracting deposits to replace any cash called upon as a special deposit.

2. Open market operations

This was another means of indirectly influencing the reserve asset ratio and also bringing about a change in interest rates. The threat of inflationary pressures in the economy will lead the Bank of England, through its broker, to increase the net sales of Treasury bills. If to a large extent they are bought by the public and non-bank institutions, payment for them will be by cheques drawn upon their respective accounts at the banks in favour of the Bank of England. This will reduce Item 2, as balances at the Bank of England will be lower, causing pressure on the reserve asset ratio. This will initiate the sequence of events that occurred with the use of a call for special deposits, and could also lead to a rise in interest rates as selling pressure developed in the market for securities.

In *Competition and Credit Control*, a document published by the Bank of England in 1971, the authorities expressed their intention of using the combination of the minimum reserve asset ratio and special deposits to influence the structure of interest rates via the more direct approach of changes in Minimum Lending Rate as described in section 5 on page 86. As has been demonstrated, open market operations could also be used to achieve a similar result. Such measures affected the price of credit, and if pursued with sufficient vigour they could also affect the availability of credit, and until 1971 the latter was often their primary objective. Special deposits were a direct means of reducing the banks' reserve assets and open market operations operated indirectly to achieve the same result. If they were conducted on a large scale the banks may eventually have been obliged to protect their reserve assets ratio by not renewing advances as they were paid off, and using the funds released to support their reserve assets. Thus a call for special deposits both raised interest rates and led to a reduction in advances as the banks took steps to restore their reserve asset ratios. The use of open market operations, which involved the increased sale of Treasury bills, would have helped to raise interest rates and banks may therefore have concentrated upon moderating advances rather than make substantial sales of securities on an already falling market. This is because the rise in interest rates in the short-term market would eventually have caused sympathetic movements in the rates earned on the securities being sold by the banks and hence their prices would already be falling. Thus not only is borrowing more expensive, but both special deposits and open market operations could result in less credit being made available, since both measures can succeed in causing an initial cash drain from the banks. There would then be a multiple contraction of credit within the banking system as a whole.

3. Directives

In this case the government may have wished to avoid a rise in interest rates and sought to take more direct action to influence the availability of credit, particularly in the form of advances. At existing rates of interest the demand for credit may have exceeded the supply, and rather than allow a rise in interest rates to ration the existing supply of credit, the government may have issued 'directives' which requested the banks to keep advances within an agreed ceiling. These quantitative measures could be reinforced by those which were qualitative, by a request that particular restraint be shown in such areas as advances to finance personal expenditure, and greater preference be given to firms that intended to use credit to help their productivity or where the firm's operations gave rise to exports or import substitutes.

4. Funding

The use of open market operations to tighten credit and interest rates could to some extent be frustrated by the banks possessing a large quantity of very liquid assets. They may, therefore, be operating comfortably within their reserve asset ratio. If this is the case, additional sales of Treasury bills could eventually be absorbed by the banks using cash or recalling funds from the discount market. The banks would not have experienced any pressure on their liquid assets as there was simply a change in the distribution of the existing total of such assets. In short, less cash and money at call was compensated for by an equivalent increase in Treasury bills. If this possibility existed, the government could conduct operations in longer-term securities which cannot be included as liquid assets and were also more likely to be absorbed by non-bank institutions. Payment for these securities by the purchasers would then be a more assured way of producing a drain of cash from the banks and make them more susceptible to the pressure to restrict lending.

Such a move by the Bank of England is known as funding and amounts to a *lengthening of the National Debt*. Government borrowing has moved in favour of selling longer-term securities at the expense of the shorter-term Treasury bills. Moreover, the falling price of longer-term securities may lead the banks to curtail advances rather than risk capital losses through the enforced sale of some of their investments held in such longer-term securities to protect their reserve assets.

5. Minimum Lending Rate (MLR)

This was formerly known as Bank Rate and was the rate at which the Bank of England would normally provide funds in its role as '*lender of the last resort*' to members of the London money market (the discount houses). It was prepared to lend against the security of Treasury bills, other approved bills or government stocks with five years or less to maturity. MLR was in fact the most important measure available to the government as a means of influencing interest rates. It was far more direct and reliable when compared with the side-effects upon interest rates of measures designed to influence the availability of credit such as special deposits and open market operations.

MLR itself was normally set ½ per cent higher than the average rate of discount for Treasury bills determined when they were last issued and rounded up to the nearest ¼ per cent. Where, however, the operation of the formula would have produced a reduction in the rate, then the Bank of England reserved the right either to leave the rate unchanged, or to change it by less than would have resulted from the operation of the formula. Prior to October 1971, when MLR was known as Bank Rate, it was determined directly by the monetary authorities. Major rates of interest such as those charged by banks for advances were automatically linked to it, so an increase in Bank Rate would bring a corresponding increase in other important rates of interest. The government decided, however, that as far as possible the new MLR should be decided by market forces as expressed by the price which the discount houses were prepared to pay for Treasury bills at their time of issue. This still enabled the Bank of England to influence market forces in order to bring about a desired change in MLR if it so wished. A deliberately instigated increase in the sale of Treasury bills on the open market or a call for special deposits would cause the banks to experience a cash drain and their immediate reaction to this was to call in money from the discount houses in order to replenish their balances at the Bank of England. Eventually of course the banks would be obliged to reduce advances and this would affect the availability of credit. What happens to the price of credit, however, is primarily determined by the reaction of the discount houses who now face a cash shortage produced by the banks' having withdrawn some of their deposits in unexpectedly large amounts. The discount houses then turn to the Bank of England as 'lender of last resort' and obtain money in exchange for bills but the Bank of England will only rediscount such bills in accordance with its MLR. This will determine how much the discount houses receive in exchange for their bills and this will most certainly be taken into account when buying new issues of both Treasury and commercial bills. They will therefore tender prices which produce a higher yield to protect themselves in the event of being obliged to meet any future cash shortage by obtaining assistance from the Bank of England at MLR. The fall in Treasury bill prices could then also have the effect of raising MLR via the application of the formula to determine its level. Thus action taken by the monetary authorities that causes the banks to experience a cash drain will ultimately produce a rise in the rate of interest associated with the holding of very short-term securities. In order to remain competitive and attract deposits the banks offer higher interest rates and then raise the interest they charge on their lending to protect their profits. A later section will describe how a similar approach was used in the early 1980s to influence interest rates which were seen by the government as the centre-piece of its monetary policy.

6. Hire purchase controls
This does not directly involve banks but rather finance houses. Expenditure financed by hire purchase agreements can be influenced by changes in the initial deposit and maximum repayment periods. For example, an increase in the initial deposit from, say, 25–40 per cent, accompanied by a reduction in the maximum repayment period from four to two years, will have a significant impact upon the demand for such items as consumer durables which are often bought on hire purchase terms.

Monetary policy in practice 1971–81

The *Competition and Credit Control* (*CCC*) document published by the Bank of England in 1971 outlined the monetary measures upon which the authorities intended to concentrate their future action in order to influence the level of lending in the economy. The commercial banks in the UK had always been obliged to maintain some minimum level of liquid assets; this document reviewed the situation and amended the previous arrangement. The result produced the situation which existed in the 1970s whereby banks in the UK had to maintain a 12½ per cent minimum reserve ratio to eligible liabilities.

Greater freedom was given to the banks in that there was to be a move away from directives of both a quantitative and qualitative nature, and the banks were to lend according to their own judgement. The Bank of England was to place greater reliance upon influencing the minimum reserve ratio via the more direct means of special deposits. The main result which they sought was a change in interest rates, as it was the price of credit rather than its availability which they viewed as a means of regulating its use to finance expenditure. Thus it was envisaged that other monetary measures, such as deliberate changes in MLR, open market operations and funding, would play a minor role in their over-all policy.

The following section will therefore review some of the factors which had previously operated to frustrate monetary policies, other issues which arose after 1971, and the extent to which the new approach as contained in the 1971 document could deal with them.

1. The money supply
In order to decide upon the direction and magnitude of monetary changes, the government needs to know what is currently happening, and changes likely to occur in the monetary system. This raises the issue of what should be regarded as money. It was always accepted that, in addition to notes and coins, such a calculation should also include existing bank deposits in sterling belonging to the private sector and transferable on demand by cheque. This produces M_1 and would seem an acceptable calculation as it covers the two most frequently used means of payment, i.e. cash and cheques drawn on a bank current account. In practice, however, deposit accounts can be very liquid

Table 5.6: Money stock 1971–7 (seasonally adjusted)

£ million

At end of period		M_1	M_3
1971	1	9,820	18,330
	2	9,890	18,740
	3	10,230	19,180
	4	10,550	20,100
1972	1	11,160	21,150
	2	11,590	23,010
	3	11,790	23,990
	4	12,290	25,670
1973	1	12,250	27,370
	2	13,010	28,590
	3	12,540	30,830
	4	13,100	32,970
1974	1	12,710	34,140
	2	13,050	34,750
	3	13,480	36,010
	4	14,460	37,230
1975	1	14,860	37,950
	2	15,570	38,200
	3	16,760	39,940
	4	17,250	40,170
1976	1	17,890	40,170
	2	18,340	42,350
	3	19,210	44,590
	4	19,060	44,470
1977	1	19,680	44,810
	2	20,460	46,520
	3	21,860	47,200
	4	23,330	48,760

SOURCE: Central Statistical Office.

and such items are included in a wider definition of the money supply known as M_3, which consists of notes and coins in circulation with the public, plus all bank deposits in both sterling and foreign currencies held in deposit or current accounts by UK citizens in both the private and public sector. Other items held at banks are included because of their liquid nature. Another definition, £M_3, excludes all bank deposits held by UK residents in other currencies.

As shown in Table 5.6, M_3 is much larger than M_1. These figures are important to the government as a basis for monetary policy and in recent years they have also been used by those economists (notably Milton Friedman from the so-called Chicago School) who argue that there is a very direct link between the money supply and the rate of inflation. Increases in the money supply beyond the expected increases in output over a period of time will simply be reflected in higher prices. Whether or not the figures are viewed from this 'monetarist' approach, or from the point of view of the more traditional causes of inflation, they provide valuable information.

If there is a fairly reliable relationship between M_1 and M_3 in terms of their relative size and movements, this may assist monetary policy, but difficulties arise if they part company as occurred after 1972 in that M_3 grew more rapidly. The choice confronting the authorities is: which of them is to be the basis of monetary measures? Severe restrictions to deal with an increase in M_3 could be misguided if changes in the figures are due to financial transactions taking place in certain assets that may not be a true indication of the over-all state of liquidity in the economy. This may result in an unnecessarily tight credit squeeze.

The issue of the growth of other financial institutions which receive deposits and make advances can also be raised, and the extent to which calculations of the money supply should take account of such activities and their future development. For example, an individual who places a deposit with a building society may well regard this as a very liquid asset and not feel obliged to alter his holding of any other assets or cut current expenditure. This gives rise to a useful definition of liquidity in terms of '*money that people think they can get hold of*'.

The building society will use such funds to make advances which immediately gives rise to an increase in the money supply. The possibility then arises that, with the widespread growth of the building society movement, some of the advance may find its way as a deposit into another account. Obviously the growth of such non-bank institutions needs to be carefully monitored if an accurate impression of total liquidity and potential spending power is to be gained. The closer they approach the commercial banks in their activities the greater the consequences they can have for monetary policy. Further definitions were then employed to take account of other liquid assets and PSL_2 (private sector liquidity) is the private sector's share of £M_3 plus holdings of very short-term securities such as Treasury bills and deposits with local authorities plus deposits with building societies and other liquid types of savings which do not take the form of a deposit.

2. Non-bank financial institutions

Among the changes instituted by the *CCC* document was the extension of monetary control to other institutions, partly to deal with the matters regarding the money supply mentioned in section 1. Finance houses, for example, now have to adhere to certain arrangements concerning their reserve assets and are susceptible to calls for special deposits. There was a recognition that previous periods of tight control over bank lending only, had driven frustated borrowers to other sources of credit which previously had not been directly influenced by monetary measures. Indeed, their operations had proved very profitable at the expense of banks at a time of high interest rates.

The problem remains, however, that the widening of the controls can still give rise to developments such as the extended use of trade credit or the growth of financial institutions that find ways of avoiding monetary measures to maintain a supply of credit to potential borrowers.

3. Sources of bank liquidity

Special deposits as a means of removing cash from the banks became necessary as it was recognised that a large part of the National Debt in the form of Treasury bills held by financial institutions left them with a very comfortable supply of liquidity. Banks could react to pressure upon their position not only by recalling money from the discount houses but by cash which could be derived from Treasury bills. Reducing the issue of Treasury bills would involve the added expense of servicing the National Debt via longer-term securities. If the authorities do follow this course of action then interest on such securities will rise even more as the banks sell existing securities to obtain cash which puts additional upward pressure on interest rates. Banks were also prepared to sell some of their holdings of shorter-term government stock as their market values are generally closer to their redemption values and thus a much reduced yield or capital loss is less likely to be experienced as a result of such sales. Moreover, the increased usage of commercial bills provided an alternative supply of liquid assets for banks, and the possibility existed of the financial system providing close substitutes for those liquid items subject to greater control. Thus, as with open market operations designed to cause a cash drain from the banks, the ingenuity of the financial network could frustrate special deposits.

4. Public Sector Borrowing Requirement (PSBR)

This has already been discussed in the context of fiscal policy, but the PSBR also has implications for the operation of monetary policy. If the total size of the National Debt is greatly reduced, this will remove from the markets a large quantity of securities which, when manipulated by the government, can help it pursue a monetary objective.

The government, however, was under pressure to reduce its annual PSBR as increased sales of government securities can lead to very high rates of interest that may reach levels that prevent the private sector from raising funds for investment. Large-scale repayment of the debt will provide cash to those holding securities and is best undertaken if the government believes there is room for a reflation of demand, as such cash would then find its way into the banks. For much of the 1970s the PSBR grew at a very rapid rate and many of the securities involved would have been held by the banks in a form which could be added to their reserve assets and at very attractive rates of interest. Thus borrowing from the domestic banking system can directly add to the money supply as it will contribute to the process of credit creation in the same way as occurs with bank lending to the private sector. Unlike advances to the private sector, however, the bank is holding a very liquid asset in the form of Treasury bills and will not therefore feel obliged to cut advances to the private sector. Moreover, as described earlier, these Treasury bills provide a very convenient source of funds in the event of the banks' experiencing a cash drain produced by an attempted squeeze by the government on the level of credit. If, however, the budget deficit is financed by the sale of longer-term securities to the non-banking private sector an increase in the money supply will be avoided, as banks will experience a cash drain since buyers of such securities pay by cheques drawn upon their accounts held by the banks. The cost of interest payable on the National Debt in 1980–1 was £9,854 million, and this must be kept in mind when deciding upon maturity dates for government securities. Longer-term borrowing will involve higher interest charges but this does mean that future beneficiaries of current government spending, on new roads for example, will be making a contribution to the costs involved. This is because future tax revenues could be used to pay interest charges or buy back securities before they mature. Moreover, if real incomes are rising, the servicing of the National Debt becomes less of a burden upon the community as a whole.

5. Directives

One of the drawbacks concerning directives was

that they could have a discriminatory impact. If, for example, the authorities requested that advances should be kept within a ceiling which was set 5 per cent above what they were twelve months ago, then banks that were underlent at that time would suffer more than those banks which had exceptionally high levels of advances. Similarly, the non-bank institutions were not included, but it was the declared intention of the authorities to refrain from the use of directives after 1971. Interest rates were to play a greater role in allocating credit but nevertheless this did imply that any selectivity that remained would be undertaken by the banks themselves. Fiscal policy, on the other hand, could be more selective because of the nature of the taxes available to the Chancellor and the wide range of areas in which to channel government expenditure.

This policy soon had to be abandoned, however, as the immediate impact of the changes contained in *CCC* was a very rapid rise in the money supply as Table 5.7 indicates. Both M_1 and M_3 grew rapidly as banks found themselves able to switch to more profitable advances which rose by 50 per cent from January 1971 to March 1972. This was a period of low industrial activity and growing unemployment and the most lucrative outlets were in property and construction companies which seemed a good hedge against inflation. Advances to this sector increased from less than £1,000 million at the end of 1971 to over £4,000 million in November 1973. Liquidity was added to by the government's need to finance the growing PSBR, and lending was also increased for personal expenditure. At times advances by banks reached 70 per cent of their deposits but those to the manufacturing sector hardly increased at all.

These activities may have been an element contributing to the acceleration of inflation in 1973–74. By August 1972 the authorities were obliged to resort once again to directives which were particularly aimed at reducing loans for consumer expenditure. Special deposits had to be called for in 1973 and 1974 to help reduce the increase in the money supply. This policy was added to by the introduction for the first time of supplementary deposits at the end of 1973 and these 'corset' controls were introduced periodically as a means of influencing bank credit.

6. Minimum Lending Rate (MLR)

The proposal that greater reliance should be placed upon interest rate policy in the years following 1971 also had to be modified. Interest rates would have had to reach abnormally high levels if they were to be used to curb the use of credit (see Table 5.7). From 5 per cent in 1971 the MLR reached 13 per cent in 1973, but in the face of rapid inflation the 'real' rate of interest was actually negative during one particular period in 1974 and the demand for credit continued. The formula for MLR was actually suspended for a period afterwards as market forces would otherwise have pushed it up to unprecedented levels that would have had severe political and economic repercussions.

Table 5.7: Minimum Lending Rate 1971–80

At end of period	*Percentage*
1971	5
1972	9
1973	13
1974	11½
1975	11¼
1976	14½
1977	5
1978	12½
1979	17
1980	14

* Until 13 October 1972 this was known as the bank rate.
SOURCE: Central Statistical Office.

7. Hire Purchase Controls

These controls also had to be re-introduced as a means of curbing credit and this is a good example of a measure that will certainly cause a rapid change in total demand. It does, however, fall very heavily upon the consumer durable industries and a tightening of HP terms will have a severe impact upon business confidence and contribute to the lack of investment which stems from the resulting 'stop–go' nature of the economy.

Within a relatively short period the authorities were forced to modify their declared policy of relying upon measures to influence the structure of interest rates, and supplement it with other measures that sought to affect the use and availability of credit more directly. For changes in MLR and other interest rates to be effective they would have had to be very large and consequently very disruptive. Large increases in interest rates, resulting from a MLR determined largely by market forces, might have shaken the financial system with very large capital losses on the sale of securities, as well as further raising the cost of financing the National Debt. Sudden large changes in interest rates can also have a disruptive effect upon business confidence and give rise to the movement of funds internationally that can have a de-stabilising impact upon relative exchange rates.

There is, in fact, a great deal of scepticism surrounding the influence which interest rates exert upon investment and consumer expenditure. It is said that consumer expenditure is more likely to be influenced by the availability of credit, and initial deposits and repayment arrangements, than by changes in interest rate. Similarly, interest charges may be of relatively minor importance for firms, for instance if investment expenditure is financed from internal sources, and they may play a very small part in total costs when compared with the annual capital repayments over short pay-off periods. If interest rates are increased, an inflationary climate will probably see them passed on in the form of higher prices.

Investment expenditure is guided by the firm's interpretation of future market prospects, and long-term plans will not be shelved because of changes in interest rates. However, if changes in interest rates are large and are an indication of prolonged deflationary policies by the government, they can be effective in changing opinions about the future market prospects. The effect upon confidence may then be cumulative and deep rooted and the government may experience great difficulty when seeking to raise private investment expenditure at some time in the future.

In 1979 the new government initiated a Review of Monetary Control Techniques in recognition of the extent to which money supply growth (M_3) had often exceeded target levels (Fig. 5.7). Then in August 1981 a revised system of control was introduced whereby the Bank of England suspended MLR and instead aimed to keep very short-term interest rates within an unpublished band. The approval of the Chancellor is needed before this band can be changed and such changes will be influenced by developments in £M_3, other money supply figures and events in foreign exchange markets. Emphasis is now placed upon an excessive demand for credit being choked off by higher interest rates and this is achieved by a greater reliance upon open market operations in the bill market where the determin-

Fig. 5.7: Monetary measures in the 1970s

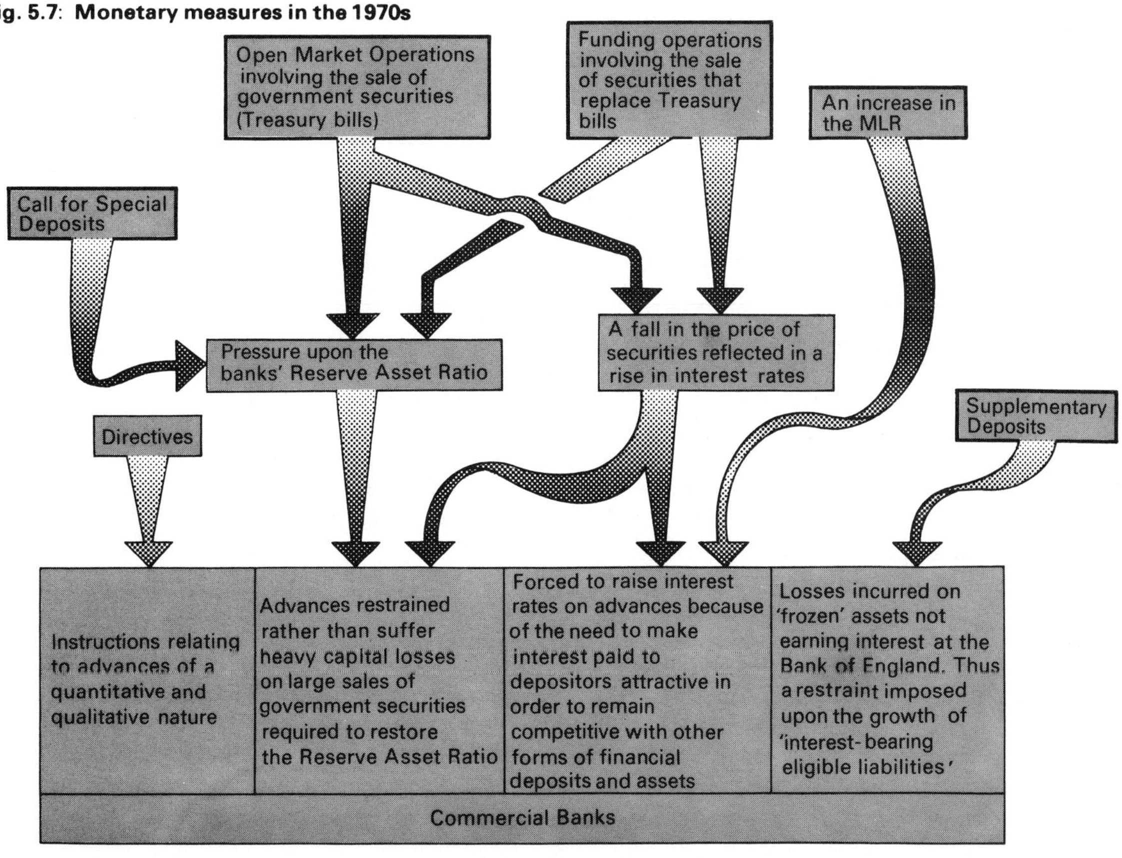

ation of short-term interest rates is now more subject to market forces. When the Bank of England now engages in open market operations it no longer quotes prices at which it will buy bills, but rather responds to the offers from the discount houses. Thus, in times of a cash shortage such dealings will produce bill prices that mean a higher short-term interest rate, and this will soon be transmitted to other rates, such as the base rate charged by the banks. On the assumption that the excessive demand for money arose out of inflationary developments in the economy, then the higher rates of interest will make it more difficult for employers to finance excessive pay rises, while also raising the price of credit to their customers faced with higher prices. Thus inflationary pressures would find it difficult to survive.

This new approach to open market operations helps the government to follow a more flexible interest rate policy. This is because interest rate objectives are no longer published and increases in interest rates become the 'fault' of market forces. This removes the political motive for delaying increases in interest rates, while the government is no longer 'blamed' for such increases.

The reserve ratio has been replaced by a **cash ratio** and recognised banks and licensed deposit-taking institutions, above a minimum size, are now required to hold cash balances on special non-operational, non-interest bearing accounts with the Bank of England. This cash ratio is equivalent to $\frac{1}{2}$ per cent of eligible liabilities, but the banks still maintain on their ordinary accounts with the Bank of England such balances as are necessary for the usual clearing purposes. This cash ratio will allow the authorities to influence bank lending as although supplementary deposits have been abandoned the technique of special deposits has been retained.

Incomes policies

The previous analysis of fiscal and monetary policies has shown how the government can seek to control the total level of demand in the economy to achieve certain objectives relating to such issues as inflation and employment. One of the serious criticisms levelled at such policies, however, was that they were not necessarily appropriate weapons for dealing with inflation which stemmed primarily from cost-push inflation, and in particular from wage push. Such policies, despite their limitations, could be used for adjusting the level of demand in the economy when demand-pull pressures were the main causes of inflation. The damaging effects of deflationary measures could be avoided, and cost-push inflation more readily tackled, with an incomes policy. During the 1970s governments placed increasing reliance upon measures designed to influence costs of production more directly via incomes policies. Indeed, the fiscal measures described in analyses of later budgets (pages 82–3) were constructed in such a way that they sought to assist the implementation of the current incomes policy. Tax cuts and improved personal allowances, for example, were made conditional to some extent upon union co-operation in moderating wage claims. Incomes policies had been in operation during some periods of the 1960s but were relatively short lived. Moreover, the growing unemployment between 1970 and 1972 did not serve to moderate wage inflation, despite the effect which this type of cost-push inflation has upon the level of employment.

The rationale of an incomes policy is relatively simple in that greater price stability can be secured if incomes are not allowed to rise faster than the anticipated rise in productivity. Reaching such an incomes policy in its purest form, as will be shown later, is a very difficult task. If a firm pays its employees an increase of 7 per cent, for example, and productivity is raised by the same amount, the increased labour costs are absorbed by the increased output and thus unit costs of production attributable to labour are left unchanged. If this practice is adopted on a large scale, other costs of production—such as raw materials and components—may also be stabilised as domestic suppliers pay wage increases in line with their respective productivity improvements.

Under such a scheme the increases in money incomes may be relatively low, but are far greater in real terms compared with very large wage rises which simply allowed individuals to keep up with increases in the cost of living due to rapid inflation. An incomes policy linked in some way to productivity will mean that increases in income do represent an improvement in real purchasing power. An increase in real income of 7 per cent a year will in fact double the living standards of the recipient in ten years.

Many of the problems of the UK economy have

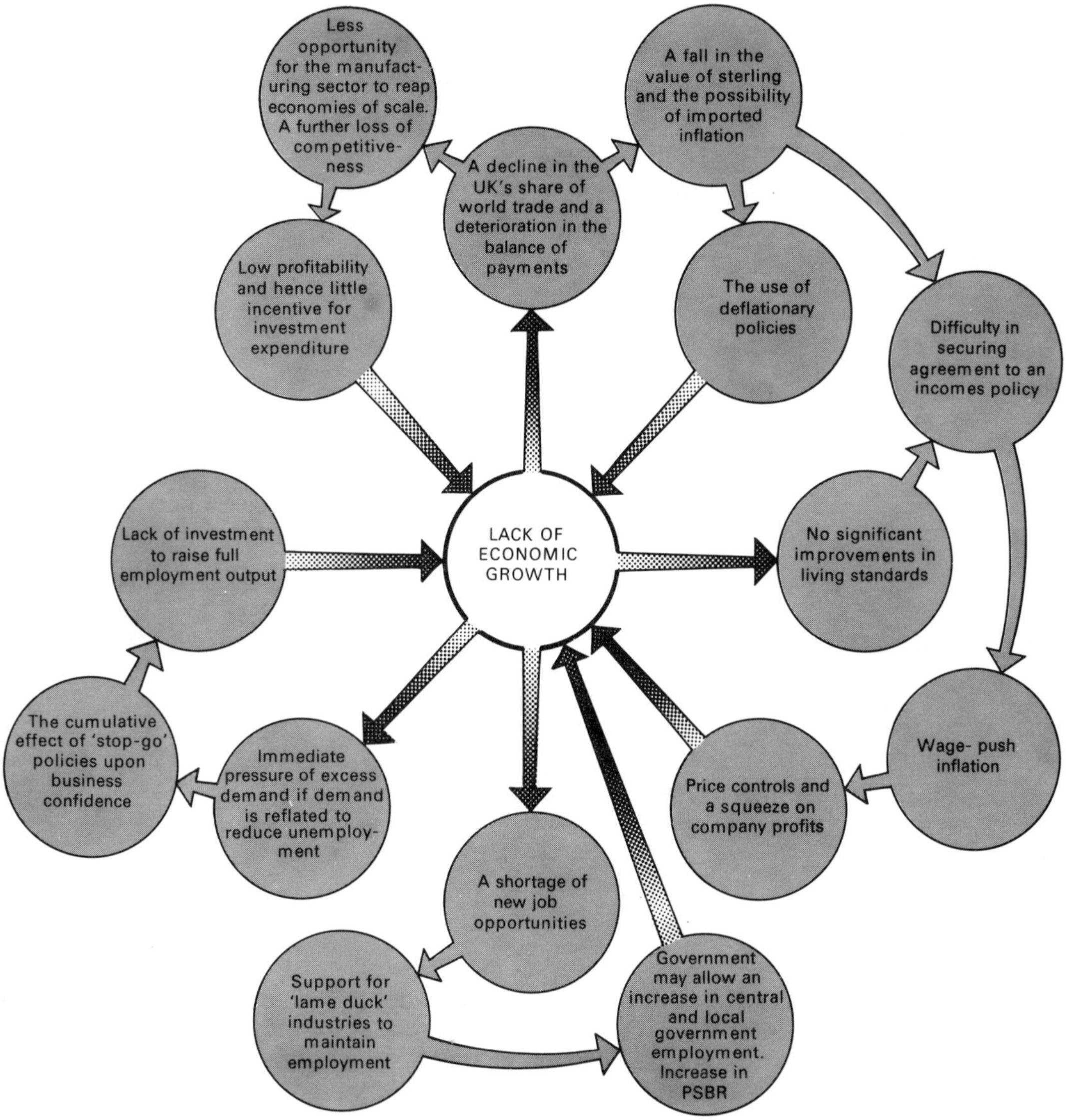

Fig. 5.8

stemmed from inflation rates which have been far in excess of those of our major overseas competitors. Moreover, this inflationary situation was tackled by the government with policies that made the prospects of economic growth, and hence improved living standards, all the more distant. For example, the strength of cost-push inflation in the early 1970s, which eventually gathered momentum, was perhaps the result of frustration among workers who had experienced no marked improvement in living standards for a period of years. This in turn was partly due to the government consistently resorting to deflationary policies to deal with inflation which in the 1960s averaged about 3½ per cent.

It is in fact important, when seeking to discover the initial cause of the rapid inflation of the 1970s, that one distinguishes between cause and effect. The greater use of collective bargaining power in these years was perhaps attributable to the lack of economic growth in the previous years, and the large wage increases negotiated in an attempt to

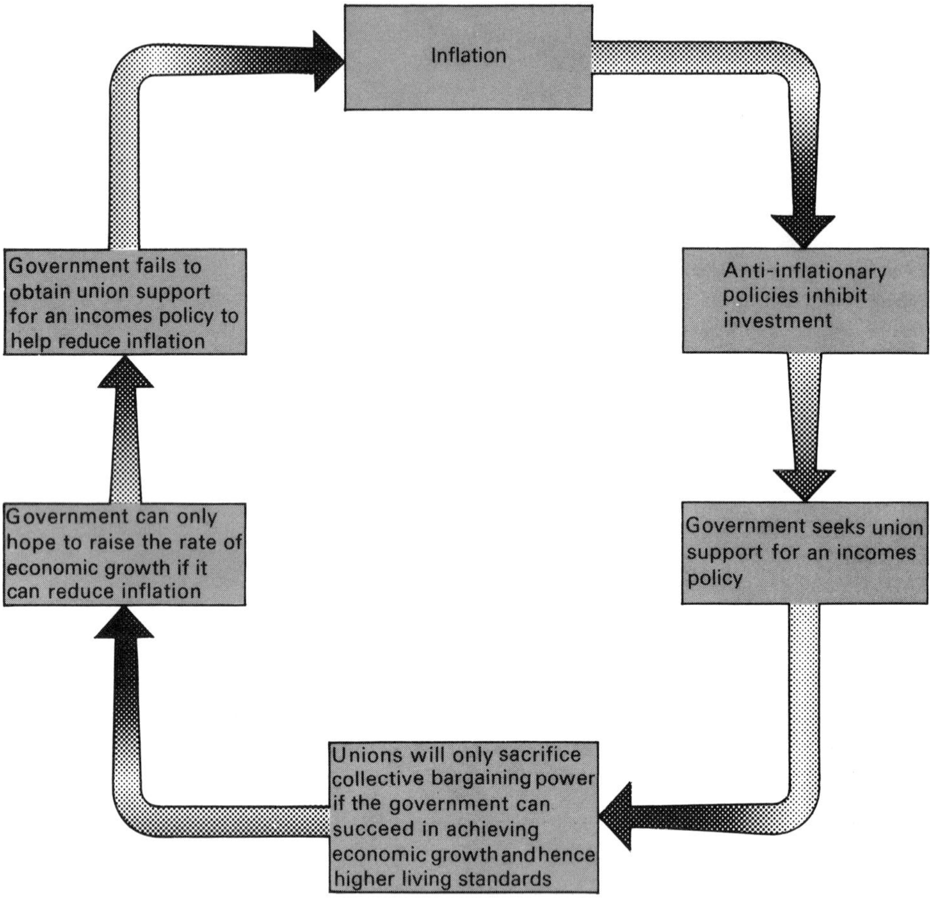

Fig. 5.9

'catch up' then helped to worsen the rate of inflation. Thus the use of deflationary policies not only inhibited investment and hence economic growth, but may also have given added momentum to inflation in the 1970s. The UK economy was left in a strait-jacket from which it became increasingly difficult to escape unless the government was prepared to place greater emphasis upon a more direct control over incomes. Some of these self-reinforcing pressures are illustrated in Fig. 5.8 (page 93).

Problems associated with an incomes policy

1. If incomes are to be restrained a decision must be taken regarding the **limits** beyond which they should not increase. The immediate problem of wage inflation may require a wage freeze followed by a period during which the policy attempts, through various stages, to reduce the percentage rise in incomes. Eventually, however, if such policies are to be linked in some way to productivity, forecasts must be made concerning, for example, the anticipated productivity improvement for the economy as a whole. This, however, raises a very distinct problem.

Trade unions may only be willing to give up well-established collective bargaining techniques and moderate wage claims if real living standards are currently rising by a significant amount. If this is not the case, then—depending upon relative bargaining positions—different groups in the economy will seek to use their power to obtain a greater share of the slowly increasing output by keeping as far as possible ahead of the rate of inflation. But a lack of investment, stemming from inflation and a general lack of business confidence further depressed by the uncertainty associated with government economic measures, can perhaps only be dealt with once inflation has been overcome. In order, however, for the government to reduce inflation, create an economic climate more conducive to investment, and thus succeed in raising living standards, it requires union co-operation in moderating wage increases, i.e. an incomes policy! Thus part of the situation illustrated in Fig. 5.7 is now further explained by the situation shown in Fig. 5.9.

The government will be confronted with a severe problem if it expects eventually to restrain wage increases in line with the rather disappointing improvements in productivity that have characterised the post-war period. Thus unions may still express a strong preference for their well-tried collective bargaining techniques during wage negotiations until the government can provide some evidence that its management of the economy has contributed to a marked improvement in the rate of economic growth. The government will also have to convince the unions that maintaining an acceptable rate of economic growth will continue to have priority over other economic objectives. Union support for the government's incomes policy may also be more readily secured if at the same time it demonstrates that it is not prepared to tackle the unemployment that results from excessive wage increases by expansionary fiscal and monetary measures. If the government displays such a discipline in relation to its fiscal and monetary policies then it will gain additional support from those groups in the economy who follow the 'monetarist' view that lax fiscal and monetary policies are the prime cause of the rapid inflation against which workers try to protect themselves by seeking large wage increases. It is for these reasons that incomes policies, in their initial stages in particular, will have to be supported by strict fiscal and monetary measures and perhaps also by statutory backing.

2. If the government intends that some form of control over incomes is to be a more permanent feature of its overall economic policy, and that this is eventually to be related in some way to the rise in national productivity, the problem then arises of the **distribution** of the permitted total among various groups in the economy.

As suggested in Book 1 (pages 81–3), this form of government intervention in the operation of the labour market as a means of allocating labour between alternative uses will have to steer a difficult path. This will be between such issues as a degree of flexibility that permits highly productive areas of the economy to attract labour into various uses more readily, the extent to which the policy is considered to be fair to those destined to receive relatively small increases, and the possible conflict with the forces arising from **wage leadership, traditional differentials,** and wage claims based upon the concept of **comparability.** To some extent the government may be tempted to use its own position as an employer in some areas of the public sector in an effort to set the trend for wage increases. This *may* be interpreted as an effort to obtain stricter adherence to its policy in the private sector, but this need not necessarily follow.

A wage freeze may be followed by a policy that then establishes a maximum permissible increase for all workers. This latter policy could involve a set amount of money or a certain percentage, but this approach, like a wage freeze, can inhibit the operation of the wage mechanism in allocating labour. A certain percentage will create pay anomalies by being particularly favourable to those on high incomes. This can also result in the lower paid reaching an income level whereby an increase in their post-tax income is more than outweighed by the loss of certain welfare payments for which their previously lower income had qualified them.

3. The government will also have to take account of **'wage drift'** as unions and groups of workers negotiate bonus schemes, working hours, overtime rates and other conditions of employment that cause actual weekly earnings to rise above what they should be according to the wage rate. Once this practice is communicated to other groups of workers, this total increase in earnings may then be regarded as the norm, and claims may be submitted on the basis of differentials and comparability because it appears that the policy has been breached by some groups. The opportunity for workers to benefit from wage drift or other allowances with a monetary value is, moreover, unevenly spread.

4. The government may eventually be obliged by both economic and political necessity to allow a greater degree of **flexibility** in wage increases when workers in particular firms or industries seek the full benefit of their respective productivity achievements. It is at this stage that the government will find its policy under the greatest pressure as workers in some key sectors or firms obtain wage increases far in excess of the norm that characterised the previous stage of the incomes policy. Although such large increases may reflect a genuine productivity deal, this may provoke strong claims on the basis of comparability.

Moreover, the government may find itself obliged to give way on its policy to a particular group of workers because of the severe disruption which industrial action may have upon the economy. The extent to which this can be avoided will depend very much upon the determination which the government displays in a potential dispute and its willingness to support its policy with fiscal and monetary policies. What happens in such a test case will set the trend for the next round of wage bargaining. All those subject to the policy must feel confident that the guidelines on pay are not going to be breached, and that if they settle within the agreed limits of the existing policy they will not witness exceptional awards at a later date. This involves both sides of industry in that employers do not permit wage drift and the TUC is able to control groups of workers with a particularly strong bargaining position.

5. The success of the policy may well depend upon its **simplicity,** since if the government sets out to control in too much detail, it may end up controlling nothing. If the government concentrates upon controlling wage settlements in key sectors, which tend to act as wage leaders, this will assist the policy at a later stage. The problem of competing claims and 'leap-frogging' can also be tackled if such unions can be persuaded to settle on a single date. This will remove the fears of strong unions who might otherwise have settled earlier but do not want to see larger increases granted afterwards.

An additional advantage of a **settlement day** for key unions is that it will help improve the accuracy and consistency of fiscal and monetary measures. This is because, for example, tax revenues can be more readily estimated, the data for future wage costs per unit of output will be more reliable, and the relative competitive positions of the economy estimated with greater confidence. This will allow the government to adopt a more certain approach to fiscal and monetary measures, and hence contribute to the restoration of confidence in the business world in that sudden and possibly de-stabilising changes in government economic measures are less likely.

6. The government may also be obliged to leave a degree of flexibility as far as the lower paid are concerned or other groups of workers which meet some criteria that qualify them as **'special cases'.** The latter may involve work which is of a particularly dangerous nature or where unsocial hours are concerned. Care must be taken that special cases are carefully defined otherwise too much flexibility will again prove self-defeating.

7. The government will have great difficulty in deciding upon the **cut-off point** from previous periods of wage negotiations that did not involve an incomes policy. There may be some groups of workers still attempting to obtain an increase and perhaps also catch up upon a previous erosion of their real income.

8. The government should also express its intention that **no definite date** will be given concerning any period during which it may attempt to operate without some form of income guideline. A terminal date for income controls will undermine the confidence of those who settle towards the end of a policy.

9. The control of incomes will be under particular pressure during a period of cost-push inflation stemming primarily from **higher import costs.** A large rise in the world price of important commodities will raise the cost of living. This however may be offset to a certain extent if the incomes policy has been successful in reducing inflation, encouraging investment, and raising the overall rate of economic growth, as this will be reflected in an appreciation of the exchange rate. Such an improvement in the value of the currency will be a reflection of real economic progress and help absorb the possible impact of higher commodity prices.

Incomes policies 1961–78

In July 1961, as part of an economic strategy to bolster sterling against pressure on the foreign exchange markets, the Chancellor at that time, Mr. Selwyn Lloyd, introduced a **'pay pause'.** The government hoped that the private sector would follow the lead which the government had taken in standing firm against claims in the public sector. The Chancellor found little union backing for his incomes policy, particularly when the nurses received a great deal of support for their wage claim which the government was refusing to meet. This approach was modified by the Chancellor in favour of a 'guiding light' norm and was continued by his successor, Mr. Reginald Maudling. However, the policy proved unworkable in the general economic environment created by reflationary measures aimed at achieving an improved rate of economic growth, since this produced excess demand pressures in the labour market.

When the Labour Government took office in October 1964 it was already committed to controls over incomes that were to be of a purely voluntary nature. This was perhaps the last occasion when an attempt was made to relate wage increases to productivity increases. The new policy was in fact based upon both sides of industry signing a **'declaration of intent'**—an undertaking that wage increases would be kept within the average productivity increase of 3–3½ per cent, as envisaged in the **National Plan**. Both these aspects of the government's economic policy stemmed from the Department of Economic Affairs headed by Mr. George Brown. Like the Department itself this voluntary policy was short lived and its failure was largely due to the very flexible interpretation of 'special cases' that allowed it to be breached by so many groups.

The government's Prices and Incomes Act 1965 had to be supported by a compulsory measure in July 1966 to freeze incomes and prices for a period of six months. This was followed by a period of **'severe restraint'** and then by a return to a voluntary approach. The devaluation of sterling in November 1967 meant that the competitive advantage had to be maintained if the balance of payments was to be quickly improved, rather than the better competitive position being rapidly eroded by inflation. The freeze succeeded in lowering inflation to 3½ per cent a year by April 1967 but the moves towards voluntary 'severe restraint' were less successful, and the large wage claims obtained by motor vehicle workers left the policy in such a weak position that it was abandoned towards the end of 1969.

The Conservative Government elected in mid-1970 abolished the Prices and Incomes Board which had been set up in 1965. The growing unemployment of the early 1970s did not have the anticipated effect of significantly moderating wage claims. The government then resorted to a voluntary policy, whereby it sought to reduce each successive claim by 1 per cent and it found the public sector again more susceptible to what became known as an **'n—1'** norm. It was an attempt to enforce the policy upon the miners, however, that precipitated its collapse, as the use of the strike weapon by miners gained them a 25 per cent wage rise. Other major unions, such as the railwaymen, sought comparable treatment and their success threatened runaway inflation.

In November 1972 the Conservative Government was obliged to introduce its first statutory wage controls. **Stage One** of this compulsory policy began with a wage freeze until April 1973, which proved successful. **Stage Two** embodied a norm which comprised a maximum percentage increase plus a flat rate component. Thus until November 1973 pay increases were limited to £1 a week plus 4 per cent, but with a maximum of £250 per year. These controls were essentially successful in moderating wage claims but anomalies were created as differentials were distorted. The lower paid would have received the largest percentage increases under Stage Two.

Stage Three was more flexible in an attempt to tackle problems arising out of distortions in the labour market, and perhaps industrial and political necessity. Wage increases were limited to £2.25 a week or 7 per cent, whichever was the larger, but the maximum permissible was £350 a year. There was also to be a rule that twelve months had to elapse before the next claim was submitted. Flexibility was reflected in that certain groups, such as the lower paid or those whose jobs were dangerous or unpleasant, could receive exceptional treatment. This stage also allowed agreements whereby workers received an extra 40p a week for every point that the retail price index rose above a certain threshold. This was a recognition that workers had become so accustomed to inflation that a claim incorporated an element that sought to protect them against future inflation. This practice was, of course, self-defeating in that it would help produce the inflation they feared, but it was hoped that this guaranteed protection against future inflation would moderate wage claims, reduce inflation and would thus only be rarely used.

Stage Three however was placed under severe pressure, as not only was there the dramatic rise in energy prices from the end of 1973 onwards, but the growth of the major manufacturing economies was producing the boom in world commodity prices. This imported inflation triggered off threshold payments which then gave inflation added momentum and produced more threshold payments. The reflationary policies of 1972 had been designed to reduce unemployment, but had led to a very substantial increase in the money supply which, after a time lag, was having an impact on the rate of inflation much in accordance with the views of the monetarists. The climax came early in 1974 when the miners used the strike weapon and caused British industry to operate on the basis of a three-day week. The Conservative

Government then lost the ensuing General Election in which they sought to win a mandate for their over-all economic policy with specific reference to income controls.

The new Labour Government dismantled statutory controls over incomes as part of its efforts to improve its relations with trade unions. Price control was, however, continued, but in the face of very rapid inflation this caused a severe squeeze on company profits. This liquidity crisis resulted in a relaxation of price controls to some extent in November 1974. Union co-operation to moderate wage claims was now dependent upon the so-called **Social Contract.** Although never precisely documented and signed, this reflected an agreement between the Labour Government and the trade union movement that the latter would moderate wage claims in exchange for the government pursuing certain social and industrial objectives. Wage claims were to be kept twelve months apart and be designed essentially to maintain real purchasing power, but exceptions were to be made in the case of the lower paid and where productivity agreements were reached. The government would respond by avoiding statutory controls over incomes, improving job security, eliminating lower pay for women, providing higher pensions and introducing taxes that sought a more equitable distribution of income and wealth. The end result, however, amounted to a very weak influence over incomes, and by February 1975 wage rates were nearly 30 per cent up on the previous year.

By July 1975 the government, with TUC support, introduced a very simple incomes policy on a voluntary basis but with legislative support held in reserve. This **Stage One** allowed a norm of a £6 per week rise for everyone with the exception of those earning more than £8,500 per year, who were not to receive any award at all. **Stage Two** the following year allowed a minimum increase of £2.50 per week, a maximum of £4.00 per week or 5 per cent within those two amounts.

Stage Three used only a percentage norm—a 10 per cent increase in earnings—but flexibility could be incorporated in the case of productivity agreements. The latter stage was combined with a budget which made some income tax cuts conditional upon trade union support for this Stage Three. Tax cuts to raise disposable income will avoid cost-push inflation although the ability of the government to make such cuts will depend heavily upon estimates regarding the PSBR. Such an approach also made the norm more difficult to calculate, as the increase in disposable income would depend upon the current tax liability of the individual concerned. Allowances for productivity deals do, however, present some groups with a means of avoiding the policy, and the government must take steps to ensure that such deals are in fact genuine, rather than the response of an employer threatened with an industrial dispute by a particular, powerful group of workers.

Stage Four in the summer of 1978 embodied a norm of 5 per cent at a time when inflation had fallen to 7–8 per cent. Again productivity deals were allowed and the government was prepared, as with Stage Three, to place sanctions upon those firms breaching the policy. In November 1978 Fords awarded their workers 17 per cent and, as had happened with much smaller firms under Stage Three, the government placed sanctions upon the company. Compared with the sanctions available to the government they did not appear very severe: only central government departments were instructed not to purchase from the Ford Company; the withdrawal of the facilities of the Export Credit Guarantee Department was not judged to be particularly harmful; while the government showed no immediate intention to withhold its financial assistance towards the new Ford investment project at Bridgend in South Wales.

The legal question which has to be resolved is whether the government can take such action. The courts must obey the statutory will of Parliament, but will challenge any arbitrary action as being *ultra vires.* The case put forward by the government, however, is that its financial assistance to firms will be forthcoming *if* such action is considered to be in the public interest. The government can therefore claim that a company breaching the pay guidelines is threatening its measures designed to reduce inflation, and is thus not operating in the public interest.

The future for Stage Four, and perhaps an eventual move to produce an incomes policy more directly linked to productivity, depended very heavily upon the government being able to prevent firms and unions from again circumventing its policy. Once a breach is made a policy can swiftly collapse and inflation then accelerates as workers attempt to catch up on the ground which they consider they lost during a policy which successfully restrained incomes. Moreover, the success of Stages Two and Three in reducing inflation may also have been attributable to a tighter control over the money supply, a strengthening of the currency, and the persistently high level of unemployment that characterised the later periods covered by incomes policies.

An incomes policy should allow the economy to operate closer to full employment output as it can also help to remove the inflationary impact of excess demand as expressed in the market for labour. The contribution of incomes policies to reducing inflation in the late 1970s does not necessarily mean, however, that such measures will be as effective during a period of rapid expansion in the economy, particularly if labour shortages appear in key sectors of the economy. But the possibility does arise that if wage inflation can be avoided during the initial period of growth, the resulting increases in living standards may eventually make income controls more acceptable to unions. The government may also be tempted to retain a more severe control over incomes in central and local government services if it wishes to ensure that the manufacturing sector in particular is able to attract more labour.

Government Economic Policy in the early 1980s

The Conservative government elected in 1979 introduced an over-all economic strategy which was essentially 'monetarist' in its approach. It followed the school of economists who firmly believed that money supply growth in excess of the growth of output was the sole cause of domestically generated inflation. This approach meant that the government eventually had to ensure that the money supply only expanded at a rate which was just sufficient to finance the increase in the volume of transactions produced by the increase in output. It sought to avoid the situation whereby the money supply expanded at a faster rate than output with the result that the increased volume of transactions was conducted at much higher money values. If for example money supply expanded by 12 per cent and output rose by only 2 per cent then this would produce 10 per cent inflation.

The government was faced with both rising unemployment and increasing inflation. If the traditional approach to fiscal and monetary policies had been employed to tackle the growing unemployment then this would have pointed to fiscal measures that sought to expand total demand via increases in government expenditure and/or cuts in taxation or monetary measures designed to ease both the availability and price of credit. The government strongly supported the view, however, that growing budget deficits and the expansion of credit in the 1970s had been the cause of rapid inflation via their effects upon the money supply. Thus traditional fiscal and monetary policies were not acceptable to a government which intended to follow the 'monetarist' approach to controlling inflation.

Inflation was seen as the root cause of unemployment because of its effects upon the UK's competitive position in the world economy. The government argued that reflationary fiscal and monetary measures might produce a reduction in unemployment in the short run but any such improvement would prove to be only temporary and would soon be followed by even higher unemployment because of the further loss of competitiveness brought about by an excessive growth in the money supply. The government also feared that any such large-scale reflation of demand would lead to a sudden and substantial increase in the import of manufactures rather than being mainly directed at domestic output. The government therefore gave total priority to reducing the rate of inflation as a means of improving the competitive position of the UK economy in anticipation of such an improvement creating both higher and more secure employment in the future and an economic environment where the level of business confidence would lead to an increase in investment to underpin the improvement in competitiveness.

The government rejected the idea of an incomes policy to control pay increases in the belief that such intervention would inhibit the workings of the labour market as a means of allocating labour. Moreover the rejection of an incomes policy was entirely consistent with its 'monetarist' view of inflation as cost (wage) push is not accepted as an independent cause of inflation as any such 'pushing' up of costs and prices can only take place if money supply growth creates an environment in which such wage increases can be granted. Thus the government took the view that an incomes policy was not necessary as long as money supply was under control and firms therefore could not readily borrow money to finance the pay increases.

The basis of the government's monetary policy became known as its 'Medium-Term Financial Strategy' (MTFS) and involved setting a series of targets for the growth in the money supply. The budget of 1980 launched the MTFS and the importance of securing a progressive reduction in the rate of growth of the money supply could be seen in the government's aim in this and future budgets of progressively reducing the volume of public expenditure and reducing the PSBR as a proportion of national income. The MTFS therefore set out a four-year path for monetary growth. The immediate target was for a growth of between 7 and 11 per cent for 1980–81 to be followed by targets of 6–10 per cent for 1981–82, 5–9 per cent for 1982–83 and 4–8 per cent for 1983–84. The budget emphasised the need for a progressive reduction in its level of spending over the same period so that by 1983–84 it would be 4 per cent lower in real terms than in 1979–80. This reduction in real terms would be achieved by increases in government spending at a rate lower than the anticipated rate of inflation, with the result that government spending would then consume less of the nation's resources. If these objectives were achieved then it was forecast that the PSBR would fall from 4¾ per cent of GDP in 1979–80 to 1½ per cent of GDP in 1983–84. The intended reductions in government spending were also in accordance with the government's declared aim of reducing the burden of direct taxation in order to promote initiative and enterprise, particularly in the small firms sector.

The strategy incorporated in the 1980 budget was in fact a recognition that monetary policy was no longer going to be used as a tool for demand management but rather as a means of promoting a general economic environment in which the economy would recover under its own momentum as the UK's competitive position improved. The experience of the 1970s had demonstrated the extent to which monetary measures, aimed at reducing the growth in the money supply, could be frustrated by the workings of a highly developed financial system which allowed institutions to maintain a healthy supply of credit to those who required it. Thus the 1980 budget and the MTFS also recognised that direct attempts to control the level of credit and hence money supply via traditional monetary measures had to be replaced by measures which would regulate the demand for money. Lending is the supplying of money to those who wish to borrow it and if borrowing can be reduced then this must mean a comparable reduction in the rate of growth of the money supply. The process of credit creation will be inhibited if financial institutions have difficulties in finding customers for the funds which other people have deposited with them. Thus the government concentrated upon reducing the demand for money. The public sector's demand for money was to be achieved via cuts in expenditure which reduced the PSBR while the private sector's demand for money was to be reduced by higher interest rates.

The new methods of monetary control introduced in 1981 reflected the government's general dissatisfaction with the previous techniques used to control the level of credit. The reserve asset ratio was abandoned as attempts to put it under pressure as a means of obliging banks to reduce the level of their advances had not proved very successful. The ½ per cent cash ratio was to be the fulcrum for monetary control as it would allow the monetary authorities to achieve its objectives in relation to interest rates. An attempt had been made in the very early part of the 1970s to allow interest rates to play a major part in monetary policy but the developments described earlier on pages 87–92 frustrated the efforts of the monetary authorities to control the money supply. The new approach meant that market forces would once again be largely responsible for the determination of interest rates in the economy so that they would move more flexibly rather than being influenced artificially by changes in MLR, which was suspended as part of the 1981 changes. The base rates charged by the banks will also now be more susceptible to market forces because developments in the money market will soon be transmitted to the banks. The actual mechanism is much the same as described on pages 86–7 dealing with MLR but with one important exception which allows market forces to operate more forcibly. When developments in the economy oblige the banks to call in money from the discount houses the latter will still be able to obtain assistance from the Bank of England by exchanging some of their bills for cash. Under the new arrangements, however, the discount houses, when offering bills to the Bank of England, will have to decide upon their own prices and the Bank will then decide which offers to accept. This is in contrast to the previous arrangements whereby the MLR ruling at the time indicated to them the rate at which they could obtain assistance from the Bank of England. The new approach means that the greater the cash shortage experienced by the discount houses the greater will be their need for assistance and this will be reflected in their willingness to offer bills to the Bank of England at correspondingly lower prices. The discount houses of course will be acutely aware of existing and future possible developments in the market for very short-term funds and thus the extent to which they may need to obtain assistance from the Bank of England in the future. Such factors will be borne in mind when taking up new issues of Treasury bills, commercial bills and other instruments which reflect short-term borrowing by both the private and public sectors. Thus when the discount houses feel that they may be obliged to seek assistance from the Bank of England on a relatively large scale they will protect themselves by offering lower prices on new bills, thus raising their yield. The government will then achieve its objective of higher interest rates in other sectors of the financial system as the banks will raise the interest paid on deposits to remain competitive and base rates charged on their lending will eventually have responded to market forces.

Between 1980 and June 1983 the rate of inflation fell from a peak of 21 per cent to 3·7 per cent and since this was the government's primary objective it is important to consider those factors which may have contributed to this change in the economic environment and other important developments which had implications for the government's over-all economic strategy during that period.

The Money Supply

The government regarded the announcement of money supply targets as an important part of its policy. Such clearly stipulated targets were seen as a means of influencing expectations concerning the future rate of inflation so that both employers and trade unions would be led to alter their attitudes towards the fixing of prices and pay settlements. It was anticipated that a progressively lower money supply target would create expectations of a lower rate of inflation and decisions concerning both prices and pay would take this into account and therefore contribute to a lower rate of inflation in the following period. If however the government fails to keep the growth of the money supply within the target range then the possibility arises that expectations concerning the rate of inflation may not be revised downwards and may even be revised upwards. The link between money supply targets and expectations also assumes that both employers and trade unions are themselves convinced that excessive money supply growth is the major cause of inflation.

Money supply targets did in fact prove to be difficult to achieve, as shown in Fig. 5.10, and the actual growth rates for £M3 were as follows: 19 per cent in 1980, 13·1 per cent in 1981, and 9·7 per cent in 1982. One of the reasons for the initial period of rapid growth in £M3 was the unexpected rate at which the economy moved into recession as shown by Figs. 5.12 and 5.13. The level of unemployment was increased by a combination of a growing world recession, cuts in government spending and rapid increases in interest rates. The immediate response of many firms was to borrow more money in order

Fig. 5.10: Monetary growth

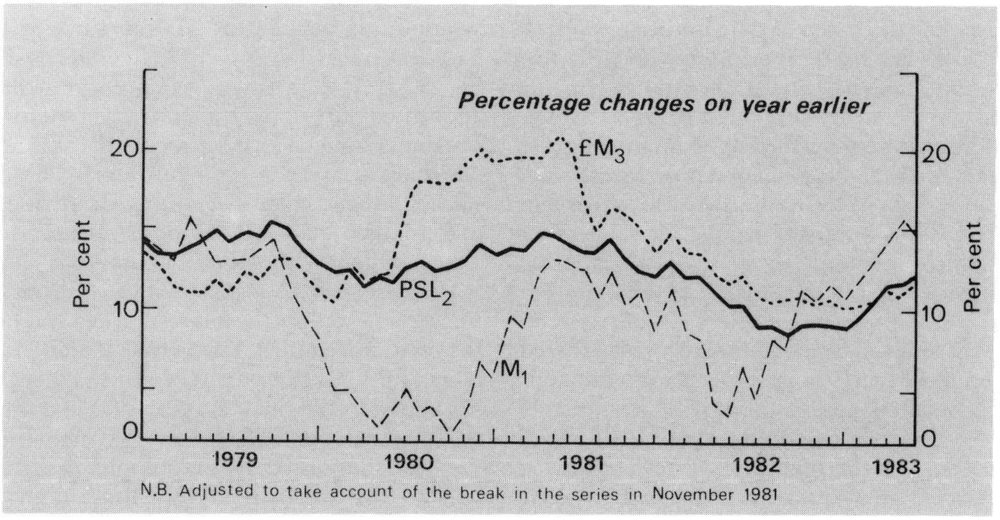

SOURCE: *Economic Progress Report*, August 1983.

to stay in business and to give themselves a breathing space in which they could formulate and then implement cost-saving programmes such as trimming down the size of their work force. Thus the deepening recession actually increased the private sector's demand for money despite exceptionally high rates of interest. Moreover during part of this period of very high rates of interest firms were faced with a situation whereby they were then obliged to increase their borrowing to meet their interest charges. The extent to which interest rates deter the demand for money will also depend partly upon the real rate of interest and in 1981, for example, base rates fluctuated between 12 per cent and 16 per cent and this has to be compared with an inflation rate of about 12 per cent for the same year. The money supply figures were also given a substantial boost by the removal of the supplementary deposit scheme in June 1980. This sudden large increase in £M_3 was proof that the financial system had devised ways of putting large-scale lenders in touch with borrowers without such funds first being deposited with the commercial banks. Such roundabout methods of finance meant that these activities did not feature in money supply figures until those lending such funds again resorted to using the banks as more convenient financial intermediaries when the supplementary deposit scheme was abandoned.

The Public Sector Borrowing Requirement

The speed and depth of the recession also had implications for the PSBR because the increased unemployment affected the government's tax revenues while at the same time involving a large increase in social security payments such as unemployment benefits. Social security payments rose from a total of £19·4 billion in 1979–80 to over £32 billion in 1982–83. Current estimates suggest that every 100,000 increase in unemployment costs the Exchequer over £450 million in terms of lost tax revenues and social security payments. Targets set for the PSBR soon had to be revised while the government sought to implement spending cuts in order to help compensate for the effects of recession upon its revenues and expenditure. This also forced the government to postpone its plans for reductions in direct taxation and its progress was largely limited to changes introduced in June 1979 which lowered some of the higher tax rates. Extra tax revenues were derived mainly from higher excise duties. In the 1981 budget, for example, the following increase in duties were applied: Spirits—60p a bottle, beer—4p a pint, wine—12p a bottle, fortified wine (e.g. sherry)—25p a bottle, petrol—20p per gallon, diesel fuel—20p per gallon, cigarettes—14p per packet of 20, and vehicle excise duty—£10. It was forecast that such increases would raise an extra £2·5 billion in a full year. In the 1982 budget excise duties were again raised to produce extra income estimated at nearly £1 billion and in 1983 such changes were designed to raise an extra £600 million in a full year. Such was the urgency to reduce the PSBR in 1981 that the government did not feel that it was in a position to increase personal tax allowances and tax bands in line with inflation and in fact in that particular year it left them unchanged.

Fig. 5.11: PSBR: percentage of money GDP

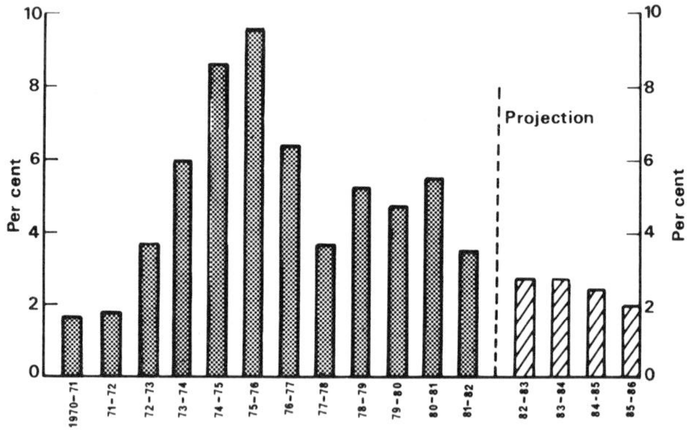

SOURCE: *Economic Progress Report*, April 1983.

At one time it was estimated that the PSBR would be $1\frac{1}{2}$ per cent of GDP in 1983–84 but this had to be revised to $2\frac{3}{4}$ per cent of GDP, as shown in Fig. 5.11. As far as the financing of the PSBR was concerned the government was successful in obtaining a much larger proportion of funds from non-bank sources. A large part was financed by the sale of longer-term government securities while index-linked National Savings Certificates proved very popular with private households. Not only were these new issues of savings certificates inflation proof, because the interest earned was linked to the retail price index, but they also offered a bonus if held for five rather than seven years. Between the beginning of the financial year 1981 and the end of the financial year 1983 National Savings schemes of various kinds raised over £7 billion towards financing the PSBR. The government also tightened its grip on spending by local authorities in order to secure a reduction in the total level of real government expenditure. It achieved this by increasing its grants to local authorities at a rate which was below the rate of inflation. Action was then taken to curb excessive rate increases as higher rates would have conflicted with the government's anti-inflationary policy and also its aim of reducing the over-all size of the public sector in relation to the economy as a whole. In particular it meant that local authorities were obliged to settle pay increases within a percentage figure which took account of the limits placed upon central government grants and to seek ways of slimming down the number of their employees.

The PSBR was also reduced by the government's policy of scaling down the financial assistance which it was prepared to make to support loss-making activities in the nationalised industries. It was hoped that this would make them commercially more viable and was part of the government's over-all policy of making such industries more susceptible to market forces in order to promote efficiency. This approach was then supported by the sale of public sector assets as either whole or parts of nationalised industries were sold off as part of the programme of 'privatisation'. This desire to stimulate market forces in key areas of the economy had the effect of reducing its expenditure while also raising revenue for the government in the year in which any such asset sales took place. The government's income and expenditure plans in relation to its 1982–83 budget are shown in Table 5.8.

Table 5.8: Government income and expenditure plans in relation to 1982–83 budget

	1982–3 Budget forecast	*1982–3 Latest estimate*	*1983–4 Forecast*
INCOME			
Central government taxation			
Income tax	30·8	30·2	31·4
Value added tax	14·7	13·9	15·5
Oil duties	5·1	5·2	5.7
Corporation tax	4·8	5·5	6·2
Tobacco	3·5	3·5	3·7
National insurance surcharge	3·4	2·8	1·7
Spirits, beer, wine and perry	3·3	3·0	3·9
Petroleum revenue tax	2·3	3·3	5·2
Supplementary petroleum duty	2·0	2·4	—
Vehicle excise duty	1·8	1·8	1·9
Taxes on capital	1·4	1·6	1·5
European Community duties	1·3	1·2	1·4
Other (including accruals)	2·6	3·6	3·3
Total	**77.0**	**78.1**	**81.5**
National insurance, etc. contributions	19·5	18·6	21·2
Local authorities' rates	12·2	12·3	13·0
North Sea oil royalties etc.	1·5	1·7	1·6
General government trading surplus and rent	3·4	3·5	3·3
General government interest and dividend receipts	2·4	2·4	2·3
Adjustments			
Accruals	0·5	−0·2	—
Public corporations transactions	3·8	3·6	3·4
Other	0·3	—	−0·5
Total receipts	**120·6**	**120·0**	**125·9**
Public sector borrowing requirement	**9·5**	**7·5**	**8·2**
Total receipts and borrowing	**130·9**	**127·5**	**134·1**

	1982–3 Budget forecast	*1982–3 Latest estimate*	*1983–4 Forecast*
EXPENDITURE			
Social security	32·0	32·5	34·4
Defence	14·1	14·4	16·0
Health and personal social services	13·6	13·9	14·6
Education and science	12·2	12·6	12·6
Scotland	6·1	6·3	6·4
Industry, energy, trade and employment	5·8	5·9	5·6
Transport	4·2	4·3	4·3
Order and protective services	4·1	4·3	4·6
Other environmental services	3·6	3·4	3·6
Northern Ireland	3·5	3·6	3·8
Housing	3·1	2·6	2·8
Wales	2·4	2·4	2·5
Overseas services	2·1	2·2	2·2
Other public services	1·7	1·7	1·7
Common services	1·6	1·6	1·0
Agriculture, fisheries, food and forestry	1·5	1·8	1·7
Government lending to nationalised industries	1·1	1·4	1·1
Arts and libraries	0·5	0·6	0·6
Local authority current expenditure not allocated to programmes (England)	—	—	0·9
Adjustments to programmes—			
PC market and overseas borrowing	−0·3	−1·1	−0·3
Special sales of assets	−0·6	−0·6	−0·8
Contingency reserve	2·4	0·3	1·5
General allowance for shortfall	—	−1·0	−1·2
Planning total in Cmnd 8789	**114·7**	**113·0**	**119·6**
Revisions since Cmnd 8789	—	−0·5	−0·3
Revised planning total	**114·7**	**112·5**	**119·3**
Gross debt interest	15·4	15·0	14·8
Planning total plus gross debt interest	**130·1**	**127·5**	**134·1**

SOURCE: *Economic Progress Report*, April 1983.

Interest rates

Higher interest rates as a means of curbing the demand for money were seen as an important aspect of the government's policy even before the new monetary measures were introduced in 1981 as can be seen in Table 5.9. In accordance with the MTFS, market forces were allowed to produce higher rates of interest as a means of choking off the excessive demand for credit. Unfortunately the initial rise in interest rates was also a factor in producing inflationary pressures within the economy as firms seek to pass on such cost increases to customers in the form of higher prices. The higher interest rates paid by the banks to attract deposits, particularly in the light of the attractive rates offered on government securities and savings certificates, also worked its way through to the building societies. In order to maintain the level of their mortgage advances the building societies raised the rates paid to savers and thus the mortgage interest charges. This had a significant impact upon the cost of living as over 50 per cent of householders in the UK are owner-occupiers. Thus the initial rise in the cost of borrowing had the effect of actually contributing to a rise in the retail price index. Any subsequent fall in interest rates, resulting from an eventual fall in the demand for money, will then have the effect of moderating the rise in the retail price index.

Table 5.9: London clearing banks' base rates

Date of change	*New rate (%)*	*Date of change*	*New rate (%)*
1979 14 Feb.	13½	*1982* 22 Jan.	14
6 Mar.	13	25 Feb.	13½
6 April	12	12 Mar.	13
15 June	14	8 June	12½
16 Nov.	17	13 July	12
1980 4 July	16	2 Aug.	11½
25 Nov.	14	18 Aug.	11
1981 11 Mar.	12	31 Aug.	10½
16 Sep.	14	7 Oct.	10
1 Oct.	16	14 Oct.	9½
14 Oct.	15½	4 Nov.	9
9 Nov.	14	26 Nov.	10
3 Dec.	14½	*1983* 12 Jan.	11
		14 Mar.	10½
		16 April	10
		14 June	9½

SOURCE: *Financial Statistics.*

Unemployment

The level of unemployment rose from 6·4 per cent in 1980 to 12·7 per cent in March 1983 and this was caused by a combination of factors. The growing recession in other major manufacturing economies resulting from the second period of large increases in the price of oil had the effect of reducing the demand for the UK's exports while the problems facing UK exporters were further aggravated by the effects of domestic inflation upon the UK's competitive position. Total demand in the economy was then also depressed by the high rates of interest which eventually had the desired effect of reducing the level of borrowing by the private sector. Firms could only reduce the amount which they borrowed by cost-saving programmes which reduced their total outlay on stocks of materials and components, and by schemes to reduce the size of their labour force. Cuts in government spending then added to the fall in total demand as some sectors of the economy, particularly the construction industry, rely heavily upon central and local government contracts to sustain the level of their business. These developments then caused further reductions in the level of demand because of the downward multiplier effect which they exerted upon the level of activity in other sectors of the economy. The result was that the level of manufacturing output (see Fig. 5.12) fell by over 15 per cent between the end of 1980 and June 1983.

Many economists regard the large increase in unemployment as shown in Fig. 5.13 as the main reason for the fall in inflation as trade union bargaining power is greatly reduced during such a severe recession and workers are less willing to take industrial action to support their pay claims. Employers also change their attitudes to wage and salary negotiations as they must pay the utmost attention to competitiveness when faced with what seems likely to be a prolonged contraction of their markets and little possibility of increasing their sales revenues. Firms therefore are forced to be more cost-conscious in order to survive and the fact that employment fell more sharply than total output indicates that employers found ways of raising the productivity of labour; this is reflected in Fig. 5.14 which illustrates a fall in unit wage costs. Thus it is widely suggested that the recession produced by a severe deflation of demand was the primary reason why inflation eventually fell. In fact inflation fell more rapidly than would have been suggested by the money supply growth which occurred in the latter period of the government's term of office.

The 'monetarist' approach anticipated that a reduction in the rate of growth of the money supply

Fig. 5.12: Output at 1975 prices

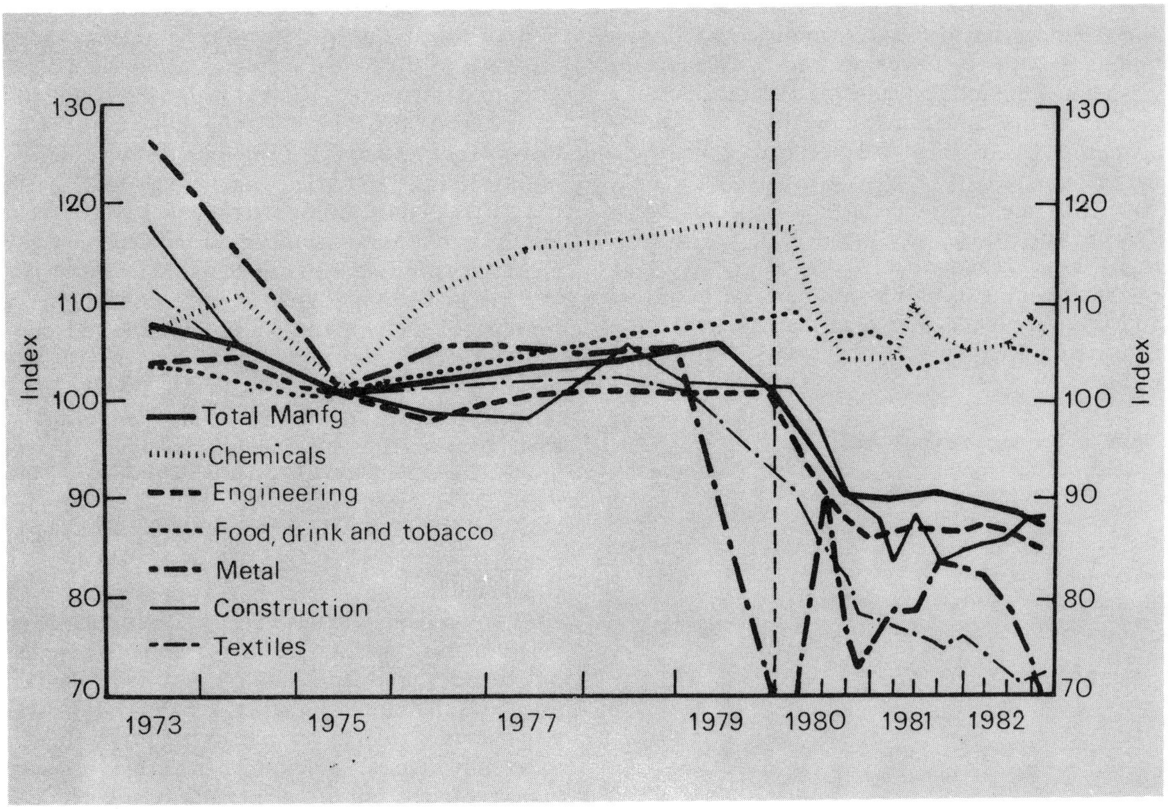

SOURCE: *Lloyds Bank Economic Bulletin*, March 1983.

Fig. 5.13: Unemployed excluding school-leavers in UK 1977–82

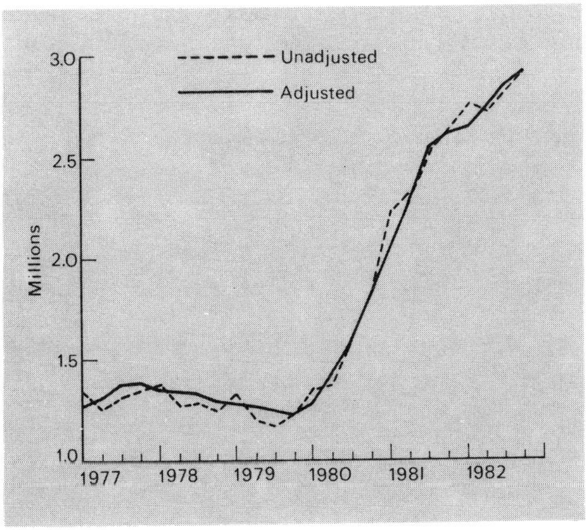

SOURCE: *Economic Progress Report*, May 1983.

would have a direct effect upon prices rather than the level of output and employment. Moreover money supply targets proved difficult to achieve and under such circumstances would not have had the desired effect of moderating people's expectations concerning the future rate of inflation. Critics

Fig. 5.14: Unit wage costs in manufacturing

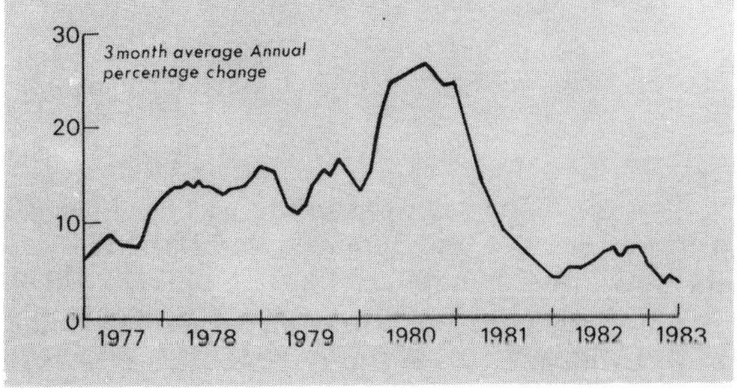

SOURCE: *Economic Progress Report*, September 1983.

of the government's monetary policy claimed that it was expectations concerning possible bankruptcy and redundancies that caused employers and trade unions to settle for lower price and pay increases. Cash limits and indirect controls over rate increases performed the same function in those parts of the economy where the local authorities were the major employers.

The exchange rate

In 1979 the exchange rate averaged £1=$2·12 but by the beginning of 1981 it had appreciated to $2·40 and its over-all position against major currencies had strengthened by over 18 per cent as can be seen in Fig. 5.15.

Fig. 5.15: Sterling exchange rates

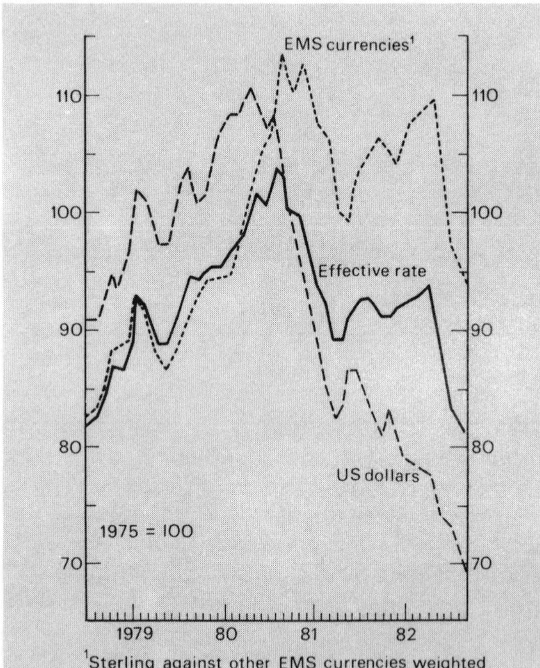

[1]Sterling against other EMS currencies weighted in proportion to their share in the effective rate index

SOURCE: *Bank Briefing*, March 1983 (Bank of England).

This rise in the value of sterling was produced by a combination of high interest rates in the UK and the anticipated benefits to the economy of North Sea oil, particularly at a time of political instability in the Middle East and future possible increases in the world price of oil. Overseas funds were therefore attracted into the UK and the increase in the demand for sterling led to an increase in its price in terms of other currencies. This over-all appreciation of sterling helped firms to moderate price increases to the extent to which they relied upon imported raw materials, semi-processed goods and components. If for example the dollar price of an import rose by 5 per cent and over the same period of time sterling appreciated against the dollar by 12 per cent then the UK importer would pay 7 per cent less in sterling for the same imported item. The rise in the exchange rate also helped to moderate the rise in the cost of living because it would have had a similar effect upon the prices of imported consumer goods. Consumers in the UK were also able to take increasing advantage of a much wider range of cheap consumer goods from the newly industrialising countries such as Taiwan, Hong Kong, South Korea and Brazil. Such developments were particularly pronounced in relation to clothing, footwear, electrical goods and other household items.

The fall in the exchange rate from the last half of 1982 onwards would have been a significant factor in stimulating inflation had it not been outweighed by other developments in the economy that helped to reduce the rate of inflation. By the end of 1983 however the fall in the exchange rate was sufficient to actually help cause an upturn in the inflation rate to nearly 6 per cent. In the meantime however the fall in the exchange rate and the general improvement in competitiveness produced a slight recovery in the level of exported manufactures and so helped to prevent an even larger decline in the level of total output and employment. The movement in the exchange rate was essentially caused by the fall in interest rates relative to those in other countries and

Fig. 5.16: Retail prices and average earnings

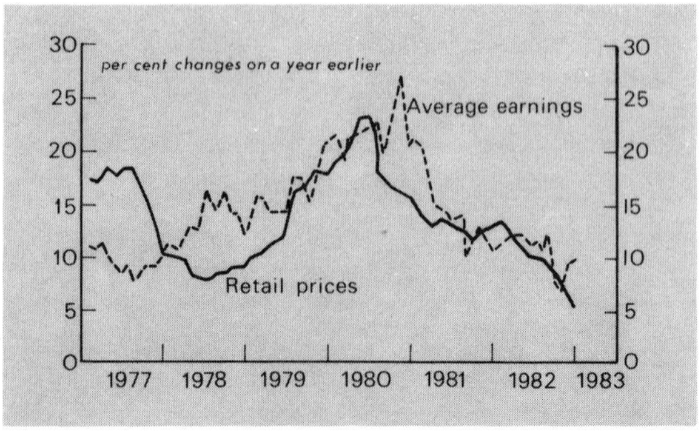

SOURCE: *Economic Progress Report*, April 1983.

revised expectations of the benefits of North Sea oil to the UK because of speculation concerning a significant reduction in the world price of oil. In the event a price war was avoided despite the world oil surplus and OPEC settled on a price of about \$29 a barrel compared with a price of \$19 in 1979 and \$35 in 1981.

Those factors which contributed to the fall in inflation and pay settlements as shown in Fig. 5.16 can now be summarised as follows:

(a) the fall in the rate of growth of the money supply

(b) the effect of recession/unemployment upon prices and pay settlements

(c) the appreciation in the exchange rate

(d) the gradual fall in interest rates

(e) proportionately smaller increases in excise duties in comparison with those of 1981

(f) the fall in energy prices

(g) the effect of smaller central government grant increases upon local authority pay settlements and lower rates increases

(h) the effect of the higher prices charged by nationalised industries in order to become less reliant upon government subsidies was less pronounced in the latter part of the government's term of office.

6. The Importance of International Trade

International trade arises because countries tend to concentrate their productive efforts upon certain areas of output that create quantities of goods and services beyond their own requirements. Surpluses are then exported and the foreign exchange earned allows them to import some of the surpluses produced in other economies. The reasoning behind this tendency for countries to specialise is basically the same as that which leads individuals to specialise in a particular activity.

The theory of comparative advantage

If people are asked what is the largest single transaction in which they are likely to be involved over their life-times, the answers given will probably relate to purchases of houses or expensive consumer durables. All these dealings, however, are dependent upon a far more important transaction—the sale of their labour as a factor service. Individuals specialise in that their occupation involves the sale of their particular skill, in return for which they receive an income. The actual use of their skill to meet their own personal requirements is probably minimal, if indeed it is ever used at all. A toolmaker or bank employee may apply their skills on very few occasions for their immediate personal benefit but sell their surplus requirements for an income. The same principle applies to households providing other factor services.

If an individual attempted to be self-sufficient, a very low standard of living, at least in material terms, would be the result. Perhaps an individual would have sufficient skills to eke out an existence in terms of basic food, shelter and clothing but anything more than that would prove increasingly difficult. A degree of self-sufficiency may be achieved in terms of food production, but as soon as surplus food production is exchanged for other products trade has taken place. The individual may recognise that he is particularly talented at growing certain produce; then a need arises for building materials, but producing these materials means his labour and other resources cannot be devoted to food production. A neighbour may be producing building materials but our individual may well believe that he can produce them more efficiently in terms of working hours. He may realise, however, that to produce building materials would involve a very high opportunity cost in terms of the food production sacrificed. This will lead him to concentrate upon growing food and the surplus produced will allow an exchange for an even larger quantity of building materials.

This same basic principle applies to the more orthodox situation where money facilitates the exchange of surpluses. People have their own personal economies in that they sell (i.e. export) their labour in return for which they receive money as a claim upon the output of others. This money can be used to buy (i.e. import) goods and services which contribute to their personal welfare. Again, a firm may believe that it can produce bought-in components more efficiently than its current suppliers in terms of man-hours, but by **specialising** in its own activity it can produce sufficient income to buy an even larger quantity of components.

For these reasons not only do individuals, firms, industries and regions tend to specialise, but also economies as a whole show a degree of specialisation rather than attempting self-sufficiency. Perhaps we could grow cotton and oranges in the UK but the cost in terms of land, labour, capital and entrepreneurial skills consumed in the process of growing them would be very high indeed. These scarce resources would be denied to other uses in which they could be employed more productively. The cost of attracting these resources into cotton- and orange-growing from alternative uses would produce very expensive cotton and oranges which reflected the high opportunity costs involved.

The principal economic force that promotes

Table 6.1

	Annual output of wheat per worker	*Annual output of chemicals per worker*
Enterprise	400 tons	200 tons
Tardis	300 tons	100 tons

specialisation stems from what economists refer to as the theory of **comparative advantage**. This theory points to countries concentrating more heavily upon those lines of output where they have a comparative advantage, and this in turn arises from their being able to supply a product at a lower **opportunity cost** than other countries. This basic theory can be demonstrated in Table 6.1, which involves two countries, Enterprise and Tardis, and indicates the output of labour in each of them in two lines of production, namely wheat and chemicals. From this information an additional chart can be established to determine where each country's respective comparative advantage lies. The opportunity cost of producing wheat and chemicals in the two countries is shown in Table 6.2.

Table 6.2

	Opportunity cost of a ton of wheat	*Opportunity cost of a ton of chemicals*
Enterprise	$\frac{1}{2}$ ton of chemicals	2 tons of wheat
Tardis	$\frac{1}{3}$ ton of chemicals	3 tons of wheat

For example, if a worker in Enterprise is producing wheat, the opportunity cost of obtaining every 400 tons of wheat is the 200 tons of chemicals which he could have produced in that alternative employment. Thus the opportunity cost of 1 ton of wheat is $\frac{1}{2}$ ton of chemicals. Similarly in Enterprise the opportunity cost of every 200 tons of chemicals is the alternative output of 400 tons of wheat which is the sacrifice to obtain the chemicals. The opportunity cost of each ton of chemical is thus 2 tons of wheat. Thus Enterprise has a comparative advantage in chemicals as the opportunity cost of each ton of chemicals is 2 tons of wheat compared with 3 tons in Tardis.

Tardis, however, has a comparative advantage in wheat production as the opportunity cost of each ton of wheat is $\frac{1}{3}$ ton of chemicals compared with $\frac{1}{2}$ ton of chemicals in Enterprise. These lower opportunity costs will be reflected in having to pay a lower price to attract resources into those areas where each has a comparative advantage. These lower costs will in turn be reflected in lower prices in that Enterprise can produce and sell chemicals more cheaply, while wheat can be produced and sold more cheaply in Tardis. These competitive strengths will attract demand for their respective products, and cause a shift of resources that leads to a greater degree of specialisation between the two countries.

Table 6.3

Re-allocation of workers	*Effect upon total output of wheat*	*Effect upon total output of chemicals*
Enterprise—10 workers moved from wheat to chemicals	−4,000 tons	+2,000 tons
Tardis—16 workers moved from chemicals to wheat	+ 4,800 tons	−1,600 tons
	+ 800 tons	+ 400 tons

Table 6.3 shows the repercussions of this re-allocation of labour in that it leads to an increase in the total output of both wheat and chemicals between the two countries. Whatever the total initial output of wheat and chemicals, more of both products in now available. Encouraged by the respective price advantages, the exchange of surpluses will give rise to international trade. Enterprise will be willing to import wheat as long as the price it pays in terms of chemicals is at a lower 'exchange rate' than that which would arise if it produced the wheat itself. Similarly Tardis is willing to import chemicals as long as the 'exchange rate' in terms of the amount of wheat is has to give up by trading is more favourable than if it produced the chemicals itself. Since both countries will be aware of the advantages of greater specialisation and the gains from trade, then eventually an 'exchange rate' will be determined from which they both benefit.

This is the basic theory of international trade. The degree of specialisation, however, suggested by the theory is not taken to extremes unless an economy has such a strong comparative advantage that alternatives are not readily available within the producing country to achieve any real degree of diversification. Some economies have concentrated upon a range of manufacturing output rather than specialising too heavily in a narrow field of manufactures and these would include countries such as the UK, Italy, West Germany, Belgium, France and Japan. The US, on the other hand, has a widely diversified output of manufactures, raw materials and food. Many developing countries are, however, heavily dependent upon just one or two products for their livelihood, such as oil, coffee, sugar, copper and other primary products.

The use of resources that give rise to **transport costs** can often outweigh the competitive advantage which a producer has achieved when seeking to export to other markets, and because of the distances, weight and mass involved many products would lose their competitive advantage in overseas markets. There are, however, man-made barriers which exist to restrict the penetration by an overseas supplier into a domestic market. Imports are faced with various barriers that artificially distort their price or availability against those ruling in the potential export market. These include import duties, import quotas, foreign exchange control on certain types of import expenditure, and subsidies to domestic producers. These barriers will prevent demand from switching to low-cost suppliers and not lead to the allocation of resources on an international scale as suggested by the theory of comparative advantage. There are many factors operating to slow down the degree of specialisation:

(a) *Governments do not wish to become too dependent upon overseas suppliers for strategically important products.*

(b) *The possible increase in monopoly power by overseas producers* can lead to higher prices and cause the government to maintain some domestic capacity for products such as energy, steel and food.

(c) *The loss of a comparative advantage can lead to heavy unemployment* that will be particularly severe in areas where the industry is mainly concentrated. The occupational and geographical immobility of labour may thus promote restrictions on imports, particularly if the country in question is not developing new lines of production in which it has a comparative advantage, and new employment prospects are limited.

(d) *Protection may be given to 'infant' industries* which potentially can develop a comparative advantage but cannot reach the scale of operation to compete with existing producers both in the domestic market and in overseas markets. The home market may thus be protected to provide a basis for its initial stages of growth.

(e) *Countries may wish to diversify their economies* as their future prosperity may be too dependent upon a single category of exports, for which world demand may be falling or rising only very slowly. This is often the case with raw materials that suffer from the development of synthetics, and where the income elasticity of demand for basic foodstuffs proves to be very low.

(f) *Diversification may be necessary because of barriers erected against that country's exports*, and this restricts its foreign exchange earnings and hence its ability to pay for imports.

(g) *Import restrictions may be proposed as a means of improving a country's balance of payments situation as well as protecting the general level of domestic employment.* The success of tariffs, however, will depend upon the price elasticity of demand for the products in question, the relative importance of non-price factors in influencing choice and, as with other forms of protection, the likelihood of retaliation.

(h) *There may be concern over the social costs involved in an economy where the living and working environment shows little variety except that associated with heavy industrialisation.*

The importance of international trade to the domestic economy

Although the UK has traditionally supported the principle of free trade, there have been periods when the government has been under substantial pressure to protect domestic firms—and hence output, employment and income—from imports. Once an economy loses its comparative advantage it becomes progressively more difficult for that country to close the competitive gap and regain its share of international trade. The setbacks which the UK has suffered in the area of international trade serve to highlight the importance of that trade to the general prosperity of the nation. The rise in living standards that has occurred over the years has largely been attributable to our ability to export those manufactures and services in which the UK has had a cost advantage. The rise in real incomes and the range of products available to households would not have been possible if the UK had relied upon domestic production to raise living standards. Indeed real purchasing power would have been much lower due to lower output and productivity in the economy as a whole.

The UK has now developed sources of energy from the North Sea but apart from this has not possessed the raw materials upon which economic progress has been increasingly based. Thus the economy has had to rely heavily upon those skills associated with manufacturing and the provision of commercial services to develop areas in which there was a comparative advantage. Raw materials are required not only to assist output for domestic consumption and fixed capital formation but also to produce exports. Exports have a dual role in that they not only earn the wealth to pay for imports of food but also the raw materials involved in the manufacture of exports themselves.

The importance of Britain's foreign trade in the economic life of the country is shown by the fact that the total value of exports of goods and services in 1982 amounted to about 20 per cent of total final expenditure on goods and services. In 1982 the UK had 8·5 per cent of the world export trade in manufactures behind West Germany (10·6 per cent), Japan (17·9 per cent), the US (17·8 per cent), and France (8·8 per cent). The earnings from non-material transactions, such as commercial services, and interest, profit and dividends earned from past overseas investment, have maintained the UK as the second largest earner of foreign exchange from such sources.

The importance of international trade to the UK is demonstrated by the emphasis placed by governments upon improving export performance by raising productivity, controlling inflation—which otherwise destroys a competitive advantage—and providing a wide range of government services to encourage export. The importance of international trade and the interdependence of trading nations is shown in Table 6.4. Even when the economy is deliberately deflated to reduce the build-up of inflationary pressures, preferential treatment is given to potential exports—perhaps by the reduction of their tax burden or by their being excepted from the general restrictions placed upon borrowing. The importance of exports to companies is shown by the fact that although in 1982 half the total exports

Table 6.4: The importance of international trade (in goods only) for some selected countries

	Total exports as % of GDP 1975	*Total exports as % of GDP* 1981	*Total imports as % of GDP* 1975	*Total imports as % of GDP* 1981
Australia	14·1	13·6	11·9	14·8
Austria	20·1	23·8	25·0	31·6
*Belgium	46·3	56·1	49·3	62·5
Canada	20·2	24·8	21·3	23·4
Denmark	24·6	27·5	29·1	30·1
Finland	20·7	28·5	28·6	28·9
France	15·6	17·8	16·2	21·2
Germany	21·2	25·7	17·5	23·8
Greece	10·9	11·7	25·3	24·3
Iceland	24·6	30·7	39·0	35·1
Ireland	41·4	46·9	49·1	63·7
Italy	20·2	21·6	22·3	26·0
Japan	11·4	13·4	11·8	12·6
*Luxembourg	46·3	56·1	49·3	62·5
Netherlands	42·4	48·7	43·3	46·9
New Zealand	17·1	22·5	24·9	22·9
Norway	25·4	31·4	34·2	27·3
Portugal	13·3	17·4	26·2	40·9
Spain	7·6	11·0	16·1	17·3
Sweden	25·1	25·4	26·0	25·7
Switzerland	23·9	28·5	24·6	32·4
Turkey	4·0	8.3	13·1	15·5
UK	19·2	20·7	23·4	20·7
USA	7·1	8·0	6·4	9·0

* Belgium/Luxembourg Economic Union.
SOURCE: Derived from *OECD Observer*, March 1983.

Table 6.5: The top ten UK exporters, 1982

Rank	*Company*	*Exports* (£000s)
1	Imperial Chemical Industries	1,552,000
2	British Aerospace	1,317,000
3	General Electric	1,097,000
4	BL	915,000
5	Ford Motors	894,000
6	Rolls-Royce	691,000
7	Distillers	425,700
8	IBM United Kingdom	419,780
9	Courtaulds	373,900
10	Hawker Siddeley	348,000

SOURCE: *The Times 1000*, 1983–84.

recorded in the overseas trade statistics was accounted for by approximately 100 enterprises, total exports were accounted for by over 2,000 firms. In addition, there are those firms processing, making components and providing services for exporting firms, so that an improved export performance will affect the output of many other firms which provide employment. The top ten UK exporters in 1982 are listed in Table 6.5 and between them they had a combined work force of approximately 720,000.

The balance of payments

Before continuing with an analysis of recent trends in the UK's trading position, it is useful to outline the general make-up of the balance of payments and the terminology which is often employed when dealing with aspects of international trade.

(i) Visible balance
This refers to trade in the tangible goods bought and sold by British residents in transaction with residents in other countries, such as the export of motor vehicles, capital goods and chemicals, and the import of such items as food and raw materials. This visible balance is often referred to as the 'balance of trade'.

(ii) Invisible balance
This deals with services and other transactions that cannot themselves be seen in the same way as the tangible goods covered by the visible trade statistics (see Table 6.8 on pages 117–18).

(iii) Current balance
Together the visible and invisible balances make up the current balance which shows whether the UK is currently earning more than it is spending overseas.

(iv) Investments and other capital transactions
This refers to a wide range of activities that centre around the need to obtain foreign exchange to finance overseas investment and other capital transactions overseas and similar activities that bring foreign exchange into the UK. Therefore this heading includes flows of investment capital such as 'direct' investment; this would include, for example, the setting up of factories or other industrial or commercial ventures. If Ford of America plan to build a plant in South Wales, this parent company will require sterling to undertake the fixed capital formation involved; the UK will obtain dollars when this exchange takes place and will therefore present a credit item under this heading. Similarly if ICI expands its activities in the US it will require dollars to do so, and this will be a debit item when the financial transactions take place. During the exploration and development stages of North Sea oil, for example, there were large capital inflows from which the UK benefited.

There is also investment in stocks and shares which is usually known as 'portfolio' investment. If overseas residents purchase stocks and shares issued by UK residents, this amounts to a credit item as the country has obtained foreign currency by 'exporting' a security of some kind. Similarly, a debit item occurs if these financial transactions take place in the other direction, as a security will then be 'imported'. There are also capital flows arising from loans between governments, trade credit to finance imports and exports, and borrowing in overseas currencies by public sector bodies such as nationalised industries. UK banks also engage in transactions in foreign currencies to finance investment abroad by UK firms. Finally, there are the changes in exchange reserves held by other countries in sterling in the form of British Government stocks, deposits in banks, local authority and finance house loans, and Treasury bills. All these transactions will give rise to some form of financial asset, and if such assets are held by overseas residents, a credit item arises; whereas if financial assets issued overseas are held by UK residents, a debit item is produced.

Investment and other capital transactions will eventually give rise to flows in the opposite direction, as in a later period they will produce invisibles in the form of interest, profit and dividends which will then appear as either credit or debit items in the current account.

(v) The balancing item
This is in effect the total of errors and omissions and is the difference between the total value of recorded transactions and the actual flow of money into and out of the Bank of England. The estimates for the current account and the flows of investment and other capital never add up exactly to the amount of foreign exchange which the country has gained or lost in the year. Few of the

transactions can be recorded precisely, and there are also differences of timing between transactions and payments which are not always identified.

(vi) Balance for official financing

The current balance, plus the investment and other capital transactions, and the balancing item, eventually give the total currency flow which has come into or gone out of the country. Official financing represents the monetary movements by which the overall balance of payments eventually 'balances'. This is produced by changes in the official reserves, net borrowing from the IMF, net transactions with other overseas monetary authorities, foreign currency borrowing by the government and by the public sector via drawings on Eurodollar facilities arranged by the Bank of England with UK clearing banks.

If the total currency flow is negative, there will be equal positive amounts under 'official financing' reflecting the funds that must be borrowed or drawn from the reserves. These positive signs exist because borrowing from overseas again represents the 'export' of a financial asset for foreign currency and therefore produces a credit item, and drawings upon the official reserves held in the Exchange Equalisation Account at the Bank of England will amount to the 'sale' of assets which help to make up the official reserves.

If the total currency flow is positive, this is the total amount which is added to the official reserves or is available to repay debts to the IMF, overseas central banks or other bodies. The headings under official financing will therefore be negative as the use of currency to repay debts and acquire overseas assets to add to official reserves will amount to the 'import' of financial assets from overseas.

These, then, are the main headings employed in describing the UK's balance of payments and the situation as it existed in 1976 and 1982 is summarised in Table 6.6.

Before the development of North Sea oil it was very rare for the UK's visible trade to be in credit. It was generally hoped that the surplus achieved on invisibles would produce an eventual surplus or at least reduce the deficit on the current account to a more acceptable level.

The large deficit on the current account in 1976 was then added to by the deficit on capital account. Direct investment was virtually in balance in 1976 and the deficit on the capital account was mainly due to large amounts of trade credit extended by UK businesses to overseas businesses. Overseas governments and other bodies also reduced the level of their sterling balances. The improvement in 1982 was mainly due to the effect of North Sea oil upon the visible trade balance.

A highly volatile part of the capital account is **'hot money'**. This is a description given to short-term capital movements from one country to another seeking a higher rate of interest. It may also represent funds moved into assets that provide safe capital values, in that the currency of the country in which assets are held is not likely to depreciate. An actual or rumoured fall in the value of the pound sterling will thus see a movement of 'hot money' as speculation develops out of the UK and into a currency which is considered stronger.

Table 6.6: The UK balance of payments 1976 and 1982

(£m)

							Official financing		
	Visible trade (f.o.b.)[1]	*Invisibles*	*Current balance*	*Investment and other capital transactions*	*Balancing item*	*Balance for official financing*	*Net transactions with overseas monetary authorities*	*Foreign currency borrowing*	*Official reserves*
1976	−3,929	+3,048	−881	−3,073	+326	−3,628	+984	+1,791	+853
1982	+2,228	+3,701	+3,948	−639	−4,593	−808	−163	+26	+1,421

f.o.b.[1] valued at prices which include carriage only as far as the port from which the goods are to be despatched, the remainder of the cost of carriage having to be borne by the purchaser of the goods.

SOURCE: Central Statistical Office.

These funds may flow back into the UK when it is believed that the pound sterling has reached a more realistic level. The fall in the value of the currency will then provide those moving back into sterling assets with greater spending power, as the pound will be cheaper to buy when conducting financial transactions. If, however, the pound sterling were to appreciate in value against other major currencies, it would attract hot money because it would provide greater purchasing power over other currencies.

Hot money is invested in very liquid assets to facilitate easy movement between currencies and it can have a de-stabilising effect as occurred in 1976 when the very rapid depreciation of the pound caused a large outflow of short-term funds which contributed to the large deficit on the capital account. The depreciation of the pound was such that it fell from an average of $2·22 in 1975 to $1·80 in 1976 and in the last quarter of 1976 averaged $1·65.

The negative total currency flow in 1976, as shown by the item 'balance for official financing' in Table 6.6, was met by transactions with overseas monetary authorities and was mainly due to a drawing from the IMF which together produced net transactions of £984 million. In addition the government borrowed £1,791 million by drawing upon previously arranged Eurodollar facilities and also used £853 million from official reserves. Thus the balance of payments eventually 'balanced' in 1976 and 1982 because of negative total currency flows being dealt with under the heading 'balance for official financing'.

The terms of trade

The prices at which exports are sold and imports are bought by an economy will have an impact upon the general welfare of an economy. Again one can give the example of an individual who has his own personal 'terms of trade'. If a person's income increases at a faster rate than the prices of the products upon which the income is spent, he will have experienced an improvement in his personal terms of trade. By selling the same amount of labour he can now buy more goods and services, or he can obtain the same quantity of goods and services as he was purchasing before the income increase, but by working fewer hours (if his terms of employment allow him to do so). Whichever of these alternatives is selected he will be better off as in the latter case he can purchase the same quantity of goods and services and take more leisure time.

The same choice would face such an individual if his income increases while prices remain unchanged, if income remains unchanged while prices fall, or if income falls at a slower rate than prices. If, however, his income rises at a slower rate than the prices of the goods and services upon which he spends his income, he will experience a worsening in his personal terms of trade. This is because the same quantity of labour will now buy less and to maintain his standard of living he must work longer hours. A similar result would arise from income remaining unchanged while prices increased, or income falling more rapidly than prices. Thus an individual's terms of trade refer to changes in the rate at which labour can be traded for goods and services.

This same interpretation can be placed upon an economy in terms of export prices and import prices, as these will influence the rate at which exports can be exchanged for imports. If, for example, there was a change in export and import prices so that a given amount of exports would now purchase a larger amount of imports, there would be a **favourable movement** in the UK terms of trade. An **unfavourable movement** in the terms of trade would occur if the changes in the export and import prices meant that a given amount of exports now purchased a smaller quantity of imports. This latter movement means that the total volume of exports must be increased if the same total volume of imports are to be maintained. Thus some goods and services previously consumed at home must be redirected to exports if extra output for export cannot be achieved.

The impact of price changes upon the UK's overall terms of trade depends upon the importance of those items changing in price in relation to total exports and imports. An increase in the world price of raw materials and foodstuffs would lead to a worsening in the UK's terms of trade, as they are a small part of exports but a major part of total imports. If, however, there was a rise in the world price of chemicals, machinery and equipment, this would result in a favourable movement in the UK's terms of trade, since such items play a much larger part in total exports when compared with total imports.

The determination of the UK's terms of trade takes account of the relative importance of various items in exports and imports by using weights to establish both an export unit value index and an import unit value index. For example, the weighting given to food, beverages and tobacco in the import unit value index is much larger than that given to such items when dealing with the export unit value index. Where manufactures are concerned, their important role in exports is reflected in a large combined weighting given to such products in the export unit value index, compared with the import unit value index.

Since the UK Government wishes to discover how the UK's terms of trade are changing, a base year is used in order to make comparisons. The terms of trade are calculated as follows:

$$\frac{\text{Export unit value index}}{\text{Import unit value index}} \times 100$$

Thus if index numbers are used, and 1975 = 100, and by 1976 this has fallen to 98, the UK's export prices must have increased less rapidly than import prices and the country will have suffered a worsening in the terms of trade. Using the same base year, the terms of trade index was 107 in 1978 which indicated a useful improvement in the UK's terms of trade. The rapid deterioration in the terms of trade that occurred in the early 1970s was largely due to a very large increase in the world price of oil and the world commodity price boom in 1974–5, as shown in Table 6.7.

The effect of a change in the terms of trade upon the UK's balance of visible trade depends very heavily upon the cause of this change. If the world demand for manufactures is expanding, the world price of such products will increase and the balance of visible trade will improve as the existing exports of manufactures will earn more foreign exchange, and the position may be further improved by an increase in the volume of exports. To a certain extent some of these increased export earnings may, however, be offset by both the price and volume of imported manufactures having increased.

If, however, the export unit value index is rising rapidly because of inflationary pressures in the UK which leads to UK export prices being higher than those of overseas competitors, this 'improvement' in the terms of trade can produce an unfavourable balance of visible trade. Not only will exports fail to increase but they could possibly decline. If the price E^d for UK manufactures is greater than one

Table 6.7: Export and import unit values of selected categories of goods, 1970–82

Index numbers 1975[1] = 100

	Export unit values					Import unit values					Terms of trade
Year	*Total*	*Food, beverages and tobacco*	*Basic materials*	*Fuels*	*Total manufactures*	*Total*	*Food, beverages and tobacco*	*Basic materials*	*Fuels*	*Total manufactures*	*Export unit value/import unit value*
Weights	1000	73	29	42	818	1,000	180	95	179	523	
1970	50.7	56	50	23	52	43·7	45	47	19	53	116
1971	53·6	59	53	26	55	45·8	48	48	24	53	117
1972	56·7	63	58	26	58	47·8	51	50	24	56	118
1973	64·0	70	71	38	64	60·8	67	66	31	68	105
1974	81·6	83	92	87	81	88·0	87	97	87	87	93
1975	100·0	100	100	100	100	100·0	100	100	100	100	100
1976	119·7	115	124	126	120	122·2	113	123	131	123	98
1977	141·6	137	144	150	142	141·1	132	145	148	142	100
1978	155·2	150	140	140	157	145·0	140	132	138	151	107
1979	171·5	159	161	203	171	159·5	145	145	175	162	107
1980	192·7	173	165	255	191	182·2	151	155	248	174	106
1981	207·0	186	163	302	205	199·8	159	159	317	181	103
1982	221·2	199	173	316	220	215·8	170	162	354	194	102

[1] These indices are weighted according to the pattern of trade in 1975. As a result of developments in oil trade, the indices give a larger weight on the import side and a smaller weight on the export side than would be the case if current trade patterns were used.

SOURCE: *Monthly Digest of Statistics.*

(i.e. elastic), total export earnings will fall. At the same time, inflation in the UK will make imported manufactures more attractive and lead to an increase in the total expenditure on imports as consumers and manufacturers increasingly switch to foreign products.

The main imports and exports of the UK

Over the last ten years there has been a continuation of an earlier trend which showed a shift in the pattern of imports. We now import relatively less food than we did and more manufactures in terms of both finished goods or semi-manufactured products for further processing. Contributory factors have been the growth in the UK's own economy which required capital goods from all possible sources, the increase in home demand for consumer goods over and above the basic necessities, and the increased efficiency of UK farmers. These trends have also been associated with a switch in the pattern of trading to more dealings with our industrialised Western European neighbours. There has also been an increase in the volume and proportion of industrial goods and semi-manufactures in exports to us from the developing countries. A general lowering of tariff barriers has also been a factor contributing to this changed pattern of international trade.

The increasing importance which finished manufactures have played in UK imports is shown in Table 6.8 (pp. 117–18). The total volume of these products imported into the UK between 1967 and 1980 has grown at an average annual rate of 13 per cent compared with an average growth of all imports of 5 per cent. As far as imports of capital goods are concerned, the figures for value can vary quite widely depending upon the movement in imports of ships, aircraft, aero engines and—more recently—North Sea production installations. When these items are excluded, the volume of other capital goods has grown at an average rate of 12 per cent between 1967–80.

Since the UK is one of many manufacturing economies, the main indicator of export performance is the trend of exports in volume terms. An increase in the prices of UK manufactures, not brought about by a general increase in the world prices of such items, will make exports less competitive. In this case the long-term increased improvement in export earnings must essentially come from an increased volume of exports. The large increase in the volume of imported manufactures, the increased price of many raw materials that occurred in the 1970s, and the need to repay international loans, required a vast improvement in the UK's export performance. This was necessary to avoid any further reductions in living standards that would result from government policies that sought to restrict consumer demand at home in order to slow down the demand for imports. Table 6.9 (p. 119) shows the export performance of the UK between 1970 and 1982. The table demonstrates the increasing significance of oil exports which have helped to sustain the growing volume of imported manufactures.

The UK's invisible trade
For the last 200 years there has nearly always been a deficit on the UK's visible trade and only in 1956, 1958 and 1971 in the post-war period was a surplus achieved on visibles before the development of North Sea oil. A current account surplus, however, was often achieved because of the regular surplus produced by the trade in invisibles. Figure 6.1 shows that invisible earnings were larger than those derived from finished manufactures and were equal to over half of the total earnings from visible exports.

The surplus on invisibles reached a record level of over £4 billion in 1981. Had it not been for this

Fig. 6.1: Current account receipts 1982

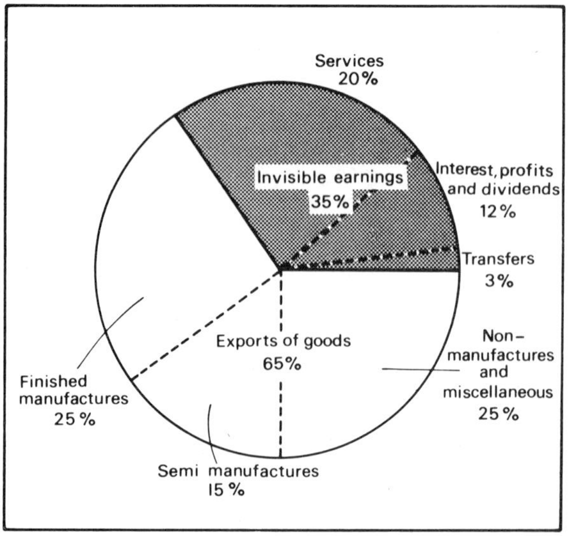

Table 6.8: Value of selected categories of UK imports and exports, 1979 and 1982 £m

Value of UK imports £m (c.i.f)[1]	*1979*	*1982*	*Jan–Feb 1983 compared with Jan–Feb 1982*
0. Food and live animals chiefly for food	5,688·5	2,496·6	+33
00. Live animals chiefly for food	88·3	179·1	−18
01. Meat and meat preparations	1,258·0	346·0	+39
02. Dairy products and birds' eggs	534·4	318·6	+216
03. Fish, crustaceans and molluscs, and preparations thereof	323·7	162·3	+50
04. Cereals and cereal preparations	668·4	773·9	+13
05. Vegetables and fruit	1,174·6	153·8	+9
06. Sugar, sugar preparations and honey	402·4	121·1	+2
07. Coffee, tea, cocoa, spices and manufactures thereof	790·8	249·9	+26
08. Feeding stuff for animals (not including unmilled cereals)	276·8	68·2	+12
09. Miscellaneous edible products and preparations	171·3	123·8	+40
1. Beverages and tobacco	828·4	1,450·7	+2
11. Beverages	477·5	1,059·3	−3
12. Tobacco and tobacco manufactures	350·9	391·4	+16
2. Crude materials, inedible, except fuels	3,865·3	1,295·0	+5
21. Hides, skins and fur skins, raw	224·6	180·5	+14
22. Oil seeds and oleaginous fruit	260·4	7·9	+1,169
23. Crude rubber (including synthetic and reclaimed)	185·2	122·8	+16
24. Cork and wood	743·0	28·6	+2
25. Pulp and waste paper	388·8	11·6	−25
26. Textile fibres (other than wool tops) and their wastes (not manufactured into yarn or fabric)	475·5	315·0	−8
27. Crude fertilisers and crude minerals (excluding coal, petroleum and precious stones)	312·3	224·6	−16
28. Metalliferous ores and metal scrap	1,077·5	346·6	+18
29. Crude animal and vegetable materials	198·0	57·3	−4
3. Mineral fuels, lubricants and related materials	5,782·2	11,193·2	+38
33. Petroleum, petroleum products and related materials	5,228·2	10,641·6	+37
32, 34 and 35. Coal, coke, gas and electric current	554·0	551·6	+63
4. Animal and vegetable oils, fats and waxes	314·6	46·5	+29
5. Chemicals and related products	3,402·2	6,119·4	+6
51. Organic chemicals	1 020·1	1,592·3	+14
52. Inorganic chemicals	452·7	694·9	+1
53. Dyeing, tanning and colouring materials	167·9	464·1	+6
54. Medicinal and pharmaceutical products	229·3	978·0	+5
55. Essential oils and perfume materials; toilet, polishing and cleansing materials	177·1	524·0	+9
56. Fertilisers manufactured	96·6	48·8	+38
57. Explosives and pyrotechnic products	6·9	36·8	+41
58. Artificial resins and plastic materials, and cellulose esters and ethers	828·1	875·3	−12
59. Chemical materials and products, not elsewhere specified	423·5	905·3	+6

Value of UK exports £m (f.o.b.)[2]	*1979*	*1982*	*Jan–Feb 1983 compared with Jan–Feb 1982*
0. Food and live animals chiefly for food	1,745·2	6,413·9	+12
00. Live animals chiefly for food	170·9	133·1	+40
01. Meat and meat preparations	275·4	1,370·9	−6
02. Dairy products and birds' eggs	226·2	567·9	+101
03. Fish, crustaceans and molluscs, and preparations thereof	146·3	404·2	−15
04. Cereals and cereal preparations	264·4	549·9	+7
05. Vegetables and fruit	148·5	1,608·3	−4
06. Sugar, sugar preparations and honey	103·6	429·5	+201
07. Coffee, tea, cocoa, spices and manufactures thereof	268·2	722·4	+3
08. Feeding stuff for animals (not including unmilled cereals)	56·9	446·5	+13
09. Miscellaneous edible products and preparations	85·0	181·1	+13
1. Beverages and tobacco	1,195·3	836·8	+32
11. Beverages	854·3	517·5	+36
12. Tobacco and tobacco manufactures	341·0	319·2	+28
2. Crude materials, inedible, except fuels	1,215·3	3,612·9	–
21. Hides, skins and fur skins, raw	221·5	189·5	−2
22. Oil seeds and oleaginous fruit	3·1	259·6	−34
23. Crude rubber (including synthetic and reclaimed)	79·2	182·9	−18
24. Cork and wood	13·5	673·5	+27
25. Pulp and waste paper	13·8	412·5	−12
26. Textile fibres (other than wool tops) and their wastes (not manufactured into yarn or fabric)	315·7	410·7	−2
27. Crude fertilisers and crude minerals (excluding coal, petroleum and precious stones)	217·7	263·5	+9
28. Metalliferous ores and metal scrap	307·0	977·5	+2
29. Crude animal and vegetable materials	43·8	243·3	+18
3. Mineral fuels, lubricants and related materials	4,323·6	7,401·2	−7
33. Petroleum, petroleum products and related materials	4,157·5	6,274·1	−8
32, 34 and 35. Coal, coke, gas and electric current	166·0	1,127·1	−1
4. Animal and vegetable oils, fats and waxes	65·7	317·0	−11
5. Chemicals and related products	4,910·9	4,181·2	+17
51. Organic chemicals	1,237·3	1,172·2	+23
52. Inorganic chemicals	681·8	539·4	−7
53. Dyeing, tanning and colouring materials	392·0	198·0	+7
54. Medicinal and pharmaceutical products	638·8	374·6	+39
55. Essential oils and perfume materials; toilet, polishing and cleansing materials	408·2	242·2	+31
56. Fertilisers manufactured	58·2	127·0	+73
57. Explosives and pyrotechnic products	31·1	10·9	+22
58. Artificial resins and plastic materials, and cellulose esters and ethers	777·0	1,017·7	−22
59. Chemical materials and products, not elsewhere specified	686·4	499·1	−1

Value of UK imports £m (c.i.f)[1]	*1979*	*1982*	*Jan–Feb 1983 compared with Jan–Feb 1982*
6. Manufactured goods classified chiefly by material	9,291.9	7,941·1	−4
61. Leather, leather manufactures n.e.s., and dressed fur skins	196·8	202·1	+11
62. Rubber manufactures n.e.s.	259·2	417·9	+2
63. Cork and wood manufactures (excluding furniture)	464·9	83·2	−23
64. Paper, paperboard and articles of paper pulp, of paper or of paperboard	1,240·3	502·9	+3
65. Textile yarn, fabrics, made-up articles n.e.s., and related products	1,691·1	1,190·8	−1
66. Non-metallic mineral manufactures n.e.s.	1,889·4	1,611·1	+16
67. Iron and steel	1,215·2	1,293·5	+12
68. Non-ferrous metals	1,564·4	1,244·7	−43
69. Manufactures of metal n.e.s.	770·7	1,394·9	−3
7. Machinery and transport equipment	12,226·4	18,097·8	−5
71. Power generating machinery and equipment	853·6	2,809·2	−13
72. Machinery specialised for particular industries	1,271·1	2,603·6	−16
73. Metalworking machinery	412·8	522·0	−20
74. General industrial machinery and equipment n.e.s., and machine parts n.e.s.	1,351·6	2,411·8	+10
75. Office machines and automatic data processing equipment	1,330·4	1,599·5	+12
76. Telecommunications and sound recording and reproducing apparatus and equipment	796·5	896·9	−10
77. Electrical machinery, apparatus and appliances n.e.s., and electrical parts thereof (including non-electrical counterparts n.e.s., of electrical household type equipment)	1,410·5	2,113·7	+5
78. Road vehicles (including air cushion vehicles)	3,943·2	3,108·4	−14
79. Other transport equipment	856·6	2,032·6	+2
8. Miscellaneous manufactured articles	4,768·1	5,157·8	+4
81. Sanitary, plumbing, heating and lighting fixtures and fittings n.e.s.	81·1	106·9	−22
82. Furniture and parts thereof	253·8	240·9	+19
83. Travel goods, handbags and similar containers	92·3	19·1	−26
84. Articles of apparel and clothing accessories	1,194·1	840·4	−2
85. Footwear	352·5	115·3	−10
87. Professional, scientific and controlling instruments and apparatus n.e.s.	634·4	1,255·2	+2
88. Photographic apparatus, equipment and supplies and optical goods n.e.s., watches and clocks	608·9	557·1	−23
89. Miscellaneous manufactured articles n.e.s.	1,55·10	2,022·9	+17
5–8. Manufactured goods	29,688·7	37,316·2	−2
9. Commodities and transactions not classified elsewhere	761·7	1,740·4	−19
Total United Kingdom imports	46,924·9	55,538·4	+7

Value of UK exports £m (f.o.b.)[2]	*1979*	*1982*	*Jan–Feb 1983 compared with Jan–Feb 1982*
6. Manufactured goods classified chiefly by material	7,761·7	9,861·2	+20
61. Leather, leather manufactures n.e.s., and dressed fur skins	223·6	154·6	+8
62. Rubber manufactures n.e.s.	363·4	326·2	+31
63. Cork and wood manufactures (excluding furniture)	76·0	436·6	−2
64. Paper, paperboard and articles of paper pulp, of paper or of paperboard	435·6	1,678·5	+4
65. Textile yarn, fabrics, made-up articles n.e.s., and related products	1,339·4	1,929·7	+15
66. Non-metallic mineral manufactures n.e.s.	1,713·7	1,520·4	+117
67. Iron and steel	1,277·6	1,369·2	−24
68. Non-ferrous metals	1,140·4	1,495·7	+22
69. Manufactures of metal n.e.s.	1,192·1	950·4	+19
7. Machinery and transport equipment	14,235·5	16,357·5	+27
71. Power generating machinery and equipment	1,789·2	1,482·7	+31
72. Machinery specialised for particular industries	2,312·7	1,485·1	+24
73. Metalworking machinery	383·9	380·5	+4
74. General industrial machinery and equipment n.e.s., and machine parts n.e.s.	1,960·3	1,633·8	+17
75. Office machines and automatic data processing equipment	1,163·7	2·122·8	+41
76. Telecommunications and sound recording and reproducing apparatus and equipment	734·4	1,586·2	+10
77. Electrical machinery, apparatus and appliances n.e.s., and electrical parts thereof (including non-electrical counterparts n.e.s., of electrical household type equipment)	1,457·4	2,180·4	+37
78. Road vehicles (including air cushion vehicles)	3,148·1	4,496·9	+35
79. Other transport equipment	1,285·8	989·2	−3
8. Miscellaneous manufactured articles	3,961·4	6,683·3	+14
81. Sanitary, plumbing, heating and lighting fixtures and fittings n.e.s.	89·9	103·6	+37
82. Furniture and parts thereof	231·2	400·1	+30
83. Travel goods, handbags and similar containers	16·7	108·6	+4
84. Articles of apparel and clothing accessories	751·2	1,500·8	+12
85. Footwear	113·3	468·5	+19
87. Professional, scientific and controlling instruments and apparatus n.e.s.	785·3	1,053·5	+26
88. Photographic apparatus, equipment and supplies and optical goods n.e.s., watches and clocks	437·0	761·8	+2
89. Miscellaneous manufactured articles n.e.s.	1,536·9	2,286·6	+10
5–8. Manufactured goods	30,869·5	37,083·2	+21
9. Commodities and transactions not classified elsewhere	1,222·4	1,275·4	+39
Total United Kingdom exports	40,637·0	56,940·3	+4

[1] c.i.f. Valued at prices covering the price ex-warehouse, and including delivery to the docks, dock dues, carriage, and insurance as far as the port to which the goods are to be consigned, but excluding delivery from the docks to the purchaser's premises.

[2] f.o.b. See note in Table 6.6.

[3] The numbers on the left-hand side of the tables refer to the Section and Division code numbers of the Standard International Trade Classification.

SOURCE: *Monthly Digest of Statistics.*

Table 6.9: Export volume index numbers (1975=100)

						Manufactures excluding erratics								
							Semi-manufactures excluding precious stones (P)			Finished manufactures excluding ships, North Sea installations and aircraft (SNA)				
	Total	Food, beverages and tobacco	Basic materials	Fuels	Total manu-factures	Total	Total	Chemi-cals	Other	Total	Passen-ger motor cars	Other con-sumer	Inter-mediate	Capital
Weights	*1,000*	*73*	*29*	*42*	*818*	*766*	*284*	*109*	*176*	*482*	*25*	*74*	*192*	*191*
1970	79·5	65	92	110	79	79	86	73	94	75	125	74	69	75
1971	85·0	71	92	110	86	86	91	80	99	82	127	79	78	83
1972	86·0	74	100	112	86	86	95	85	101	80	110	83	80	75
1973	97·2	88	106	117	98	97	111	103	116	89	107	93	94	80
1974	102·3	91	111	109	103	104	117	122	114	95	107	99	98	90
1975	100·0	100	100	100	100	100	100	100	100	100	100	100	100	100
1976	108·6	103	121	120	109	109	116	124	112	104	109	121	100	100
1977	117·7	111	127	165	117	115	127	141	119	108	104	134	103	103
1978	121·0	132	139	200	116	117	132	154	118	108	111	138	107	97
1979	123·8	124	147	277	116	116	134	157	120	106	88	133	108	96
1980	125·9	131	165	290	117	116	127	149	113	110	81	130	116	99
1981	124·3	137	155	353	112	112	123	150	107	106	78	127	111	96
1982	127·1	140	150	391	113	113	125	157	106	105	73	122	113	96

SOURCE: *Monthly Digest of Statistics.*

substantial increase in invisible earnings in recent years, the large current account deficits brought about by the huge deficit on visible trade would have been decidedly worse. Fig. 6.2 shows that the UK has the second largest share of the world trade in invisibles.

Fig. 6.2: How Britain compares: invisible accounts (SDR billion) 1980

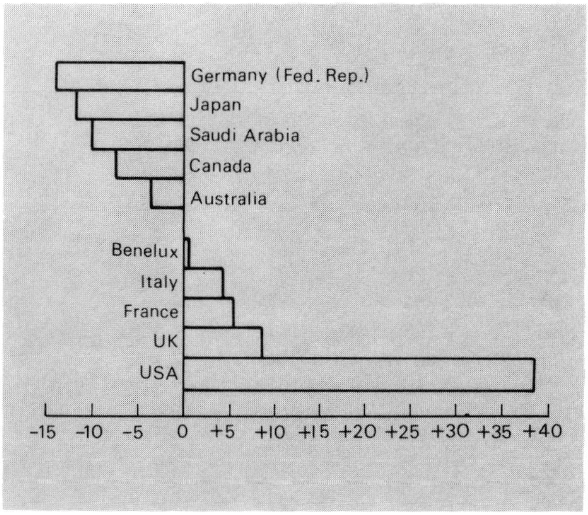

SOURCE: *Economic Progress Report*, May 1983.

Table 6.10 provides details of the UK's invisible earnings and payments over the last few years and the following sections will describe those factors which would have influenced the various categories of invisible trade.

Sea transport

The demand for UK shipping services will be very much influenced by the level of world trade and the extent to which UK operators can offer competitive freight rates. The recent world recession in world trade left many countries with excess shipping capacity and there has been fierce competition between shipping companies. This has provided an advantage to those overseas shipping lines which are able to make full use of an abundant supply of relatively cheap labour to crew their vessels. Thus both UK importers and exporters have increasingly opted for overseas shipping operators. The data under this heading also involves the payments made by UK operators to various overseas authorities in connection with port, handling and repair charges, for example. Their vessels will also need to purchase fuel and other supplies while they are in foreign ports. A rise in the price of fuel obviously has a significant impact upon such debit items. Similar payments by overseas shipping companies while their ships are visiting the UK will represent credit items as far as invisible trade is concerned.

Table 6.10: UK invisible transactions overseas

£m

	1979	*1980*	*1981*	*1982*
Credits (amounts received from overseas)				
Private services:				
Sea transport				
Dry cargo	2,038	2,200	2,155	2,163
Tankers	1,766	1,616	1,629	1,414
Total	3,804	3,816	3,784	3,577
Civil aviation				
Fares, freight, etc.	1,114	1,255	1,258	1,361
Disbursement of o/seas airlines	641	955	1,101	1,110
Total	1,755	2,210	2,359	2,471
Travel	2,797	2,961	2,970	3,229
Financial services	1,588	1,601	1,954	2,132
Other services	4,150	4,758	5,170	5,657
Total private services[1]	14,094	15,346	16,237	17,066
General govt. services	344	381	439	410
Interest, profits + dividends	7,879	8,289	10,089	10,027
Transfers				
Private	796	808	844	967
General govt.	550	958	1,658	2,157
Total	1,346	1,766	2,502	3,124
Total credits	23,663	25,782	29,267	30,627
Debits (amounts paid overseas)				
Private services:				
Sea transport				
Dry cargo	2,201	2,434	2,536	2,831
Tankers	1,482	1,247	1,351	1,130
Total	3,683	3,681	3,887	3,961
Civil aviation				
Fares, freights etc.	694	910	987	1,077
Disbursements abroad	773	905	935	1,003
Total	1,467	1,815	1,922	2,080
Travel	2,109	2,738	3,271	3,637
Other services	2,080	2,278	2,470	2,785
Total private services[1]	9,339	10,512	11,550	12,463
General govt. services	1,141	1,139	1,065	1,312
Interest, profits + dividends	6,987	8,562	9,078	9,790
Transfers:				
Private	982	1,083	1,119	1,207
General govt.	2,608	2,790	3,364	4,135
Total	3,600	3,873	4,483	5,342
Total debits	21,067	24,086	26,176	28,907
Net balances				
Sea transport	+121	+135	−103	−384
Civil aviation	+288	+395	+437	+391
Travel	+688	+223	−301	−408
Financial services	+1,588	+1,601	+1,954	+2,132
Other services	+2,070	+2,480	+2,700	+2,872
General gov't. services	−797	−758	−626	−902
Total services	+3,958	+4,076	+4,061	+3,701
Interest, profits + dividends	+892	−273	+1,011	+237
Transfers	−2,254	−2,107	−1,981	−2,218
Net invisible balance	+2,596	+1,696	+3,091	+1,720

[1] Includes public corporations

Interest, profits and dividends from and to overseas

£m

	1979	*1980*	*1981*	*1982*
Credits: overseas earnings on:				
Direct investment exc. oil	2,815	2,914	3,597	3,147
Portfolio investment	450	679	796	936
Export credit + sterling lending by UK banks	741	970	1,343	1,648
Interest on UK borrowing + lending in foreign currencies (net)	−44	352	1,010	1,454
Interest on bank deposits and lending overseas	283	432	584	539
Other (including oil companies)	3,634	2,942	2,759	2,303
Total credits	7,879	8,289	10,089	10,027
Of which:				
Private sector + public corporations	7,063	7,346	9,141	9,212
General govt.	816	943	948	815
Debits: earnings due to overseas residents on:				
Direct investment exc. oil	2,149	1,982	2,106	2,245
Portfolio investment	747	899	971	1,066
Sterling liabilities	911	1,529	1,902	2,282
Foreign currency borrowing by general govt.	576	518	489	402
Foreign oil companies investment in UK	1,940	2,965	2,774	2,850
Other	664	669	836	945
Total debits	6,987	8,562	9,078	9,790
Of which:				
Private sector + public corporations	5,631	7,005	7,458	8,109
General govt.	1,356	1,557	1,620	1,681
Net balance				
Private sector + public corporations	+1,432	+341	+1,683	+1,103
General govt.	−540	−614	−672	−866
Total	+892	−273	+1,011	+237

SOURCE: *British Business*, 15 April 1983, p. 91.

Civil aviation

Credit items include receipts by the British airlines from overseas residents for passenger fares and for the movement of freight. Approximately 17 per cent of the value of the UK's import and export trade is conducted using air transport, and UK airlines have a large share of such trade. Air freight, however, only accounts for about 3 per cent of imports and exports when measured in terms of volume.

The competitive position of UK airlines is obviously important in determining its share of such trade but international agreements do influence the fares charged on a large number of routes. An upturn in the level of economic activity in major manufacturing economies will increase the demand for business travel while higher real incomes will increase the demand for overseas holidays. A very large number of UK residents go abroad for their holidays but a very large proportion of the flights involved in package tours are operated by the well-established charter airlines in the UK and this helps to keep down the total of civil aviation debits. Other payments and receipts under this heading involve landing charges, servicing and fuel, for example, and Heathrow Airport therefore earns large quantities of foreign exchange from overseas airlines that helps to offset similar costs incurred by UK airlines using foreign airports.

Travel

This covers personal expenditure by UK residents in overseas countries and by overseas residents in the UK. In 1977 this particular account recorded a surplus of over £1 billion but since then it has moved into a deficit. The rate of inflation in the UK and the exchange rate are important factors in making the UK an attractive tourist and conference destination and these operated in favour of the UK until 1977. The rapid deterioration on the travel account was produced by increasing inflation and the rise in the value of currency which not only affected earnings from overseas visitors but also encouraged more UK residents to holiday abroad. The more recent fall in inflation and the lower exchange rate has arrested the decline to some extent and the future demand by UK residents for foreign holidays may also be reduced by the high level of unemployment. The effect of the recession upon real incomes will also influence the amount of money spent on holiday abroad.

Financial services

The earnings under this heading stem from the highly developed services provided mainly by the City of London, where the financial and allied institutions display an expertise which is recognised throughout the world. These services include banking, brokerage, commodity trading, merchanting, underwriting of capital issues, risk underwriting and other insurance. Many of these services are linked to the level of world trade while such earnings are also largely insulated against inflation because many charges are based upon the actual value of the financial transactions being handled.

Other services

Other services provided to overseas residents include telecommunications and postal services, royalties, films and television, advertising, consultancies associated with construction work, other consultancy work of a non-financial nature, importing and exporting agencies and other services which give rise to credits such as the earnings of UK entertainers working abroad, UK road hauliers, UK computer services and the services associated with the exploration and production of oil and natural gas. This heading also includes the expenditure of overseas students in the UK and the personal expenditure of overseas military personnel stationed in the UK and also the money spent by their establishments on goods and services from the private sector.

General government services

This covers the amount spent abroad in maintaining and staffing UK embassies, consulates and diplomatic missions. The largest debit item however is the cost of maintaining UK military forces overseas and in 1981 the foreign exchange cost of these forces was over £1 billion. Credit items arise mainly from services which the UK government provides on behalf of the EEC and payments by the US government to the UK government in connection with the USAF bases.

Interest, profits and dividends (IPD)

IPD credits and debits are defined to include all interest, profits and dividends received by UK residents from abroad or payable by UK residents to overseas residents. Profits and dividends flow into the UK as a result of overseas investment by UK companies. Such investment may for example have taken the form of setting up a productive unit abroad in order to manufacture a particular product or to supply a service. Alternatively the expansion overseas may have involved a merger or takeover with a foreign enterprise. Financial institutions in the UK are also free to invest their funds in the shares of foreign companies and this will also give rise to dividend payments from abroad. This heading also includes all interest flows between UK residents and non-residents and therefore covers for example payments and receipts of interest by UK banks, interest payments by the public sector on securities held by overseas residents, interest receipts by the public sector on any loans which it makes abroad and on its holdings of foreign currency assets which make up the UK's foreign currency reserves, interest payments on their overseas borrowing and interest receipts by private UK residents on bank deposits abroad.

Many UK companies have built up large overseas investments and the return on such assets will be influenced by the profitability of the enterprises involved. Until 1979 this type of investment regularly gave rise to a large surplus but the position has now been reversed, mainly due to the return which is now accruing to overseas companies involved in North Sea oil.

When interest rates in the UK are higher than those in other countries this tends to attract large inflows of funds which are then deposited within the banking system or in other types of financial assets which are of a relatively liquid nature. Such flows will also be encouraged by speculation concerning a possible appreciation in the exchange rate. Assume for example that the exchange rate is £1=$1·60 and the interest on a certain type of financial asset in the UK is 10 per cent. In this case a US investor with $160,000 will be able to obtain a sterling asset of £100,000. If these assets are then converted back into dollars at the end of one year and the exchange rate has risen to £1=$1·80, the US investor will receive £110,000 which will then allow him to purchase $198,000. Thus the total return on the investment is 23·75 per cent.

When the government is obliged to offer attractive rates of interest in order to finance the PSBR this may attract foreign investors and the subsequent interest payments will represent debit items on this account. Overseas governments also hold part of their foreign currency reserves in sterling assets such as UK government stock while also maintaining some reserves in more liquid sterling assets. Similarly the UK government holds its foreign currency reserves in assets which earn interest in other parts of the world and the total level of such foreign currency reserves depends largely upon the trading position as they can be built up during times of a surplus.

Transfers

These refer to transactions in which one of the parties does not receive anything in return. Government transfers include grants to overseas countries as part of the government's international aid programmes and contributions to the European Community; in 1982 the latter amounted to £2·9 billion. These debits, however, were offset to some extent by receipts from the EEC for various agricultural and regional schemes worth £1·1 billion, and during that same year the UK negotiated a refund of £1·0 billion, having successfully argued that its total contribution to the EEC was too large. Private transfers deal with gifts of goods sent by parcel post, payments by UK residents to their dependants overseas and transfers by missionary societies, relief organisations and other charities. Private transfers usually produce an over-all deficit which reflects the number of overseas workers in the UK and the activities of organisations such as Oxfam.

The surplus on invisibles, and that by private services in particular, demonstrates the skills of 'invisible exporters' in adapting to the changing pattern of world trade that emerged after the massive transfer of wealth to oil-producing countries. These exporters are assisted by various bodies such as the **British Overseas Trade Board** which, through the Department of Trade, provides an Export Intelligence Service to 'invisible exporters'. At the same time the **Committee on Invisible Exports** brings together representatives of the main contributors to the UK's earnings from invisibles with representatives from government departments and the Bank of England to suggest and implement measures for the encouragement of invisible earnings.

Direct investment and the UK balance of payments

In 1976 the heading 'Investment and other capital transactions' in the summary of the UK balance of payments showed a deficit of £3,073 million. This negative sum, however, should not be taken as indicating a massive outflow of capital from the UK for investment overseas at the expense of GDFCF at home. It is often assumed that these 'investments' can be compared with machinery, plant and buildings in the UK and therefore that the size of this outflow means fewer jobs in the UK and a large drain upon the UK's reserves.

This item in the balance of payments, however, includes not only direct investment in productive capacity but also stockbuilding, stock appreciation and other transactions of a financial nature, such as additions to or repayment of working capital, other loans, trade credit and transactions in securities. For example, 'banking and money market liabilities' are included under this general heading and in 1976 amounted to a credit balance of £1,421 million. This essentially means that there was a net outflow from the UK of short-term capital funds, which had previously been held in liquid financial assets such as deposits and short-term securities, to obtain what may have been a favourable rate of interest by international standards. The fall in the exchange rate in 1976, however, created a large switch out of sterling assets. Another large amount was represented by export credits which amounted to £1,178 million and meant a debit item as UK banks and businesses were in effect providing loans to overseas buyers. Export credits are provided to assist exports but do amount to a capital outflow on the balance of payment accounts. But not only will these credits promote exports but they will eventually be paid for and in the meantime may earn some form of interest.

Direct investment by UK companies in their overseas branches, subsidiaries and associates includes fixed capital formation but also includes the re-investment of retained profits which arise out of overseas operations. In 1976 UK private investment overseas amounted to £2,154 million, compared with £2,062 million in the form of overseas investment in the UK private sector. Is it the build-up of UK investments overseas that has given rise to substantial foreign exchange earnings in the form of interest, profits and dividends.

By 1977 however investment and other capital transactions produced a positive currency flow of £4,169 million. This was partly accounted for by a fall in UK private investment overseas while the prospects for North Sea oil encouraged investment by overseas oil companies while also stimulating purchases of British government securities. The UK would be better placed to withstand a possible oil shortage and speculation concerning a strengthening of sterling also encouraged inflows of 'hot money'.

If companies are prevented from expanding their activities abroad there is no guarantee that controls on the export of capital will force these companies to increase their fixed capital formation in the UK.[1] The removal of foreign exchange controls, combined with reduced investment in the North Sea now that the industry was well established, led to a deficit on overseas investment of £6,359 million in 1982. Such outflows, however, will produce foreign earnings in the future in the form of interest, profits and dividends on the invisible account. As far as the destination of UK overseas direct investment is concerned North America is the largest recipient and in 1980 £1,896 million was invested in that area of the world compared with £483 million in the EEC, £117 million in other countries of Western Europe, £97 million in oil-exporting countries, £424 million in other developed countries and £474 million in the rest of the world. Direct investment in the UK again showed the dominance of North America with a total of £1,760 million compared with £157 million from the EEC, £228 million from other countries of Western Europe, £23 million from oil-exporting countries and £204 million from the rest of the world.

[1]At one time there were certain restrictions on the export of capital but on 24 October 1979 the Chancellor of the Exchequer removed all foreign exchange restrictions. Thus outward portfolio investment and direct investment can be financed quite freely in terms of foreign exchange.

Export markets and sources of imports

After the US, the largest customers and suppliers are our nearest neighbours in Europe. Table 6.10 (p. 120) gives a detailed breakdown of UK exports, while Table 6.11 (p. 121) shows that the EEC is the most rapidly-growing market for UK exports. This highlights the fact that world trade is expanding most rapidly between manufacturing economies, as the general increase in real incomes in these economies produces a demand for a wide range of consumer goods. This in turn requires fixed capital formation and provides markets for plant, machinery and equipment. This creates fundamental problems for those countries relying upon food exports, for which the income elasticity of demand is relatively low, and for those producing raw materials being replaced by synthetics. It was because of the more slow-growing markets in the old Commonwealth that the UK has had to concentrate more heavily upon the rapidly-growing markets of Western Europe, and the EEC in particular.

Even before Britain joined on 1 January 1973, trade with the original six members of the EEC was becoming of increasing importance to the UK and continued to grow during the transitional period for the removal of the trade barriers, although this was a relatively slow process. The UK was becoming a growing market for manufactures and as a result a small visible surplus which existed with the EEC in 1970 was turned into large deficits in the late 1970s, but oil exports to the EEC have recently helped to improve our trading position with other members.

Table 6.11 shows that among the developed countries of the world the UK's exports are making little impression upon South Africa, Australia and New Zealand. Japan also seems to be a developed economy where exports do not appear to be making much progress and this largely accounted for the visible deficits with 'other developed economies'.

The oil-producing countries have become a

rapidly growing market, and it was the recycling of oil revenues to manufacturing economies via imports that allowed the oil-consuming countries gradually to recover from the initial impact of higher-priced oil imports in the late 1970s. Table 6.12 shows that prior to 1975 these oil-producing countries were relatively small export markets, but since then they have been using their foreign exchange earnings to finance the imports of capital goods to develop and diversify their economies.

Since the conception of the **United Nations Conference on Trade and Development** in the early 1960s, the underdeveloped countries of the world have been seeking more favourable terms for their exports of manufactures and primary

Table 6.11: UK exports and imports by area.

£m

	1979	*1982*	*1979*	*1982*
	Exports	*(f.o.b.)*	*Imports*	*(c.i.f.)*
Total trade	40,637·0	55,538·4	46,924·9	56,940·3
European Community:				
total	17,479·4	23,117·9	20,887·6	25,252·1
France	3,026·6	4,486·5	4,015·8	4,269·1
Belgium and Luxembourg	1,890·6	2,298·1	2,272·9	2,861·8
Netherlands	3,061·3	4,653·4	3,442·8	4,474·7
Germany, Federal Republic	4,217·6	5,414·7	5,778·1	7,414·1
Italy	1,463·1	2,022·7	2,478·8	2,745·1
Irish Republic	2,544·9	2,890·5	1,681·4	2,000·0
Denmark	1,015·3	1,096·6	1,079·6	1,335·6
Greece	260·1	255·3	138·0	151·7
Rest of Western Europe:				
total	2,559·1	6,713·9	7,192·0	8,346·6
Norway	773·2	924·7	1,316·9	2,023·4
Sweden	1,536·9	1,935·3	1,600·2	1,673·2
Finland	410·6	513·6	792·2	849·9
Switzerland	1,249·2	1,196·2	1,835·1	1,669·9
Austria	257·3	251·0	345·2	404·3
Portugal	305·4	430·7	338·1	379·9
Spain	567·3	870·4	706·4	956·9
Yugoslavia	173·8	158·9	51·3	52·1
Turkey	135·6	218·1	65·8	207·8
Other countries	149·8	215·1	140·8	129·1
North America: total	4,791·4	8,335·2	6,197·2	8,112·7
Canada	767·2	851·7	1,272·2	1,439·6
United States	4,003·1	7,457·1	4,883·6	6,638·3
Other countries	21·1	26·4	41·4	34·8
Other developed countries: total	2,474·8	3,241·2	3,042·7	4,436·1
South Africa	715·7	1,192·9	648·9	745·8
Japan	606·2	681·5	1,488·2	2,658·0
Australia	840·8	1,043·6	489·7	493·2
New Zealand	312·1	323·2	415·9	539·1
Oil exporting countries:				
total	3,648·1	6,447·0	3,212·7	3,454·8
Algeria	108·9	199·2	83·4	176·3
Libya	248·7	260·9	58·4	342·5
Nigeria	627·2	1,225·2	176·3	356·8
Gabon	6·5	14·2	10·9	27·6
Saudi Arabia	808·3	1,361·7	1,000·6	1,447·8
Kuwait	224·8	333·2	736·9	104·8
Bahrain	110·8	152·3	9·3	35·5
Qatar	101·7	245·4	40·5	34·0
Abu Dhabi	154·9	272·9	90·3	184·3
Dubai	303·2	254·0	141·7	57·5
Sharjah, etc	23·5	32·1	1·1	25·2
Oman	122·3	265·3	26·0	46·4
Iraq	201·2	875·2	393·5	79·8
Iran	231·8	333·7	242·7	226·0
Brunei	22·8	41·8	0·4	2·4
Indonesia	75·8	212·1	56·1	91·7
Trinidad and Tobago	104·6	158·4	41·2	65·2
Venezuela	137·7	148·7	97·3	141·9
Ecuador	33·5	60·8	6·2	9·3
Other developing countries: total	5,353·8	6,571·9	5,104·4	5,899·8
Egypt	253·1	338·6	237·7	412·8
Ghana	87·8	66·7	89·9	78·4
Kenya	170·3	153·9	115·4	104·3
Tanzania	121·4	72·0	40·4	19·5
Zambia	85·5	61·2	101·4	40·0
Cyprus	97·6	111·9	87·3	89·9
Lebanon	65·7	67·6	9·4	24·2
Israel	270·8	224·4	219·3	275·1
Pakistan	139·9	199·2	68·0	81·5
India	455·8	805·3	365·5	379·2
Thailand	94·4	104·8	49·9	76·5
Malaysia	187.5	210·8	221·7	185·2
Singapore	270·9	406·2	185·3	245·5
Taiwan	103·1	125·2	213·5	335·5
Hong Kong	439·5	732·5	689·3	872·5
South Korea	145·2	167·8	263·6	321·7
Phillipines	104·3	97·9	81·3	127·1
Jamaica	44·7	56·0	82·1	92·8
Mexico	134·8	162·9	35·5	106·1
Chile	43·1	56·9	131·2	111·2
Brazil	285·8	158·8	399·3	444·0
Argentina	128·4	37·3	144·2	58·7
Other countries	1,624·2	2,153·9	1,273·2	1,418·0
Centrally planned economies: total	1,185·6	973·9	1,196·0	1,326·9
Soviet Union	416·2	355·7	491·6	645·1
German Democratic Republic	57·0	63·7	109·7	133·9
Poland	260·1	133·3	227·4	151·7
Czechoslovakia	73·8	70·1	96·8	82·0
Romania	70·3	115·2	65·9	51·5
Other countries	308·2	235·9	204·6	262·6
Low value trade	144.9	137·5	92·3	111·3

SOURCE: *Monthly Digest of Statistics.*

Table 6.12: UK trade by area—percentage of total value of exports and imports[1], 1970–82

Year	*EEC*		*North America*		*Rest of Western Europe*		*Other developed countries*		*Oil-exporting countries*		*Rest of world*	
	Exports	*Imports*	*Exports*	*Imports*	*Exports*	*Imports*	*Exports*	*Imports*	*Exports*	*Imports*	*Exports*	*Imports*
1970	28·9	28·3	15·0	20·9	17·1	14·9	12·0	10·1	5·8	7·2	21·1	18·6
1971	27·7	30·7	15·6	18·1	16·8	15·9	11·9	9·7	6·4	8·7	21·6	16·8
1972	30·0	33·8	16·4	16·1	17·0	16·2	9·9	10·7	6·7	7·6	20·0	15·8
1973	32·5	35·4	15·4	14·9	17·0	16·1	9·9	9·2	6·5	7·7	18·5	16·1
1974	33·7	35·0	13·7	13·6	16·7	14·3	10·4	7·4	7·4	15·8	18·1	13·8
1975	32·2	38·3	11·8	13·0	15·9	13·8	9·5	8·2	11·6	13·1	19·0	13·5
1976	35·5	38·4	12·1	13·4	15·7	13·8	7·6	6·6	12·5	17·1	16·6	14·4
1977	36·8	40·0	11·9	13·5	14·5	14·1	6·5	7·7	13·6	10·0	16·5	14·6
1978	38·0	43·3	12·0	13·5	12·5	14·3	6·5	7·4	13·3	8·3	17·5	13·2
1979	42·5	45·2	11·7	13·3	13·9	15·6	6·1	6·3	9·0	6·7	16·6	12·9
1980	43·1	42·3	11·1	15·0	14·4	14·9	5·6	6·2	10·1	6·2	15·5	12·5
1981	41·3	42·4	14·0	14·8	12·4	15·2	5·7	7·2	11·6	7·2	14·6	12·9
1982	41·6	44·3	15·0	14·2	12·0	14·2	5·8	7·8	11·6	6·0	13·6	10·9

[1] Figures do not sum to 100% because of rounding.
SOURCE: *UK Balance of Payments*, Central Statistical Office.

products in order to secure the foreign exchange to finance their economic development. The possibility exists therefore that they could also become a market for UK exports, perhaps assisted by the creation of producers' associations for their primary products which would help to raise their foreign exchange earnings. Capital goods in the form of machinery and transport equipment account for 50 per cent of the UK's exports, and industrialisation in these developing economies gives rise to the possibility of important export markets for capital goods. During the 1970s earnings from construction work overseas also made a significant contribution to invisibles as they grew from £160 million in 1971 to £1,000 million in 1981 and much of this was earned in OPEC countries.

Balance of payments problems and policies

The following sections will deal with balance of payments problems arising in an economy which is running with a balance of payments deficit, and as such will initially tend to concentrate upon the experience of the UK in the years before 1972, when governments followed a policy of 'fixed' exchange rates and before the UK's trading position was supported by the benefits derived from North Sea oil.

Overseas borrowing

A 'temporary' disequilibrium in the balance of payments can arise because earnings from exports and payments for imports will not be sufficiently synchronised to avoid periods when additional foreign exchange is required to meet exceptional payments for imports. To meet such a possibility, governments seek to maintain official reserves of gold and foreign currencies upon which they draw when required. In the UK, for example, regular payments for imported military aircraft, repayment of previous loans from international financial institutions, and the seasonal demand for overseas holidays, may give rise to certain peaks in the demand for foreign currencies. Fluctuations in commodity prices may also produce a correspondingly larger foreign exchange requirement. At other times the UK may be in receipt of exceptional earnings as overseas buyers of capital goods, for example, make periodical payments to manufacturers in the UK. To even out what may prove to be unjustified fluctuations in the exchange rate, the **Exchange Equalisation Account** at the Bank of England would 'step into the market' and either sell or buy gold and foreign currency to maintain the value of sterling.

At times, however, the temporary disequilibrium may have proved to be exceptionally large and lasted for a longer period. A sudden upturn in the level of industrial output in the UK will increase the demand for a wide range of imported raw materials and perhaps also capital goods, particularly if firms are low on stocks and domestic manufacturers of plant and equipment have insufficient capacity to meet this increase in demand. This increase in imports will need to be financed until some of the output is exported. The strain on the reserves may need to be supported by seeking additional funds from the **IMF** and other central banks from countries within the **Group of Ten** which will, in co-operation with the **Bank for International Settlements**, provide the UK with assistance to support sterling through the use of **'swap'** facilities. When a central bank seeks the aid of other central banks the Bank for International Settlements acts as an intermediary. The 'swap' may be for gold, securities, dollars, or some other currency. In the first place the transfer is generally for three months.

These financial institutions have contributed towards the growth of international trade by providing a source of international liquidity. They reduce what may be unwarranted speculation against a country's currency which could otherwise lead the government involved to take action to restrict imports in order to prevent a fall in the value of its currency. On occasions the simple presence of potential loans in the form of **'standby arrangements'** may be sufficient to reduce the speculative pressure, which originates from fears that the deficit country has insufficient official reserves and promotes rumours of a devaluation.

Speculative pressure during what may have been a temporary disequilibrium in the balance of payments has been particularly severe in the case of the UK during much of the post-war period when sterling still played a significant role as a **key** or **reserve currency** in that it was used as a means of international exchange. Large sterling balances held by overseas residents could soon promote a 'run' on the pound as they were sold in order to move out of a currency under pressure. This would reduce the UK's reserves as the Bank of England was forced to support its value.

The role of sterling as a key currency produced a belief that the UK had a moral obligation to maintain its value. At a time when other sources of international liquidity were not sufficiently developed, this caused the UK Government to follow domestic policies restricting the general level of demand at home in order to curtail the growth of imports rather than resorting to a devaluation. For this reason, attempts by the government to raise the level of economic activity in the economy were often cut short by this immediate pressure on the balance of payments, the value of sterling and the reserves.

The importance of tackling fundamental economic problems

The use of reserves and other sources of international liquidity to assist the balance of payments are, however, eventually exhaustible in that they cannot deal with a 'fundamental' disequilibrium. This occurs when the economy is running a persistent deficit in its balance of payments because it is losing its competitive advantage in world markets, with the result that exports are losing ground while perhaps at the same time imports are increasing. Foreign loans may still be secured, but they will probably be supplied only if the institutions concerned believe that the recipient government is adopting policies which will tackle the fundamental problems that are producing the persistent deficits.

There are several ways in which a government can seek to deal with the immediate problem of a serious balance of payments deficit. These policies may succeed in improving the payments position but are essentially a means of tackling the symptoms of the problem and not the underlying economic ills that may have given rise to the persistent deficits. They amount to policies that provide a breathing space during which the government should implement measures aimed at the source of the disequilibrium. In the case of the UK, this has included not only measures to reduce inflation but also to encourage investment in order to raise productivity, develop industries that still have a competitive future, promote more efficient import-substitute industries, and pursue policies that raise the mobility of labour so that the growth of potentially competitive firms is not frustrated by labour shortages in certain skills.

There has also been a recognition that in a highly competitive market it is also important that due emphasis is placed upon non-price factors such as delivery dates, quality and after-sales services. None of the policies described below can directly contribute to the solving of these fundamental problems. Some of them can relieve the immediate pressure on the balance of payments, and allow the government to pursue relevant domestic policies without having to pay undue attention to the external position that may otherwise cause them to reverse these domestic policies and introduce a general deflation of demand.

Restrictions on imports

During the inter-war period tariffs were adopted by many countries in an effort to protect domestic employment and the balance of payments but since many countries were suffering from the same problem this amounted to the 'exporting' of unemployment. This led to retaliation that then contributed to a further decline in the level of world trade. In the post-war period the UK, as an economy that depends upon large imports of raw materials and food, has not resorted to tariffs as a means of tackling balance of payments problems. Even when imported manufactures started to penetrate the home market such measures were not adopted as they can lead to retaliation and are directly against the spirit of the General Agreement on Tariffs and Trade (GATT), and the UK would find it difficult to discriminate against specific overseas suppliers. Membership of the EEC would make the introduction of tariffs a very difficult policy to negotiate for acceptance by other EEC countries in particular.

The UK has not generally used import quotas to protect the balance of payments, although they may be used on some products to assist employment in certain industries, such as textiles. However, for a short time in 1968 a system of **import deposits** was used to discourage imports. This required importers to place a sum of money equivalent to a certain percentage of the value of the imports with the customs authorities. This was seen as a means of reducing imports from those sources which provided the UK firm with trade credit so enabling them to pay after they had received sufficient income from selling their imported products on the UK market. This was a short-lived measure, however, and it was particularly unpopular with our EFTA partners.

The role of tariffs as a means of improving the balance of payments is mainly through reducing imports, as they do nothing directly to promote exports and may therefore have to be in force for a long period before the position improves. The possibility does exist, however, that the enlarged, protected home market may create greater confidence among industrialists, so that investment and expanding output may then render some manufactures more competitive in overseas markets. If tariffs are going to be used the government must be sure that the industries selected for protection do have a viable future, so that when the tariffs are removed they prove able to face foreign competition. The possibility always exists that protection from imports leads to complacency in home industries so that inefficiency and increasing labour costs are then supported by tariffs. The removal of tariffs will have a severe effect upon such industries unless complacency is avoided by clearly stipulating that the tariffs are a purely temporary measure and the time-table for their gradual removal is strictly adhered to.

The added difficulty facing the UK is that the demand for imported manufactures may prove relatively inelastic so that the tariffs may need to be very high, in which case they may provoke retaliation. As an alternative, the government has generally sought some form of **voluntary quota** from overseas suppliers such as those attached to the import of consumer durables from Japan in 1977 and 1978. This, however, raises the problems associated with the multilateral nature of international trade. If a country is to accept a voluntary or more formal restraint on its exports, this may cause it to concentrate its attention on other overseas markets which may react in the same way. If, however, it fails to maintain its foreign exchange earnings in the face of such quotas, this may reduce exports from other countries and so the threat of more widespread restrictions increases.

It is also possible that the use of a tariff can actually have a harmful effect upon exports and be regressive in its effect. For example, a tariff on imported components may raise the production costs of all user industries, some of which may have been producing final products for exports. Moreover, if it is considèred to be in the national interest that tariffs should be introduced, the cost of protecting the balance of payments falls mainly upon those who still purchase imported products at the higher price, and those obliged to purchase the high-price domestic output because the previously cheaper import is priced beyond their reach.

If the nation as a whole is eventually to benefit from the use of temporary measures to protect the balance of payments, there is a case for all individuals contributing to the cost of the protection according to their ability to pay. This would suggest using a subsidy to give home producers a temporary advantage, while seeking to implement investment and rationalisation programmes that would then allow the removal of the subsidy. Since subsidies can be raised from a variety of taxes designed to be progressive, this could lead to a more equitable distribution of the costs of protection. Moreover, subsidies will not affect the competitive position of user industries.

The use of a subsidy also means that industries can maintain their position in overseas markets where they will be in constant touch with the changing tastes and preferences in competitive markets rather than producing essentially for a tariff-protected home market. A tariff can thus lead to a bias in the product that may not comply with foreign demand.

It is also difficult to assess the costs of protecting these home producers if a tariff is used, whereas the amount of the annual subsidy can be readily calculated and any increase in the required amount is likely to promote investigations as to why this has arisen.

Deflation as a means of improving the balance of payments

In 1949 and 1967 the UK devalued sterling to alleviate a fundamental disequilibrium in the balance of payments. Until 1972 the UK had adopted the **'adjustable peg'** system of exchange rates, whereby the value of sterling was fixed but could be altered if the seriousness of the balance of payments situation left little other alternative. Between 1949 and 1967 the UK had tackled deficits by relying mainly upon policies designed to deflate the level of domestic demand. Other economies were more tolerant of such policies in that they may hasten the government's implementation of policies that seek to improve the competitive position of the economy. It is in the long-term interests of other manufacturing economies that the UK does eventually embark upon a more sustained period of economic growth, in order that the resultant increase in real incomes in the UK provides these other countries with larger markets. It is after all more profitable to sell in rich markets than poor markets.

Moreover, deflation will produce unemployment by reducing home demand and so there will be no significant improvement in average living standards. This may cause the government to experience the repercussions of these measures at the next election as deflation will of course be unpopular among the electorate. This should produce a greater determination on the part of the government to tackle the underlying problems. A period of deflation, however, may then lead to an economic climate that makes raising productivity via increased investment all the more difficult because of the effect upon business confidence. It is this which has led to the phenomenon of 'stop-go' policies in the UK, dealt with in greater detail in Chapter 5.

Deflation may have to be both severe and prolonged as it seeks to improve the balance of payments by lowering the level of domestic demand, and hence output, so reducing the demand for imported inputs and also consumer goods. There was also the belief that a deflated home market would force producers to seek export markets. Such policies were in general use between 1964 and 1967, but the worsening balance of payments position and the lack of improved economic growth, in addition to the urgent need to repay large overseas loans eventually led to a devaluation of sterling in November 1967. This was an attempt to achieve a swift and large turnabout in the balance of payments.

Currency adjustments and the UK's balance of payments

Since most major European manufacturing economies had healthy payments positions there was little likelihood of retaliation in 1967 so long as the UK did not devalue by an undue amount. The pound was devalued from \$2·80 to \$2·40 and the effect of this was to make UK products cheaper in overseas markets while making imports more expensive. If, for example, a UK motor vehicle was priced at £2,000, the cost to a US buyer would fall from \$5,600 to \$4,800. The pound, being devalued, is therefore cheaper to buy when conducting such transactions. The UK motor vehicle manufacturer still receives £2,000, but note that the UK has earned less foreign currency on the sale.

This devaluation also means a fall in the exchange rate between sterling and other currencies, and UK exports will have a similar competitive advantage in other markets. As far as imports are concerned, an item of office equipment from the US priced at \$4,200, for example, will now be raised in price on the UK market from £1,500 to £1,750, and the same applies to imports from other economies which do not devalue at the same time. The devaluation means that more pounds are now needed to purchase the same quantity of foreign exchange involved in such transactions.

A devaluation in fact amounts to a deliberate worsening in the UK's terms of trade as more must now be exported to pay for the same quantity of imports, and the success of such a move will therefore depend very heavily upon the elasticity of demand for both exports and imports. If the value of the price elasticity of demand for UK exports is greater than one (i.e. elastic), the lower foreign exchange earned per unit exported will be more than outweighed by the increased volume of sales and the consequent increase in total foreign exchange earnings from exports. The demand for imports in the UK, which take the form of raw materials and food, is essentially inelastic and thus it was not expected in 1967 that any marked improvement in the balance of payments would stem from the import side. Nevertheless, when the 1967 devaluation occurred it was hoped that the demand for imported manufactures would prove relatively elastic.

It was recognised that a time lag would occur before the benefit of the devaluation on the UK balance of payments was felt, since it would be some time before both domestic buyers and those overseas could adjust to the situation when considering new contracts. Table 6.13 shows that UK exports did eventually respond and grew much more rapidly in the next two years. The 1967 devaluation, however, did coincide with a rapid growth in world trade during these years and the combination of these events allowed the UK to arrest the decline in its share of the world trade in manufactures.

In order to support the devaluation, the government also continued to deflate domestic demand to ensure that productive capacity was released to cope with the anticipated increase in exports and in demand for output to replace some imports. In the years following this currency change the export of manufactures grew at an annual rate of nearly 13 per cent as against an annual rate of $2\frac{1}{2}$ per cent in the previous ten years.

By the beginning of 1972, however, the gain in competitiveness was all but lost and until then the position had been maintained by a continued deflation of the economy. Policies aimed at reducing the rate of inflation in the economy were largely unsuccessful and had still left the UK with an inflation rate above that of its main competitors. Neither had this breathing space succeeded in raising over-all productivity by an amount that

Table 6.13: Summary of the UK balance of payments, 1966–82. Index numbers 1975=100

£m

Year	*Exports (f.o.b.)*	*Imports (f.o.b.)*	*Visible balance*	*Invisible balance*	*Current balance*	*Volume index of manufactures Export*	*Volume index of manufactures Import*	*Volume of world trade in manufactures*	*UK share of world trade in manufactures (%)*
1967	5,241	5,840	−599	+330	−269	60	50	51	12·3
1968	6,433	7,145	−712	+468	−244	69	59	57	11·6
1969	7,269	7,478	−209	+714	+505	78	62	66	11·3
1970	8,150	8,184	−34	+857	+823	79	66	72	10·8
1971	9,043	8,853	+190	+934	+1,124	86	71	77	10·9
1972	9,437	10,185	−748	+995	+247	86	85	84	10·0
1973	11,937	14,523	−2,586	+1,605	−981	98	103	95	9·4
1974	16,394	21,745	−5,351	+2,078	−3,273	103	110	104	8·8
1975	19,330	22,663	−3,333	+1,812	−1,521	100	100	100	9·3
1976	25,191	29,120	−3,929	+3,048	−881	109	110	112	8·7
1977	31,728	34,012	−2,284	+2,243	−41	117	119	117	9·4
1978	35,063	36,605	−1,542	+2,481	+939	116	136	123	9·5
1979	40,678	44,136	−3,458	+2,595	−863	116	159	130	9·7
1980	47,389	46,211	+1,178	+2,028	+3,206	117	154	137	10·3
1981	50,977	48,107	+2,870	+3,091	+5,961	112	160	140	8·6
1982	55,545	53,317	+2,228	+1,720	+3,948	113	178	137	8·5

SOURCE: Central Statistical Office.

would provide a more permanent advantage. Investment in manufacturing capacity requires the prospect of a large sustained market. Export markets are vital to achieve levels of output where economies of scale can be exploited. The competitive advantage which results provides larger sales and hence both the confidence and profits that promote further investment. Once export markets are increased this provides the means by which the initial competitive advantage is improved still further.

The 1967 devaluation did not therefore provide any lasting benefit to the balance of payments since, apart from rising inflation, the increased export market was largely offset by the reduced home market because of the accompanying deflation to ensure a rapid improvement in the balance of payments. Consequently, the government's attempts to raise over-all productivity to secure a competitive future were frustrated by the belief that because there was not a sustained and growing total market substantial increases in investment by the manufacturing section in particular were not justified.

From the beginning of 1972 the visible balance deteriorated rapidly and at the same time the government was faced with growing unemployment. Expansion of demand at home was bound to worsen the balance of payments even further and so the government decided to adopt a **floating exchange rate** which was seen as a means of securing export-led growth. The government was prepared to absorb the impact of higher imports on the balance of payments resulting from a general expansion of home demand by allowing the currency to depreciate. The fall in the value of sterling would encourage exports, and so it was hoped the growth in the economy would be export orientated. Since the government was no longer giving priority to maintaining the value of sterling, it hoped to reduce expectations held by firms that deflation would be used to protect the balance of payments.

The value of sterling would in future be determined by the forces of demand and supply operating in international exchange markets. The demand for sterling depends upon the extent to which overseas residents wish to buy UK exports or invest in the UK, as these transactions will eventually necessitate the purchase of sterling. The supply of sterling will come from UK residents wishing to buy imports or invest overseas, since this will involve the sale of sterling to obtain foreign currency. As with other free markets the price of sterling in terms of other currencies will then move to a level which produces an equilibrium whereby the demand for sterling is equal to the supply of sterling. If the UK is running a balance of payments deficit, this implies that the supply of sterling exceeds the demand and so sterling will depreciate. This amounts to a gradual devaluation, thus making exports more competitive and imports more expensive, and this should contribute to an improvement in the balance of payments.

In the event, the immediate impact of the general expansion of the economy in 1972 was a continued deterioration in the balance of payments because imports of manufactures as well as raw materials increased rapidly, as Table 6.12 indicates. At the same time some exports may have been redirected to meet the growing home demand.

The decision to float could be viewed as a means of allowing an opportunity to adapt the UK economic structure to a higher growth in the demand for manufactures. An improved position in international trade, however, requires a change in the volume of capital investment and its increasing reallocation into the manufacturing sector with export potential. These more permanent changes may have resulted from a depreciating exchange rate that reduced the necessity to deflate home demand. The UK economy, however, was not equipped to cope with the sudden increase in home demand and imported manufactures supplied this excess demand and inflation continued.

As Table 6.13 indicates, exports performed better in 1973 but failed to match the growth of imports at a time when world trade in manufactures was expanding rapidly. The already deteriorating position was then dramatically worsened by the exceptional rise in world commodity prices in 1974 and 1975, and the rise in the price of oil from the latter part of 1973 onwards. Exports held up well in 1974 and imports of manufactures slowed down. Whether or not the fall in the value of sterling would have eventually improved the situation is now solely the subject of speculation because in Britain, as in all other major economies, a period of recession followed the oil crisis and world trade fell.

The floating exchange rate, designed to protect the balance of payments, now became a source of additional inflation. The massive depreciation of sterling between 1975 and 1976 as the balance of payments continued in deficit contributed to what was termed 'imported' inflation. Higher import prices were made even more inflationary in their impact upon the economy by the fall in the exchange rate. In the last quarter of 1976 the daily **spot rate** for sterling averaged $1·65. The resulting rise in the cost of living provoked additional wage and salary increases, so contributing to the payments deficit and a further fall in the value of sterling.

In general, major economies did not engage in measures to improve their balance of payments in the period immediately following the oil crisis, which would simply have shifted the problem from one to another. The UK arranged loans from international financial institutions to assist the balance of payments situation.

The general improvement in the UK balance of payments in 1977 was largely a reflection of the reduced rate of domestic inflation and the competitive advantage provided by the floating exchange rate. The position was further supported by a loan of $3,900 million from the IMF which prevented further speculative pressure on sterling and funds returned to the UK. The rapid improvement in the visible balance, and the implications of North Sea oil for the balance of payments, had by early 1978 led to an appreciation of sterling. This actually provoked some fears that UK exports would start to lose the competitive edge they had previously gained. This provided support for those who believed that the floating pound should be 'managed' by the selling of sterling to prevent a larger appreciation.

If sterling is kept undervalued, however, this can lead to inflows of purely speculative funds that can have a de-stabilising effect upon the economy if they are used to support the growth of domestic credit facilities. Thus the decision to allow sterling to appreciate, and the possible effect on export competition, was taken largely to prevent what may have been an inflationary impact on domestic prices. In addition, the improvement in the exchange rate would contribute to lower import prices for raw materials, but this in turn must be considered in the light of continued penetration of the UK market by imported manufactures.

The actual appreciation in the exchange rate was much greater than was anticipated as large inflows of capital were encouraged because of the high interest rates which could be earned. Export competitiveness was therefore affected by a combination of high earnings, low productivity and an over-valued pound on foreign exchange markets. Table 6.14 relates the total increase in labour costs since 1975 to hourly earnings and productivity growth for the five major manufacturing economies with whom the UK must compete in both the domestic and world markets. This lack of competitiveness has now produced the situation whereby the UK actually imports more finished manufactures than are exported. In 1981 imports of finished manufactures were £18,370 million compared with exports of £19,444 million but an actual deficit in trade in finished manufactures occurred in 1982 as the imports were £22,073 million while exports totalled £21,369 million.

Table 6.14: Unit labour costs 1975–82

	Total increase (%)				
	US	*UK*	*France*	*West Germany*	*Japan*
Earnings	+86	+182	+161	+70	+56
Productivity	+11	+22	+38	+28	+52
Unit labour costs	+68	+131	+90	+32	+3
	Unit labour costs 1980–82				
Earnings	+20	+29	+33	+13	+12
Productivity	+ 1	+11	+ 7	+ 4	+ 3
Unit labour costs	+18	+16	+25	+ 8	+ 8

SOURCE: *Economic Progress Report*, July 1983.

The position of the UK in terms of competitiveness has been much better when the period 1980–82 is analysed. The fall in unit labour costs has been largely due to the productivity growth which resulted from the labour 'shake-out' in manufacturing industry when firms were faced with the deflationary impact of government policies upon their markets. More recently the fall in the exchange rate (see Fig. 5.15 on page 106) has added to these developments and UK exports of manufactures have held up relatively well considering the depressed level of world trade as shown by Fig. 6.3. A change in cost-competitiveness can arise from a change in the exchange rate, in earnings or in productivity. From the point of view of the long-term prospects of the economy, however, a rise in productivity is the most desirable. The ultimate factor in determining productivity is not simply a 'shake-out' of labour as this approach has definite limits, but the level of investment in new and improved capacity. If this does happen on a sufficiently large scale UK industry will be in a better position to take full advantage of any recovery of world trade produced by an upturn in economic activity in other major economies. Future investment, however, will depend upon the government's economic policies aimed at creating an economic environment in which firms will be prepared to undertake long-term investment projects involving many millions of pounds. Table 6.15 indicates those markets in the UK where imports have steadily increased their share. Both user industries and consumers do of course benefit from competitively priced products from abroad but such a state of affairs can only be sustained if exports are improved. The UK economy will not always be able to support its trading position by relying upon the benefits derived from North Sea oil. Neither can it rely upon a fall in the exchange rate to help offset a lack of competitiveness as this will contribute to a worsening in the UK's terms of

Fig. 6.3: Trade volumes (excluding oil and erratic items)

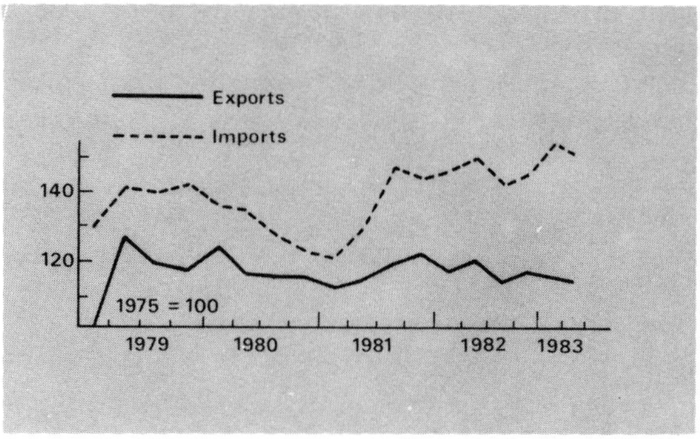

SOURCE: *Economic Progress Report*, July 1983.

trade. If this did happen then the UK would effectively be offering overseas residents a larger claim upon the output of goods and services in exchange for a fixed quantity of their goods and services. The effect upon living standards in the UK would be the

Table 6.15: Import penetration and export sales ratios for products of manufacturing industry

		Imports/Home demand		*Exports/Manufacturers' sales*	
		Twelve months ending			
		Dec. 1976	*Jun. 1982*	*Dec. 1976*	*Jun. 1982*
SIC Order					
III	Food and drink	18	16	6	6
IV	Coal and petroleum products	15	18	14	16
V	Chemicals and allied industries	25	33	34	41
VI	Metal manufacture	24	32	18	28
VII	Mechanical engineering	29	36	45	49
VIII	Instrument engineering	54	63	56	63
IX	Electrical engineering	32	46	37	42
X	Shipbuilding and marine engineering	39	21	33	23
XI	Vehicles	29	46	43	48
XII	Metal goods n.e.s.	11	16	16	18
XIII	Textiles	26	41	26	33
XIV	Leather and leather goods	30	45	27	35
XV	Clothing and footwear	26	36	15	20
XVI	Bricks, pottery, glass, cement, etc.	8	11	13	14
XVII	Timber, furniture, etc	28	29	6	7
XVIII	Paper, printing and publishing	22	23	10	11
XIX	Other manufacturing industries	15	25	20	23
III–XIX	Total manufacturing	23·0	28·8	23·7	27·2

SOURCE: *The Monthly Digest of Statistics*, March 1983.

same as would arise if an individual regularly agreed to work increasingly longer hours for the same income. Both such developments lead to a progressive decline in welfare as a fall in the exchange rate offers price reductions to overseas buyers in order to maintain exports, and in the case of a longer working week it amounts to a reduction in the price at which an individual is willing to offer his or her labour in order to keep a job. There is obviously a limit to this method of maintaining competitiveness.

7. Community Pressures on the Business Organisation

Consumer pressure

Large companies, multinationals, nationalised industries, local authorities and government departments do appear to be all-powerful in relation to individual consumers of their products and services. Of course, as we have seen, legislation lays down a framework of rights within which organisations must operate. But unless individuals know of their rights or are prepared to pursue them, then much of the legislation is ineffective.

Organisations can, however, be pressurised into abiding strictly by law, and indeed even providing guarantees and codes of practice in excess of what is required by the existing legal framework.

In the competitive market even firms benefiting from a certain brand loyalty can never be assured of their continued marketing success. Companies must continue to provide quality products or services, otherwise customers will eventually be lost. Persuasive advertising can maintain sales levels, but if the reputation of a company begins to suffer, or if goods are not competitively priced, or if tastes begin to change, then no amount of marketing effort will uphold existing sales levels. A good example is the disastrous effect on sales of tinned salmon of the outbreak of botulism in 1978, even though it was confined to one tin of salmon. This can be seen from the statement in the press some months after the scare (Fig. 7.1). Obviously in this particular instance the company could not have foreseen this problem arising and it is probable that no negligence was involved. However, it is a pointer—perhaps extreme—to the fact that companies must be aware of their market image.

It may appear that individuals do not carry much weight as complainants. Letters of complaint to organisations are usually answered in standard form with profuse apologies and occasionally with some enclosed free gift as a means of appeasement. But most companies do investigate internally any customer complaint. Because of the competitiveness of the market, and the possible adverse effect of bad publicity, organisations are concerned about complaints, and often go to the trouble of having a specialist department to deal with consumer problems.

The Office of Fair Trading (OFT) generally recommends that the individual personally pursues a complaint as the first stage of the proceedings. In its information leaflet called *Car* in the 'For Your Protection' series, the OFT suggests that if an individual has a problem regarding defects in the car he has purchased or has recently had repaired, and the dispute cannot be settled with the parties directly involved, he should 'make a formal complaint, preferably in writing to the manager, director or any other senior member of the firm concerned. Keep a copy of any letter you send. If a dealer cannot help with a problem about a new car, you should then contact the manufacturer.'

If there is a breach of a contractual situation, the individual has the opportunity of taking court action. There is evidence that this does not happen as often as it should because of the cost and time of litigation. The establishment of the **Small Claims Court of Arbitration** within the County Courts has provided a cheaper, quicker means of resolving consumer complaints if the sums involved are less than £500. However, even if a consumer is prepared for eventual litigation, his perseverance of a just claim usually results in out-of-court settlements, especially when insurance companies are concerned with the settlement of the claim.

Associations

Organised pressure has a better opportunity of influencing the policy of organisations. There has developed over the years a large number of associations which represent various aspects of our society. Complaints from and to these associations are likely to be taken much more seriously than any individual pressure.

Fig. 7.1

ADVERTISEMENT

CANNED SALMON IS CLEARED!

On 27th September, 1978 The Department of Health cleared all canned salmon, except, as a precaution, production from one Alaskan cannery. All responsible retailers will by now have removed such salmon from sale.

You can now buy salmon again with confidence.

But just check your larder for USA cans which bear the code with the letter F in the second place of the top line as follows:
Return any cans with □ F □ □
this code to your retailer. □ □ □ □ □

Canning remains one of the safest forms of food preservation.
This statement has been issued in the public interest by the British Association of Canned and Preserved Foods Importers and Distributors in co-operation with the Canned Salmon Industry in the USA and Canada and the Can Making Industry of North America and the United Kingdom.

It has also been agreed by the Department of Health and Social Security in the UK.

SOURCE: Department of Health and Social Security.

Some examples of associations are:

1. **National Consumer Protection Council** is responsible for the safety aspects of consumer protection.
2. **Advertising Standard Authority** investigates complaints covering advertising standards and special offers.
3. **Federation of British Carpet Manufacturers** investigates complaints about woven carpets.
4. **British Vehicle Renting and Licensing Association** deals with complaints about car hire firms.
5. **British Electrotechnical Approvals Board for Household Equipment** will investigate complaints about approved appliances found to be technically unsafe.
6. **Electricity Board Consumer Consultative Councils** which take up complaints about their Area Board. (A similar Council has been established for each Gas Board.)

Each of these associations—and others not mentioned here—will take up complaints from consumers. Many of the associations are established by the business organisations themselves, which is further evidence of the importance they place on maintaining goodwill amongst their customers.

Many organisations have, under pressure from the OFT, adopted or revised **voluntary codes of practice,** for example:

The **Mail Order Publishers Authority** (MOPA) which has been in operation for several years but has responded to suggestions from the OFT. Members now advertise their wares much more precisely so that all details of the offer are given, including items like postage and whether the customer has the right to reject the goods after a reasonable period of examination.

The **Association of British Travel Agents** (ABTA) has improved its code of practice for its members after a period of bad publicity. For instance, liability for misrepresentations cannot be included in the booking terms. Surcharges should be clearly stated, and currency surcharges are not to be imposed less than 30 days before the start of the holiday. Attempts must be made not to overbook and in the case of unavoidable bookings, suitable alternative accommodation should be offered. ABTA also runs a conciliation and arbitration scheme for disgruntled holidaymakers.

If all companies were members of such associations many of the consumer complaints would be dealt with more effectively and standards of trading would improve.

Citizens Advice Bureaux and media pressure

Individuals can always seek advice from the Citizens Advice Bureaux (CABx), who have established a network of centres in most localities (approximately 700 in England). They exist with the support of government-backed local authority grants and rely to a certain extent on voluntary help. Their use is mainly in giving advice to people with problems; for instance, they can show an individual the most effective way of dealing with a consumer complaint. In some cases they may be prepared to support an individual complaint, e.g. by helping to complete a letter or by putting them in touch with a solicitor. Many CABx have conscripted the help of local solicitors who, on a voluntary basis, give legal advice on a rota system. The future may see some changes in the neutral stance taken by CABx. Because of the difficulty in obtaining legal representation for minor issues it has been suggested that the CABx should begin to positively assist in case presentation.

Information on adverse trading practices can be passed to the Director-General of Fair Trading. He will investigate such complaints, and most organisations are prepared to abandon or alter their trading methods on the advice of the OFT, without waiting for legislation to enforce such advice.

Bad publicity is an excellent deterrent to any firm or organisation engaging in unfair or unsavoury trading practices, maladministration or simply inefficiency. The press have always been good campaigners for the rights of the individual. Any scandalous activity by organisations is potentially good news, and may be covered by a local or national newspaper, either provoked by an individual complaint to the editor by a member of the public, or through the resources of its own investigation teams. There is of course no compulsion for organisations to respond to any allegations made in the press, but such adverse publicity usually elicits some form of public statement, even if only to deny any untoward practice. At best it causes organisations to examine internally those areas concerned in the complaint.

The BBC and the independent television companies are also useful for investigating unfair trading practices. Many programmes are shown with a view to educating the public by exposing and highlighting problem areas. The 'World in Action' team has won several awards for its documentaries probing interferences with and intrusion into people's fundamental rights.

A very powerful counter to persuasive and often misleading advertising—which merely advertises the strong points of any available product or service—is the Consumers Association publication '*Which?*'. Independent of organisational pressure, relying heavily on donations and subscriptions, this magazine organises intensive tests of consumer goods and services and makes searching and well-documented comparisons, all of which assist buyers in obtaining value for money. The Consumers Association has also helped to build up a more discriminating public. It also publishes a number of specialist supplements, such as *Motoring Which?*, *Holiday Which?*, *Money Which?*, etc.

With over a quarter of a million subscribers, the Consumers Association represents an effective body of opinion which no manufacturer or supplier can afford to ignore. In particular, the

Association has influence with MPs and a voice on many influential committees.

The local politicians

The local Member of Parliament carries considerable weight in drawing the attention of the public and of Parliament to problems raised within a constituency. The advantage of contacting an MP is that results can often be obtained with private firms, nationalised industries or local authorities, because if they do not respond he or she can take up the matter with the minister responsible, and if the problem is more serious, it can be raised in the House.

Local councillors can also be lobbied over a wide range of local matters, including the way that revenue is spent. The local authority has considerable current and capital revenue; approximately two-thirds of this is supplied by the central government which has a considerable influence on how it is spent. But the local authority can use its discretion as long as those services laid down by law are provided. Elected councillors can be put under pressure to spend the money wisely, although it must be remembered that most financial planning is long term and so pressure must be applied to change plans and policies possibly five years in advance.

Self-help pressure groups

In recent years there has been a development of self-help associations specially formed within the community to combat a specific threat to community life from the activities of an organisation. For instance, a section of the community may attempt to dissuade a firm from expanding its premises or from continuing a nuisance, such as creating excessive noise or pollution. Interested parties may combine together to bring pressure to bear on the organisation in a variety of ways, for example, by setting up a petition, hiring legal advice to scrutinise all the plans and modes of operation of the organisation, holding protest demonstrations and public meetings, rallying the support of trade unions from within the organisation under attack, attending council meetings and finally pursuing any legal rights that might exist. The variety of interest groups is enormous, and it should be remembered that in any pluralist society not all the pressure groups will have equal status and power. Even the most persistent group may not achieve its objectives, despite wide media coverage, if other interests remain more powerfully dominant, or are supported by the existing political structure which is not prepared to alter its stance or be flexible on a particular issue.

The hiring of legal representation is one of the most effective means of bringing pressure to bear on the organisation. Without necessarily incurring the cost of litigation, a relatively small fee will hire the services of a solicitor to write letters to the organisation on behalf of the complainant. This gives the complaint authenticity and authority, and firms will respond more readily to a solicitor's letter than to a personal letter. If the complaint seems to be made on substantial grounds, a large firm may realise that it will lose the case if it should go to court and will usually prefer to settle the dispute rather than risk the attendant bad publicity of a court case.

Legal services

Problems which cannot be overcome with formal letters may need to be resolved legally. Many people have a good understanding of their legal rights but are unable to pursue them because of inadequate means. The Legal Aid Act 1974 allows solicitors to give advice and do work up to the value of £25 under what is known as the Green Form Scheme, which can then be claimed from the Legal Aid Fund, depending on the financial position of the complainant.

If a court case proves necessary, a person may be entitled to free legal aid or contributory legal aid, subject to financial status, although financial limits are stringent and the applicant must satisfy a panel of lawyers that he has a reasonable chance of succeeding in his case. The major principle behind the legal aid scheme is to ensure that an individual's just claim in law is not defeated by penury. There have still been difficulties in keeping at an acceptable social rate the financial levels for which free legal aid or aid based on contributions is granted. The Legal Aid Act 1979 markedly improved the provisions available. However, criticisms can still be levelled at the scheme, in particular, the fact that no aid is yet available to contest a case at tribunals despite their increasing status and workload. Neighbourhood **Law Centres**, which are backed by local authorities and by charities and have developed in many urban areas, provide an additional service to those unable to secure aid. For nothing or for very low fees solicitors will assist those with legal problems and, subject to the Law Society's approval, act for their clients in court cases.

Complaints to the correct authority
There is now a wealth of legislation protecting the individual in all aspects of community life, which does not entail the individual taking action himself, but simply requires notice of the complaint or dispute being sent to the correct authority, many of which were described in Chapter 1. For instance, if a consumer purchases a tin of food which is short in weight, the sum of money involved makes a nonsense of litigation. Yet if any difficulty is incurred in obtaining a replacement from the store, an officer at the local Trading Standards department will be interested in the complaint as it constitutes an offence under the Weights and Measures Act 1963. A prosecution would be undertaken on the consumer's behalf.

If food is purchased which is not fresh, the Chief Environmental Health Officer may feel that a breach of the Food and Drugs Act 1955 has occurred.

If an individual's life is being disrupted by excessive noise from a small factory close to his dwelling, the prospect of a civil action may be daunting, but the burden can be passed on to the Environmental Health Department. If the noise is excessive and a danger to health it may contravene legislation enacted to allow people to live without the nuisance of noise (Public Health Act, 1936, the Control of Pollution Act 1974). A statutory abatement order can be issued against the factory, giving it a time limit within which the nuisance must be stopped. Failure to comply with this order can lead to a prosecution and a fine, with a recurring penalty for each day the nuisance is continued. Usually the mere presence of the Environmental Health Officer brings about some improvement. The Environmental Health Officer's services can also be used to prevent abuses under the Clean Air Acts 1956–68 if smoke is emitted which is an offence to the inhabitants of an area.

The Parliamentary Commissioner for Administration

Consumers can always make use of the Parliamentary Commissioner (Ombudsman). He is an independent officer of the Crown investigating complaints referred to him by MPs either on their own behalf against the alleged unjust actions of a government department, or on behalf of a member of the public who has raised a complaint. Virtually all government departments are within the jurisdiction of the Ombudsman, but some public affairs are excluded from his powers, such as inter-government dealings, and the conduct of civil or criminal proceedings. His powers are extensive in that he can examine all documents relevant to any claim of maladministration, but the action he can take is limited, being mainly a report to a Select Committee plus the value of any adverse publicity. The report is referred to the Member of Parliament who made the complaint and an annual report is made to Parliament on cases dealt with.

This system of the Ombudsman, which was established in 1967 for central government, was extended in 1974 to include local government. Commissions were established for England, Wales and Scotland, and can deal with all manner of complaints against any local authority, its committees and officers.

A further development of the concept of ombudsman occurred with the reorganisation of the National Health Service by the National Health Service Reorganisation Act 1973. Separate Health Service Commissioners were appointed with a brief similar to that of the parliamentary Commissioner.

Index

The letter-by-letter system has been adopted.
Acronyms in common use, i.e. EEC, have been dealt with as such.
To avoid proliferation of the terms used in business affairs the index contains a number of principal subjects as follows:

consumer, *containing all aspects of business affecting, including trade except international trade and finance.*
economy
finance, *containing all aspects of, in its widest sense.*
government *means central (i.e. 'Whitehall' in its broadest sense); departments; policy, etc.*
international organisations
international trade, *containing methods; systems; practices and some financial aspects.*
Law—*this subject is divided into separate entries for Acts of Parliament; courts; Parliament.*
local authority, *containing any subject not within the purview of central government.*